Computer Organisation and Architecture

Computer Organisation and Architecture
An Introduction

Second Edition

B.S. Chalk, A.T. Carter and R.W. Hind

First published 2004 by
PALGRAVE MACMILLAN
Houndmills, Basingstoke, Hampshire RG21 6XS and
175 Fifth Avenue, New York, N.Y. 10010
Companies and representatives throughout the world

PALGRAVE MACMILLAN is the global academic imprint of the Palgrave
Macmillan division of St. Martin's Press, LLC and of Palgrave Macmillan Ltd.
Macmillan® is a registered trademark in the United States, United Kingdom
and other countries. Palgrave is a registered trademark in the European
Union and other countries.

ISBN 1–4039–0164–3

This book is printed on paper suitable for recycling and made from fully
managed and sustained forest sources.

A catalogue record for this book is available from the British Library.

10 9 8 7 6 5 4 3 2 1
13 12 11 10 09 08 07 06 05 04

Printed and bound in China

Contents

Contents

Contents

Preface to the second edition

A great deal has happened in the world of computing since the publication of the first edition of this book. Processors have become faster and the number of transistors contained in the processor chip has greatly increased. The amount of memory, both primary and secondary, in the standard personal computer has increased and become faster. New peripheral devices have come onto the scene and some of the old ones have almost disappeared. Networked computers are the norm, as is connection to the Internet for almost all home computers. Having said all the above, the basic von Neumann architecture has not been superseded yet.

This second edition of *Computer Organisation and Architecture, An Introduction*, builds on the first edition, bringing the material up to date and adding new chapters on 'Networking and what's next'. After considerable thought, we have decided to use the Intel family of processors rather than the Motorola 68000 for our examples. This is because the availability of Intel based personal computers (PCs) tends to be greater than machines based on the Motorola 68000, taking into account that many people, especially students, have a PC at home. Our change must not be seen as a criticism of the Motorola processors, but simply a matter of expedience for experiential learning.

Many of our examples make reference to PCs, but all the basic principles apply to all sizes and shapes of computers. There are still a large number of powerful high-end computers being used in big organisations and it must be remembered that the world of computing is not just PCs.

The target audience for this edition has not changed and with the addition of the networking chapter, we hope that the area of appeal will have widened.

We have included Chapter 12 in order to look briefly at some developments. Some are a few weeks away while others are experimental or just proposals. With the rate of development we are seeing, it is difficult to imagine where computing will be in say five years time. We live in exciting times.

Suggested answers to a number of the end of chapter exercises are available on the WEB site associated with this book.

A.T. Carter, R.W. Hind

Acknowledgements

Tony and I wish to thank Bernard Chalk for allowing us to produce a second edition of his book and for his helpful comments on our proposed changes. We also express grateful thanks to Dave Hatter of Palgrave Macmillan, without whose assistance, both technical and editorial, this edition would not have reached completion.

Thanks must also be extended to our wives, Deb and Margaret, for their patience and understanding.

A.T. Carter, R.W. Hind
March 2003

List of trademarks

AMD, Athlon XP, Duron are trademarks of Advanced Micro Devices, Inc.

ANSI is a trademark of American National Standards Institute.

Apple Mac is a trademark of the Apple Corporation Inc.

Ethernet is a trademark of Xerox Corporation.

IBM is a trademark of International Business Machines.

Intel 80x86, Intel386, Intel486, Pentium, MMX, Xeon, Celeron and Pentium are registered trademarks of Intel Corporation.

Java, Sun, Sun Microsystems are trademarks of Sun Microsystems Incorporated.

Microsoft, DOS, MS-DOS, Windows, Windows 95, Windows 98, Windows 2000, Windows NT, are trademarks of Microsoft Corporation.

Motorola 68000 is a registered trademark of Motorola, Inc.

MIPS is a trademark of MIPS Technologies.

Novell is a trademark of Novell Incorporated.

SPARC is a trademark of SPARC International, Inc. Products bearing SPARC trademarks are based upon an architecture developed by Sun Microsystems, Inc.

UNIX is a registered trademark, exclusively licensed through X/Open Company, Ltd.

Other product names mentioned herein may be trademarks and/or registered trademarks of their respective companies.

Introduction

Not all that many years ago, the only places where one would be able to see a computer would have been the central offices of large organisations. The computer, costing at least £500000, would have been housed in a large, temperature controlled room. The computer would have been run by a team of people, called operators, working on a shift system which provided 24-hour operation. Users of the computer would have a terminal, consisting of a TV screen and a keyboard, on their desk and they would use the facilities of the computer by means of on-screen forms and menus. These computers were called *main frame computers* and in fact there are still many of these in operation today. Today, almost every home has a computer either in the form of a *Personal Computer* (PC) or *games console* and the cost is well under £1000.

There is a vast array of different types of computers between the two types mentioned above, varying in size, cost and performance. However, the majority of these computers are based on a model proposed by John von Neumann and others in 1946. In Chapter 1, we describe the von Neumann model and relate its logical units to the physical components found in a typical PC. This will provide a foundation for a more detailed discussion of computer organisation in subsequent chapters. There are two approaches to investigating a complex system. One, known as the top-down approach, looks at the system as a whole with particular attention being applied to what it does, in other words, the functions the system performs. Then each function is investigated in more detail with the intention of gaining an understanding of how the system performs the function. The level of detail considered increases until the individual component level is reached, at which point the operation of the whole system should be understood in minute detail. The alternative approach, known as the bottom-up approach, considers individual components and then looks at ways in which these can be connected together to provide the functions required of a system.

In this book, we will start by using the top-down approach to get an understanding of what basic functions a computer can perform, then we will use the bottom-up approach to show how basic components can be interconnected to provide the required functionality.

1.1 Computer functionality

The mighty computer can do little more than add two numbers together. Everything else we see the computer being used for, be it playing a graphics game, word processing a document or running a payroll, is a sequence of operations that mainly involves adding numbers together. 'Wait a minute' you say, 'computers can subtract, multiply, divide and do many other things too'. We will deal with these simple functions here and the rest of the book will cover many other aspects. Take subtraction, if we wish to subtract 20 from 30 all we need to do is change the sign of 20 and add the two numbers to give 10. So we have done subtraction by using addition.

$$30 + (-20) = 10$$

Multiplication is successive addition so if we wish to multiply 25 by 3 we can carry out the following calculation:

$$25 + 25 + 25 = 75$$

Division is successive subtraction, which is successive addition with a sign change.

TQ 1.1   How would you use the above system to check if two numbers were equal?

Let us see how the addition function can be achieved.

1.2 The von Neumann model

A key feature of this model is the concept of a *stored program*. A *program* is a set of *instructions* that describe the steps involved when carrying out a computational task, such as carrying out a calculation or accessing a database. The program is stored in memory together with any *data* upon which the instructions operate, as illustrated in Figure 1.1.

To run a program, the CPU or *Central Processing Unit* repeatedly fetches, decodes and executes the instructions one after the other in a sequential manner. This is carried out by a part of the CPU called the *control unit*. The execution phase frequently involves fetching data, altering it in some way and then writing it back to memory. For this to be possible, an instruction must specify both the *operation* to be performed and the location or *memory address* of any data involved. Operations such as addition and subtraction are performed by a part of the CPU called the *Arithmetic and Logic Unit* (ALU). Input and Output devices are needed to transfer information to and from memory. To sequence these transfers and to enforce the orderly movement of instructions and data in the system, the control unit uses various control lines.

Figure 1.1 The von Neumann model

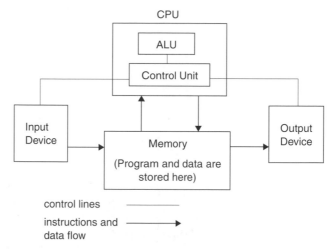

control lines ─────────
instructions and ───────▶
data flow

Figure 1.2 Basic PC system

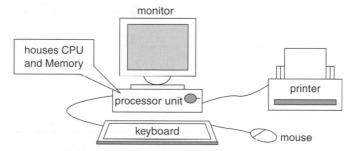

1.3 A personal computer system

Figure 1.2 shows some of the basic *hardware* of a 'stand alone' personal computer (PC) system. The *processor unit* houses the bulk of the electronics, including the CPU and memory. Attached to this are various *peripheral devices*, such as a keyboard, a mouse, a *monitor* which can be a TV type screen or a flat Liquid Crystal Display (LCD) and a printer. These devices provide the Input/Output (I/O) facility. If we open the processor unit and take a look inside, we find a number of electronic components mounted on a *large printed circuit* board known as a motherboard, as shown in Figure 1.3. The components are connected together by conducting *tracks* for carrying electrical signals between them. These signals carry information in digitized or digital form and are therefore referred to as *digital signals*.

Most of the electronic components are in the form of *integrated circuits* (IC), which are circuits built from small slices or 'chips' of the semiconductor material, *silicon*. The chips are mounted in plastic packages to provide for connecting them to the motherboard. One of the largest and most complex ICs on the board is the *microprocessor*, normally referred to as the *processor*, which is the CPU of the system. This chip contains millions of electronic

Figure 1.3 A typical motherboard (reproduced with permission from EPOX Electronics)

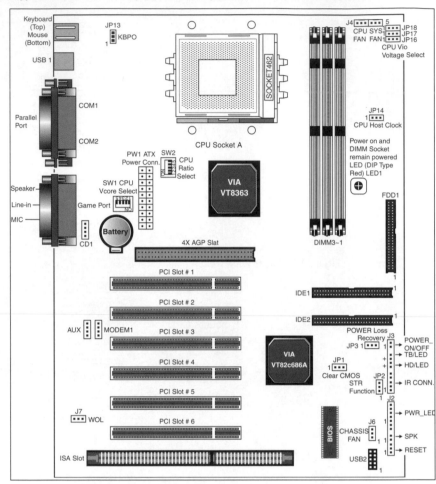

switches called *transistors* organised in the form of *logic gates*, the basic building blocks of digital circuits. These logic gates are used to implement the control unit, the ALU and other components of the CPU such as its *register set*. Logic gates are discussed in Chapter 3.

There are two basic types of semiconductor memory on the motherboard, *Random Access Memory* (RAM) which is a read–write memory and *Read Only Memory* (ROM). These form the fast *primary* or *main memory* of the system and both store information in *binary form* (1s and 0s). RAM is often provided in the form of *memory modules*, each module containing a number of memory chips. The modules are plugged into sockets on the motherboard. Because RAM can be read from and written to, it is suitable for storing programs and data. Unfortunately RAM chips are normally *volatile* and therefore lose their content when the computer's power is switched off. ROMs on the other hand, are *non-volatile* and are used for storing various *system programs* and data that needs to be available when the computer is switched on. Non-volatile means that the ROM does not lose its content even when the power is removed.

TQ 1.2   Why is ROM unsuitable for storing user programs?

In addition to a fast main memory, the PC also has a large but slower *secondary* memory, usually in the form of a *hard disk* and one or two *floppy disk* units and a *CD or DVD read/write unit*. Programs are stored on disk as *files* and must be loaded into main memory before they can be executed by the processor. Computer memory is discussed in Chapters 6 and 7.

The processor is connected to memory and the other parts of the system by a group of conducting tracks called a *system bus*, which provides a pathway for the exchange of data and control information. Logically, a system bus is divided into an *address bus*, a *data bus* and a *control bus*. To co-ordinate activities taking place inside the processor with those taking place on the system bus, some form of timing is required. This is provided by a crystal controlled *clock*.

Input/Output (I/O) *cards* are plugged into the *sockets* shown in Figure 1.3. The sockets are connected to the system bus. The cards are used for connecting peripheral devices to the system. In general, peripheral devices operate at much slower speeds than the CPU and so the I/O cards will have special *interface chips* mounted on them for connecting the peripheral devices to the system bus. Interfacing is discussed in Chapter 8.

It is worth mentioning that although PCs are very common and there are many millions in use today, two other types of small computer are becoming very popular, namely the small *laptop* or *portable* computer and the even smaller, *palmtop* or *personal data assistant* (PDA) computer. Both laptop and PDA computers are single unit devices with the monitor, keyboard and mouse built into the single unit. Other than size and a slightly higher price, there is little difference between a laptop and a PC. PDAs have a restricted keyboard and sometimes a stylus is used to actuate the keys rather than fingers. They also tend to have somewhat limited capability.

1.4   Representing memory

We can visualise main memory as a series of storage boxes or locations, as shown in Figure 1.4. Each location is identified by an *address* and can be used to store an instruction or some data. For example, the instruction *move* 4, is stored at address 0 and the datum, 2, is stored at address 5. The first instruction, *move* 4, copies the 'contents of address 4' or number 1, into one of the processor's registers. The second instruction, *add* 5, adds the 'contents of address 5' or number 2, to the first number stored in the register. The third instruction, *store* 6, stores the 'contents of this register' or the sum of the two numbers, into address 6. Finally the last instruction, *stop*, halts or prevents any further execution of the program.

Figure 1.4   A representation of memory

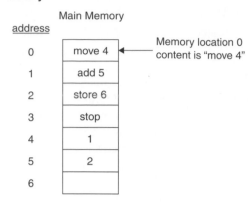

1.5 High- and low-level languages

Instructions such as *move* and *add* are called *machine instructions* and are the only instructions the processor can 'understand' and execute. Writing programs at this level requires a knowledge of the computer's *architecture*, which includes amongst other things, details of the processor's registers, the different instructions it can execute (*instruction set*) and the various ways these instructions can address memory (*addressing modes*). Programming at machine level is called *low-level language* programming and some examples of this can be seen in Chapters 4 and 5.

When we wish to write programs to solve particular problems, it is often easier to write them in English-like statements using a *high-level language* (HLL), such as Java or C.

For example, the HLL statement:

$$Sum := A + B;$$

gives the same result as our previous program while being easier to follow. The fact that the *variables* A, B and Sum refer to memory addresses 4, 5 and 6 or some other locations, is hidden from the programmer and allows him or her to concentrate on the logic of the problem rather than the organisation of the computer.

Because the machine cannot directly understand or execute HLL program statements, these statements must be translated into *machine instructions* before the program can be executed. Translating a HLL program into a *machine language* program, often called *machine code*, is the responsibility of a piece of *system software*. Two approaches to the process of translating HLL into machine code are common. One is called *Interpretation*, where each HLL statement is in turn converted into machine code statements which are then *executed*. The other is called *Compilation*, where the whole HLL program is converted into machine code statements and placed into a file called an *executable* file. After the compilation process is completed the executable file is then executed. Interpretation is ideal for the software development stage. Compilation is best for a fully developed program as it runs faster.

Figure 1.5 Different user interfaces (a) graphical (b) command driven

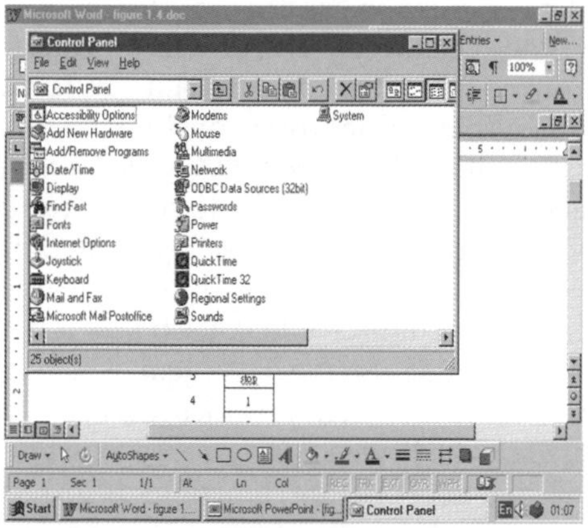

(a)

```
Microsoft(R) Windows 95
  (C)Copyright Microsoft Corp
1981–1996.


C:\WINDOWS>
```

(b)

1.6 The operating system

As well as software for solving user problems (applications software), software is needed for carrying out various system tasks, such as controlling the monitor, reading the keyboard, loading files into memory from the hard disk and so on. These programs are part of a powerful piece of systems software called the *operating system.*

When we switch on a PC, we are presented with some form of user interface. The interface might be graphical, as shown in Figure 1.5(a), or command driven, as shown in Figure 1.5(b). In either case, the operating system creates an environment for the user conveniently to examine files and run programs. For a Graphical User Interface (GUI), this is done by 'clicking' on icons using a pointing device such as a mouse, while for a Command Driven Interface (CDI), it is done by entering special commands and file names from the keyboard. The fact that we do not have to know where a file is stored on disk or the main memory locations in which a program is loaded, is simply due to the operating system.

Many operating system functions are either invisible to the user, or become apparent only when things go wrong, such as when an error occurs. The operating system is often referred to as a resource manager as part of its job is to control the use of the processor, memory and file system. It is also responsible for controlling access to the computer itself by providing a security mechanism, which might involve user passwords. We will return to the topic of operating systems in Chapter 9.

1.7 Networked systems

Very few office or college PCs are stand-alone systems. They are connected to a network, which means that users of PCs can communicate using e-mail or share resources such as printers, scanners and other PC's disk systems.

There are two basic network configurations, peer-to-peer and server-based networks. Peer-to-peer networks consist of a number of PCs connected together in such a way that each PC is of equal standing. Each PC can, providing permission has been granted, access disks and peripheral devices of any other PC directly. This is ideal if the number of PCs on the network is small, say up to 10, but it is a difficult configuration to manage and keep secure. *Server-based* networks consist of a number of PCs connected together and also connected to a special PC called a *server*. The server provides a central file store and a machine to control printing and network access. To use the network, a PC user must 'log on' to the server, which involves security and access checking. The PC user can then access the server file system and the peripherals connected to it. Each user is normally allocated his or her own area of storage on the file system, which is only available for that user. A common file area is often provided, available for all users, into which work to be shared can be loaded. Server-based networks are ideal for larger networks. Server-based networks are sometimes incorrectly referred to as client/server networks. Client/server systems are more to do with distributed computer systems than the Local Area Networks (LANs) commonly found. We will cover networks in more detail in Chapter 11.

Answers to in text questions

TQ 1.1   Subtract one number from the other and see if the answer is zero. If the answer is zero, the numbers are equal. The ALU can easily tell if a register contains all zeros.

TQ 1.2   Because they can only be read from and not written to, they cannot be loaded with user programs.

EXERCISES

1   Explain what the letters CPU, RAM, ROM and LAN stand for.

2   Write down the main features of a von Neumann style computer.

3   Explain why ROM is needed in a PC system.

4   Explain what is meant by the terms machine instruction and instruction set.

5   State the parts of the CPU that are used for (a) fetching and interpreting instructions (b) performing arithmetic operations such as 'add'.

6   Briefly explain the benefits of programming in a HLL.

7   Software can be classified as either application software or systems software. Give an example of each type.

8   When it is required to run a piece of software designed to run on one type of machine on another type of machine, the software needs to be recompiled. Explain why this is so.

9   From the time you 'double click' on an icon for a text document in a GUI, to the time it appears on the screen and you are able to edit it, the operating system must perform a number of tasks. Outline what you think these might be.

10   Networks allow users to share peripherals and file stores. Explain the security risks that this might involve.

11   Explain why a laptop computer may cost more than a PC with a similar specification.

12   There is a growing trend for desktop PC users to want LCD displays rather than TV type monitors. Explain why you think this is.

13   In a peer-to-peer network it is possible to send a message from one PC to another PC directly but this is not possible in a server-based network. Does this mean that server-based networks can not be used for e-mail? Explain.

14   What is the effect if one PC in a peer-to-peer network fails or is switched off?

15   What is the effect if the server machine in a server-based network fails?

Data representation and computer arithmetic

Data is represented and stored in a computer using groups of binary digits called *words*. This chapter begins by describing binary codes and how words are used to represent characters. It then concentrates on the representation of positive and negative integers and how binary arithmetic is performed within the ALU. The chapter concludes with a discussion on the representation of real numbers and floating point arithmetic.

2.1 Bits, bytes and words

Because of the two-state nature of logic gates, see Chapter 3 for more details on logic gates, the natural way of representing information inside an electronic computer is by using the digits 0 and 1 called binary digits. A binary digit or *bit* is the basic unit from which all information is structured. Computers store and process information using groups of bits called words, as illustrated in Figure 2.1.

In principle, the number of bits in the word or word length can be any size, but for practical reasons, modern computers currently standardise on

Figure 2.1 Words stored in memory

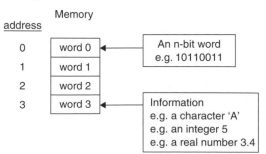

multiples of 8-bits, typical word lengths being 16, 32 or 64 bits. A group of 8 bits is called a *byte* so we can use this unit to express these word lengths as 2 bytes, 4 bytes and 8 bytes, respectively. Bytes are also used as the base unit for describing memory storage capacity, the symbols K, M, G and T being used to represent multiples of this unit as shown in the following table:

Multiple	Pronounced	Symbol
1024	kilo	K
1024 × 1024	mega	M
1024 × 1024 × 1024	giga	G
1024 × 1024 × 1024 × 1024	tera	T

Thus K or KB represents 1024 bytes, M or MB represents 1048576 bytes, G or GB represents 1073741824 bytes and T or TB represents 1099511627776 bytes.

In this book, we will use the lower case b to represent bits. Thus Kb means Kbits and so on.

2.2 Binary codes

With an n-bit word there are 2^n different unique bit patterns that can be used to represent information. For example, if $n = 2$, there are 2^2 or four bit patterns 00, 01, 10 and 11. To each pattern we can assign some meaning, such as:

$$00 = \text{North}, \quad 01 = \text{South}, \quad 10 = \text{East}, \quad 11 = \text{West}$$

The process of assigning a meaning to a set of bit patterns defines a particular *binary code*.

TQ 2.1   How many different 'things' can we represent with 7 bits ?

(1) ASCII code

The *ASCII code* (American Standard Code for Information Interchange), is a 7-bit character code originally adopted for representing a set of 128 different symbols that were needed for exchanging information between computers. These symbols include *alphanumeric* characters such as (A–Z, a–z, 0–9), special symbols such as ($+$, $-$, &, %, etc.), and *control* characters including 'Line Feed' and 'Carriage Return'. Table 2.1 illustrates some of the printable ASCII codes such as 'A' = 1000001 and '%' = 0100101. $b_6, b_5, \ldots, b_0$ are the seven bit positions, numbered from left to right.

Table 2.1   ASCII codes for, 'A', 'z', '2' and '%'

Character	ASCII Codes						
	b_6	b_5	b_4	b_3	b_2	b_1	b_0
A	1	0	0	0	0	0	1
z	1	1	1	1	0	1	0
2	0	1	1	0	0	1	0
%	0	1	0	0	1	0	1

Control codes, such as 'Carriage Return' = 0001101 and 'Line Feed' = 0001010, are called non-printing characters. The full ASCII table is given in Appendix 3.

In addition to providing a code for information exchange, the ASCII code has also been adapted for representing characters inside a computer. Normally characters occupy a single byte of memory: the lower 7 bits being used to represent the ASCII code and the upper bit being set to 0 or 1, depending upon the machine. The extra bit can also be used to provide additional codes for storing graphic characters, or as a *parity bit* for checking single bit errors.

TQ 2.2   By referring to the ASCII table in Appendix 3, write down the ASCII codes for the characters – 'a', 'Z' and '*'.

Binary codes can also be used to represent other entities, such as instructions and numbers. To represent numeric data we require a set of rules or *numbering system* for assigning values to the codes.

2.3 Number systems

(1) Decimal number system

We represent decimal numbers using strings of digits taken from the set {0, 1, 2, 3, 4, 5, 6, 7, 8, 9}. Moving from left to right, each symbol represents a linearly increasing value. To represent numbers greater than 9 we use combinations of digits and apply a weighting to each digit according to its position in the number. For example, the decimal integer 126 is assigned a value of:

$$1 \times 100 + 2 \times 10 + 6 \times 1 = 100 + 20 + 6$$

Figure 2.2 Weightings used in the decimal number system

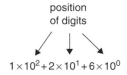

$$1\times 10^2 + 2\times 10^1 + 6\times 10^0$$

The weighting applied to these digits is 10 raised to the power of the position of the digit, as shown in Figure 2.2.

The position of a digit is found by counting from right to left starting at position 0.

Fractional or *real* numbers use a decimal point to separate negative powers of 10 from positive powers of ten. For example 52.6 represents:

$$5 \times 10^1 + 2 \times 10^0 + 6 \times 10^{-1}$$

The reason for using 10 is that there are ten different digits in this representation, which we call the *base* or *radix* of the system. Other positional number systems use different sets of digits and therefore have different bases. To distinguish one number system from another, we often subscript the number by its base, such as 126_{10}.

(2) Binary number system

The binary number system uses just two digits $\{0, 1\}$ and therefore has a base of 2. The positional weighting of the digits is based on powers of 2, giving the number 1011_2, for example, a decimal value of:

$$1 \times 2^3 + 0 \times 2^2 + 1 \times 2^1 + 1 \times 2^0 = 8 + 0 + 2 + 1 = 11_{10}$$

This system of weighting is called *pure binary*, the binary digit furthest to the right being the *least significant bit* (lsb) and the one furthest to the left being the *most significant bit* (msb).

TQ 2.3   What is the decimal value of the number 11.1_2?

(3) Hexadecimal number system

The hexadecimal (Hex) number system is a base-16 system and therefore has 16 different symbols to represent its digits. By convention the symbols adopted are $\{0, 1, 2, 3, 4, 5, 6, 7, 8, 9, A, B, C, D, E, F\}$, where:

$$A = 10_{10}, \quad B = 11_{10}, \quad C = 12_{10}, \quad D = 13_{10}, \quad E = 14_{10} \text{ and } \quad F = 15_{10}$$

In this system the weighting is 16 raised to the power of the position of the digit. For example $A1F_{16}$ has a decimal value of:

$$A \times 16^2 + 1 \times 16^1 + F \times 16^0 = 10 \times 256 + 1 \times 16 + 15 \times 1 = 2591_{10}$$

Table 2.2   Comparison of binary and hexadecimal number systems

binary	hexadecimal
0000	0
0001	1
0010	2
0011	3
0100	4
0101	5
0110	6
0111	7
1000	8
1001	9
1010	A
1011	B
1100	C
1101	D
1110	E
1111	F

(4)   Binary to hexadecimal conversion

Table 2.2 compares the first sixteen digits of the binary number system with the hexadecimal number system.

From the table we can see that a single hexadecimal digit is capable of representing a 4-bit binary number. Because of this fact, we can convert a binary number into hexadecimal by grouping the digits into 4's, replacing each group by one hexadecimal digit, as shown below:

$$\frac{1011}{B} \quad \frac{0011}{3} \quad \frac{1010}{A}$$

The binary number 101100111010_2 expressed in hexadecimal is therefore $B3A_{16}$. To convert a hexadecimal number into binary, we reverse this operation and replace each hexadecimal digit by a 4-bit binary number. One reason for using hexadecimal, is that it makes it easier for humans to talk about bit patterns if we express them in their Hex equivalent. Try this experiment with a friend. Read out a 16-bit binary number quite quickly and get the friend to write the number on paper. Very few will be able to do this correctly. Now convert the binary number to Hex and read out the Hex value, again asking the friend to write the number down. Almost certainly, they will get the number down correctly this time.

TQ 2.4 Convert the hexadecimal number $ABCD_{16}$ into binary

2.4 Negative numbers

The binary system described so far is unable to represent negative integers and for this reason we call it *unsigned* binary. To support the use of negative numbers it is necessary to modify our representation to include information about the sign as well as the magnitude of a number. In this section we will consider two ways of doing this.

(1) *Sign and magnitude representation*

In this representation, the leftmost bit of the number is used as a *sign bit* and the remaining bits are used to give its magnitude. By convention, 0 is used for positive numbers and 1 for negative numbers. For example, using an 8-bit representation the numbers -5_{10} and $+20_{10}$ are 10000101 and 00010100 respectively.

TQ 2.5 What do 10001111 and 01010101 represent?

Unfortunately, representing numbers in this way makes binary addition and subtraction, which is performed by the Arithmetic and Logic Unit (ALU), more awkward to deal with. When performing addition, for example, the sign bits must be checked before the magnitudes are separated out and added. If the sign bits are different, then a binary subtraction must be substituted for an addition, and before completing the operation, an appropriate sign bit must be reinserted. These extra processing steps add to the complexity of the ALU and increases the execution time of the operation.

TQ 2.6 How is zero represented in this system?

(2) *Two's complement representation*

In this representation, there is only one representation of zero and it is more flexible than sign and magnitude in that it allows binary addition and subtraction to be treated in the same way. Rather than separating the sign from the magnitude, the 'negativeness' of the number is built into it. This is accomplished by giving the most significant bit position of an n-bit number a weighting of -2^{n-1} instead of $+2^{n-1}$ that we use with unsigned binary.

Figure 2.3 Showing the weighting of two's complement numbers

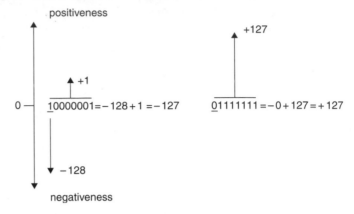

Therefore with an 8-bit representation, the numbers $+127_{10}$ and -127_{10} are given by:

$$+127 = 01111111 = -0 \times 2^7 + 1 \times 2^6 + 1 \times 2^5 + 1 \times 2^4 + 1 \times 2^3$$
$$+ 1 \times 2^2 + 1 \times 2^1 + 1 \times 2^0$$
$$= -0 + 64 + 32 + 16 + 8 + 4 + 2 + 1$$
$$-127 = 10000001 = -1 \times 2^7 + 0 \times 2^6 + 0 \times 2^5 + 0 \times 2^4 + 0 \times 2^3$$
$$+ 0 \times 2^2 + 0 \times 2^1 + 1 \times 2^0$$
$$= -128 + 0 + 0 + 0 + 0 + 0 + 0 + 1$$

We can visualise these two numbers as shown in Figure 2.3, where the most significant bit provides a large negative contribution and the remaining seven bits provide a positive contribution.

Any two's complement number where the most significant bit (msb) is equal to 1, must have an overall negative value. The msb therefore acts as both a sign bit and a magnitude bit.

With an 8-bit two's complement representation, we can represent numbers between -128_{10} and $+127_{10}$ as shown in Table 2.3.

TQ 2.7 What would the number 10000111 represent?

From the table we can identify a connection between the bit pattern of a positive number, such as $+2 = 00000010$, and the bit pattern of its opposite number, $-2 = 11111110$. If we reverse all the bits of the number $+2$, exchanging *1 bits* for *0 bits* and vice versa, we get the bit pattern 11111101. This is called finding the *one's complement*. If we now add '1' to the lsb of this number we get:

$$
\begin{array}{r}
11111101 + \\
1 \\
\hline
11111110 = \text{two's compliment} \\
\hline
\end{array}
$$

Table 2.3   8-bit two's complement representation

-128	10000000
-127	10000001
-126	10000010
-2	11111110
-1	11111111
0	00000000
$+1$	00000001
$+2$	00000010
$+126$	01111110
$+127$	01111111

TQ 2.8   What is the two's complement representation of the number -3_{10}?

Worked example   What is the decimal value of the two's complement number 11110000 ?

Solution   Because the sign bit is 1, we know that it must be a negative number. If we represent this number as $-X$, then its two's complement must be $-(-X) = +X$. The two's complement of 11110000 is 00010000 as shown below:

$$\begin{array}{r} 00001111\ + \\ 1 \\ \hline 00010000 \end{array}$$

Because this is $+16_{10}$ then the decimal value of 11110000 is -16_{10}

Another worked example   How do we represent -25?

Solution

The 1's complement of this is
add 1 to get the two's complement

$$\begin{array}{l} +25 = 00011001 \\ 11100110\ + \\ \quad\quad\quad 1 \\ \hline 11100111 \end{array}$$

So 11100111 is how -25 is stored in two's complement form.

Table 2.4   Rules for binary addition

Digits added	Sum	Carry-out
$0 + 0$	0	0
$0 + 1$	1	0
$1 + 0$	1	0
$1 + 1$	0	1

2.5 Binary arithmetic

(1) Binary addition

The rules for adding pairs of binary digits are given in Table 2.4. Using these rules, we add the binary numbers 1010 and 0011 by adding the digits together in pairs, starting with the least significant pair of digits on the far right, as shown in the following example. Note that the second pair of digits when added produce a carry forward which must be added in with the third pair of digits.

$$\begin{array}{r} 1010\ + \\ 0011 \\ \hline 1101 \\ \hline 1 \lrcorner \end{array}$$

The carry forward or carry-out generated when adding the second pair of digits is shown in table row four. This gets included as a carry-in to the sum of the next most significant pair of digits, just as we do with decimal addition. Table 2.5 makes this more explicit and shows how the sum (S) and carry-out (Co) depend upon the digits (A and B) being added and the carry-in (Ci).

(2) Two's complement arithmetic

We add two's complement numbers in the same way as we add unsigned binary. For example, $12 + 20 = 32$ as shown below:

$$\begin{array}{r} 12 = 00001100\ + \\ 20 = 00010100 \\ \hline 00100000 = 32 \end{array}$$

We can also add negative numbers, such as $-1 + (-2) = -3$, provided that we ignore the bit carried-out of the sum:

$$\begin{array}{r} -1 = 11111111\ + \\ -2 = 11111110 \\ \hline 11111101 = -3 \end{array}$$

(ignore) $1 \lrcorner$

Table 2.5 Rules for binary addition with carry-in included

A	B	Ci	S	Co
0	0	0	0	0
0	1	0	1	0
1	0	0	1	0
1	1	0	0	1
0	0	1	1	0
0	1	1	0	1
1	0	1	0	1
1	1	1	1	1

If we add large positive or large negative numbers together, we sometimes get the wrong answers, as the following examples illustrate:

$$64 = 01000000\ +$$
$$65 = 01000001$$
$$\overline{10000001} = -127 \text{ (should be } +129)$$

$$-64 = 11000000\ +$$
$$-65 = 10111111$$
$$\overline{01111111} = +127 \text{ (should be } -129)$$

(ignore) ↵

These are examples of *arithmetic overflow*, which occurs whenever a sum exceeds the range of the representation. In the first example, the sum should be $+129$ and in the second it should be -129. From Table 2.3, we can see that these results are both out of range, because the largest and smallest numbers that can be represented are $+127$ and -128. Overflow is a consequence of two's complement arithmetic and can only occur when we add two numbers of the same sign. If the sign bit of the sum is different from that of the numbers being added, then overflow has taken place. The ALU signals this event by setting the *overflow flag* in the *Flags Register*.

One of the main advantages in using a two's complement representation, is that the ALU can perform binary subtraction using addition. For example, $7 - 5$ is the same as $7 + (-5)$, so to perform this operation we *add* 7 to the two's complement of 5. This is shown below:

$$00000111\ +$$
$$11111010$$
$$1$$
$$\overline{00000010} = +2_{10}$$

(ignore) 1↵

Figure 2.4   BCD representation of decimal number 9164

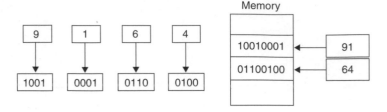

Do you remember what we said in Chapter 1 about computers only being able to add?

2.6 Binary Coded Decimal (BCD)

When entering decimal data into a computer, the data must be converted into some binary form before processing can begin. To reduce the time needed to perform this conversion, we sometimes use a less compact but easily converted form of binary representation called Binary Coded Decimal (BCD).

To convert a decimal number into BCD, we use a 4-bit positional code for each decimal digit. It is usual to weight these digits in the normal 8-4-2-1 way, so that the decimal digits 1, 2, 3, … are replaced by the BCD codes 0001, 0010, 0011, Figure 2.4 illustrates how the decimal number 9164 is encoded and stored in two consecutive bytes of memory.

TQ 2.9   Which 4-bit binary codes are left unused by the BCD representation?

Because of these unused or invalid codes, we cannot perform arithmetic on BCD numbers in the same way as we do with pure binary. For example, 9 + 1 would give 1010, which is an invalid code. To overcome this problem most computers include special logic in the ALU for performing BCD or decimal arithmetic.

2.7 Floating point representation

In the decimal number system we frequently represent very large or very small numbers in *scientific notation* rather than as a fixed point number. For example, the fixed point decimal numbers 299800000 and 0.0000000000000000001602 can be represented as $2.998 \times 10^{+8}$ and 1.602×10^{-19}, respectively. The power to which 10 is raised, such as +8 or −19, is called the *exponent* or *characteristic*, while the number in front is called the *mantissa*.

Figure 2.5   A simple floating point format

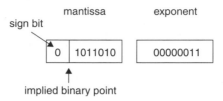

By substituting the base 2 for the base 10, we can use a similar notation for representing real numbers in a computer. For example, the decimal number 5.625 could be represented as 1.01101×2^2 or 1011.01×2^{-1}, where each exponent specifies the true position of the binary point relative to its current position in the mantissa. Because the binary point can be dynamically altered by adjusting the size of the exponent, we call this representation *floating point*.

(1)   Storing floating point numbers

To store a floating point number we need to record information about the sign and magnitude of both the mantissa and the exponent. The number of words used to do this and the way this information is encoded is called a *floating point format*. Figure 2.5 shows how 1.0011010×2^2 might be represented and stored using two bytes or 16-bits of storage space.

With this particular format, a sign and magnitude representation is used for storing the mantissa and a two's complement representation is used for the exponent. Before storing this number it must be *normalised* by adjusting the exponent so that the binary point is immediately before the most significant digit. The normalised form of the number 1.011010×2^2 is therefore given by 0.1011010×2^3, so the digits 1011010 and the two's complement representation of the exponent $+3$, which is 00000011, are stored in their respective bytes.

TQ 2.10   What is the largest number we can represent using this format?

The *range* of numbers we can represent with an 8-bit exponent is approximately 10^{-39} to 10^{+39} and the *precision* we get with a 7-bit mantissa is about 1 part in 10^3. We can increase the precision by using more bits to store the mantissa, but with a 16-bit mode of representation, this can only be done by reducing the range. To overcome this type of problem, most machines support two modes of precision, *single precision* and *double precision*, as illustrated in Figure 2.6.

TQ 2.11   How would the number 5.125_{10} be stored in single precision format?

Figure 2.6   Single and double precision formats

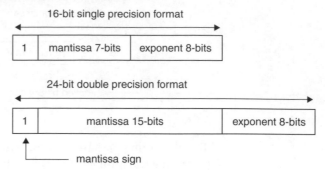

Figure 2.7   Floating point addition

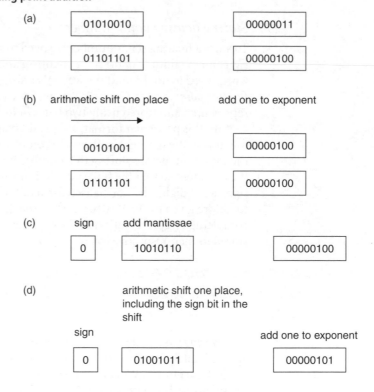

(2)   *Floating point arithmetic*

Floating point arithmetic is more complicated than integer arithmetic. To illustrate this, we will consider the steps involved in performing the operation 5.125 + 13.625, using single precision arithmetic. We will assume that these numbers have been normalised and stored in memory, as shown in Figure 2.7(a).

The first step in this operation involves aligning the binary points of the two numbers, which is carried out by comparing their exponents and arithmetically shifting the smaller number until its exponent matches that of the other. In Figure 2.7(b), the mantissa of the smaller number 5.125, is shifted one place to the right so that its exponent becomes the same as that of the number 13.625. Notice that a zero has been inserted in its most significant bit position.

Having the same exponents, the sign bits are separated and the mantissae are added, as shown in Figure 2.7(c). Because the result now occupies 8 bits, it must be *re-normalised*, by shifting the bits one place to the right and incrementing the exponent. Finally, the sign bit is reinserted as shown in Figure 2.7(d), to produce a sum of $+0.1001011 \times 2^5$ or 18.75_{10}.

Floating point multiplication and division operations also involve a number of steps including adding/subtracting the exponents, multiplying/dividing the mantissae and re-normalising the result. Remember that multiplication and division can be carried out by successive addition and successive subtraction, respectively. These operations can be carried out either by using software routines or by employing special hardware in the form of a floating point *coprocessor*. Floating point or numeric coprocessors improve the performance of compute intensive applications, by allowing any floating point arithmetic to take place in parallel with the CPU. When the CPU detects a floating point instruction, the operands are passed to the coprocessor, which performs the arithmetic operation while the CPU proceeds with another activity.

2.8 Summary

Computers store and manipulate information as n-bit words. An n-bit word can represent 2^n different entities, such as characters and numbers. A group of 8 bits is called a byte and can be used to store a single ASCII character. The binary number system uses a positional weighting scheme based on powers of 2. The hexadecimal number system uses a positional weighting based on powers of 16. The hexadecimal number system provides a useful shorthand for representing large binary numbers. Negative numbers are often represented in binary form using the two's complement representation. This representation allows subtraction to be carried out using the same basic circuitry used for addition. When adding two's complement numbers with the same sign, a condition called overflow can occur. An overflow condition is automatically flagged in the Flags Register. Real numbers can be represented as floating point numbers. Floating point numbers use a particular format to represent the mantissa and the exponent. Floating point arithmetic involves more steps than with integer arithmetic and can be performed using either software routines or by employing additional hardware in the form of a coprocessor. Floating point coprocessors can execute floating point operations in parallel with the CPU.

Answers to in text questions

TQ 2.1 With n = 7 there are $2^7 = 128$ unique bit patterns that can be used to represent different 'things'.

TQ 2.2 'a' = 1100001, 'Z' = 1011010 and '*' = 0101010

TQ 2.3 $1 \times 2^1 + 1 \times 2^0 + 1 \times 2^{-1} = 2 + 1 + 0.5 = 3.5_{10}$

TQ 2.4 1010 1011 1100 1101

TQ 2.5 10001111 represents -15_{10} and 01010101 represents $+85_{10}$

TQ 2.6 Zero can be written as either 1000000 or 00000000

TQ 2.7 This number would represent $-128 + 7 = -121$

TQ 2.8 (a) Write down the 8-bit representation of the number, $+3_{10} = 00000011$ and find its one's complement, 11111100
(b) Add 1 to the lsb

11111100 +
       1
_____
11111101 = two's compliment

TQ 2.9 Because only 10 of the 16 possible 4-bit binary codes are used, we are left with the six invalid codes.

1010, 1011, 1100, 1101, 1110, 1111

TQ 2.10 The largest number is $+0.1111111 \times 2^{+127}$

TQ 2.11 $+5.125_{10} = 101.001 \times 2^0 = 0.101001 \times 2^{+3}$ when normalised. It would therefore be stored as:

sign bit ↓

01010010	00000011

EXERCISES

1 How many binary codes can we generate with 16 bits?
2 Convert the following decimal numbers into binary:
(a) 16   (b) 127 and   (c) 255
3 Convert the following binary numbers into decimal:
(a) 0111   (b) 101101000011 and   (c) 1011.0111
4 Convert the following binary numbers into hexadecimal:
(a) 101011101011   (b) 11100110 and   (c) 010100011

5   Perform the following binary additions:

(a) 00101 + 10110 and   (b) 100111 + 100101 + 000001

6   If a byte addressable RAM occupies the hexadecimal addresses A000 to BFFF, then how many KB of storage space is available?

7   Perform the following operations using 8-bit two's complement arithmetic. In which cases will arithmetic overflow occur?

(a) 100 + 27   (b) 84 + 52   (c) 115 − 64   (d) −85 − 44

8   Represent:

(a) $+101.1111 \times 2^{+5}$ and   (b) $-0.0001 \times 2^{+6}$

using the simple floating point format given in Figure 2.5.

Boolean logic

In Chapter 1 we mentioned that logic gates are the basic building blocks of a digital computer. This chapter describes these gates and how they can be used to build useful circuits.

3.1 Logic gates

Integrated circuits such as microprocessors, memory, interface chips and so on, are manufactured by putting hundreds, thousands or millions of simple *logic gates* on to a silicon chip. The chip is then packaged to provide pins for connecting the circuit to the rest of the system, as illustrated in Figure 3.1.

Each logic gate generates an output that depends on the electronic logic level applied to its input(s). For two-state logic devices, the logic levels are described as one of: true/false, high/low, on/off or 1/0. Only a few basic types of gate are needed to build digital circuits, each gate performing a particular *logic function* such as AND, OR, or NOT. We represent these gates using special symbols, as shown in Figure 3.2.

The input and output logic levels applied to these gates are represented by *boolean variables*, such as A, B and X. These variables can take only the values 1 or 0. For simplicity we have only considered dual-input gates, but it should be remembered that apart from the NOT gate, all other gates can have two, three or more inputs, the upper limit depending upon the technology used to implement the gate. The function of each logic gate is described by a *truth table*, which relates its input logic state to its output logic state. For example, the truth table of the AND gate shows that the two inputs can take the values 00, 01, 10 or 11 and that the output value is 1 only when the input is 11.

TQ 3.1 What is the output value of an Exclusive-OR gate if just one of its inputs is at logic 1?

TQ 3.2 If the output value of a NAND gate is 0, then what can we deduce about its inputs?

TQ 3.3 Sometimes we describe a NOT gate as an inverter. Why?

Figure 3.1   Relationships between chip, logic gate and package

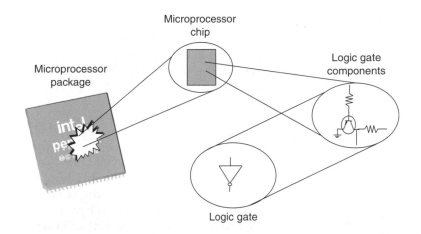

Microprocessor
chip

Microprocessor
package

Logic gate
components

Logic gate

Figure 3.2   Digital logic gates

FUNCTION		SYMBOL	TRUTH TABLE

NOT
$f(X) =$ 'A
or $\overline{A}$
or   !A
or   NOT A

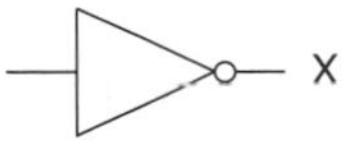

A ▷○ X

A	$\overline{A}$
0	1
1	0

AND
$f(X) =$ A.B
or   A & B
or   A AND B

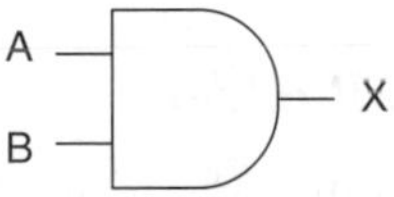

A B	A.B
0 0	0
0 1	0
1 0	0
1 1	1

NAND
$f(X) =$ $\overline{A.B}$
or   A NAND B
or   NOT(A AND B)

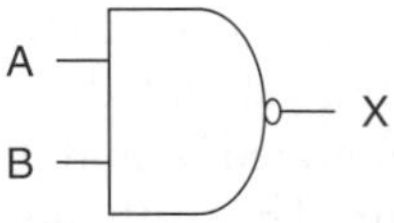

A B	$\overline{A.B}$
0 0	1
0 1	1
1 0	1
1 1	0

OR
$f(X) =$ A+B
or   A I B
or   A OR B

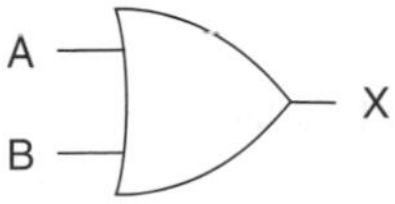

A B	A+B
0 0	0
0 1	1
1 0	1
1 1	1

NOR
$f(X) =$ $\overline{A+B}$
or   A NOR B
or   NOT(A OR B)

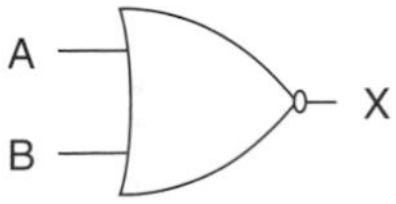

A B	$\overline{A+B}$
0 0	1
0 1	0
1 0	0
1 1	0

eXclusive-OR
$f(X) =$ $A \oplus B$
or   A XOR B

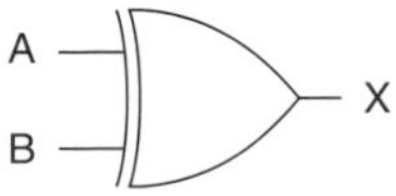

A B	$A \oplus B$
0 0	0
0 1	1
1 0	1
1 1	0

3.2 Combinational logic circuits

By connecting simple logic gates together in various ways, we can build a whole range of useful circuits. In this section we will illustrate this with a few simple examples. Binary addition is covered in Section 2.5 but in the following two sections we will look at how circuits can be built to perform the addition function.

3.2.1 Half-adder

Figure 3.3(a) illustrates a circuit called a *half-adder*, which can be built using an AND gate in combination with an Exclusive-OR gate. The circuit has two inputs, labelled A, B and two outputs, labelled S, C. From the AND and Exclusive-OR truth tables, we can see that when A and B are both at logic 0, both S and C are also at logic 0. If we now take B to logic 1, then S also goes to logic 1, while C remains at logic 0.

TQ 3.4 Complete the truth table in Figure 3.3(b).

The half-adder, represented symbolically in Figure 3.3(c), is used as a building block for a more useful circuit called a *full-adder*.

3.2.2 Full-adder

A full-adder is shown in Figure 3.4(a). It is a combinational logic circuit with three inputs, labelled A, B, C_i and two outputs, labelled S and C_o. The circuit is used to find the sum S of a pair of binary digits, A and B. C_o is 1 if a carry-out is generated and is 0 otherwise. C_i or carry-in, is used to allow any carry generated by adding a previous pair of binary digits to be included in the sum. The truth table for the full-adder circuit is given in the Table.3.1.

Figure 3.3 **Half-adder**

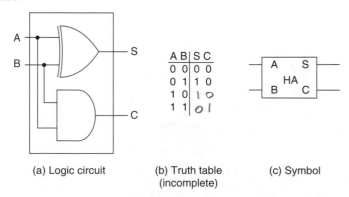

A B	S C
0 0	0 0
0 1	1 0
1 0	1 0
1 1	0 1

(a) Logic circuit   (b) Truth table (incomplete)   (c) Symbol

Figure 3.4   Full-adder

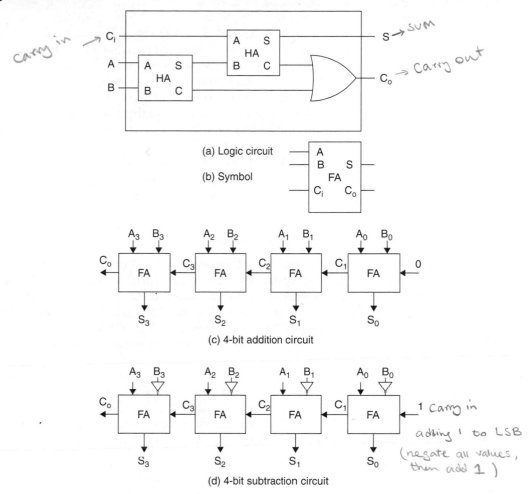

(a) Logic circuit

(b) Symbol

(c) 4-bit addition circuit

(d) 4-bit subtraction circuit

Table 3.1   Truth table for full-adder

A	B	Ci	S	Co
0	0	0	0	0
0	1	0	1	0
1	0	0	1	0
1	1	0	0	1
0	0	1	1	0
0	1	1	0	1
1	0	1	0	1
1	1	1	1	1

A chain of these full-adders can be used to add binary numbers together as in Figure 3.4(c) where a 4-bit addition unit is built from a series of four full-adders. In Section 2.5 two's complement arithmetic was introduced. With two's complement arithmetic it is possible to perform subtraction using adder circuits. Figure 3.4(d) demonstrates how a 4-bit subtraction unit can be built from a series of full-adders with the B input negated and the carry-in to the first full-adder set to 1.

TQ 3.5   Why is the carry-in set to 1 in Figure 3.4(d)?

3.2.3 A 2-to-4 decoder

Another useful circuit is the 2-to-4 line decoder shown in Figure 3.5, which can be built from a combination of NAND and NOT gates. The NOT gates are arranged in such a way that each of the four input combinations 00, 01, 10, 11 activates a different NAND gate, by taking both of its inputs 'high'. This forces the output of the NAND gate to go 'low'. The inputs A, B are therefore used to select one and only one of the outputs $\overline{S0}, \ldots, \overline{S3}$ by forcing it to go low.

This circuit can be used to select one device from a choice of four. The select lines in such devices are often active low, that is, the device is selected when the control input is 0. This is due to the electrical characteristics of the circuits whereby a more efficient circuit can be designed with an active low control input. This circuit can be used for address decoding, which we discuss in Section 6.4.

Figure 3.5   A 2-to-4 decoder

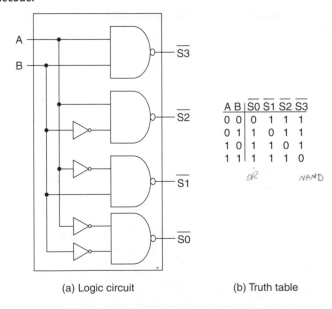

(a) Logic circuit

A B | $\overline{S0}$ $\overline{S1}$ $\overline{S2}$ $\overline{S3}$
0 0 | 0   1   1   1
0 1 | 1   0   1   1
1 0 | 1   1   0   1
1 1 | 1   1   1   0

(b) Truth table

Figure 3.6 2-input multiplexor

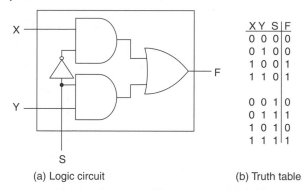

X Y S	F
0 0 0	0
0 1 0	0
1 0 0	1
1 1 0	1
0 0 1	0
0 1 1	1
1 0 1	0
1 1 1	1

(a) Logic circuit   (b) Truth table

3.2.4 A 2-input multiplexor

The circuit in Figure 3.6 has three inputs X, Y, S and one output F. From the truth table you will notice that when S = 0, the output F is the same as the input X, and when S = 1, the output F is the same as the input Y. In other words, the circuit acts as a logic switch, the output F being connected to X or Y depending upon whether S = 1 or S = 0.

When designing logic circuits the result is often a very long and complex expression. In order to simplify these logic expressions, algebraic techniques of minimisation or Karnough maps may be used. These techniques are explained and demonstrated in Appendix 1.

3.3 Sequential logic circuits

Combinational logic circuits, where the output depends solely on the current state of the input, are useful for implementing functional units such as adders or switches. However, for memory elements and other functional units that have outputs that depend upon their current input and the current state of the circuit, we need to use sequential logic elements. The simplest form of sequential logic circuit is the *flip-flop*.

3.3.1 R-S flip-flop

Figure 3.7 illustrates a NOR gate version of an R-S flip-flop, the NOR gates being labelled G1 and G2. The circuit has two inputs, labelled R, S and two outputs, labelled Q and $\overline{Q}$. The bar over the latter Q (pronounced 'not Q'), indicates that this output is the complement or inverse of Q.

The circuit can exist in one of two stable states by virtue of the fact that its outputs are cross-coupled to its inputs. For this reason we call this type of circuit a *bistable* device.

With the inputs and outputs shown in Figure 3.8(a), the circuit is in the first of its two stable states. We can check this by referring to the truth table of the NOR gate given in Figure 3.2, and noting that the output of a NOR

Figure 3.7   R-S flip-flop

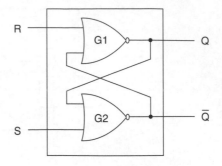

Figure 3.8   Operation of an R-S flip-flop circuit

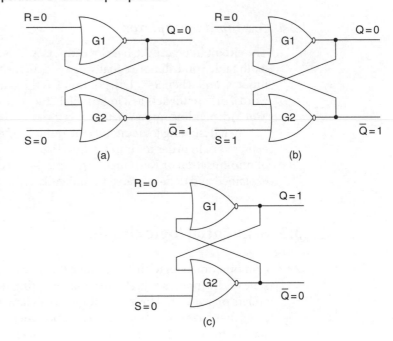

gate is always 0 if either or both of its inputs are at logic 1. Because the output Q, from gate G1, is also an input to G2, then when Q = 0 and S = 0 the output $\overline{Q}$ is 1. This output is fed-back to G1 and holds Q = 0, irrespective of whether R = 0 or R = 1.

When S is taken to logic 1, as shown in Figure 3.8(b), $\overline{Q}$ goes low forcing the Q output of Gl to 1, since both its inputs are now low. The output of Gl is fed-back to G2 and holds $\overline{Q}$ low, so that when S is restored to 0, as shown in Figure 3.8(c), the outputs remain in this second stable state.

TQ 3.6   Describe what happens if R is now taken high then low.

Figure 3.9 Clocked R-S flip-flop

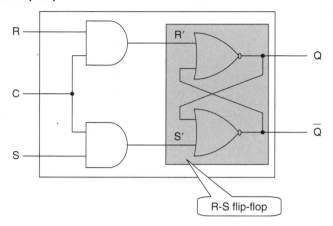

R-S flip-flop

The R or *Reset* input is used to restore the circuit to its original state (Q = 0), while the input S is called *Set*, because it sets the circuit into a second stable state (Q = 1).

3.3.2 Clocked R-S flip-flop

A clocked R-S flip-flop circuit is shown in Figure 3.9.

In this circuit, inputs R and S are ANDed with a third *clock* input C. The outputs of the AND gates (R′ and S′) then act as inputs to the R-S flip-flop.

TQ 3.7 When C = 0, what will the values of R′ and S′ be?

Only when C = 1 do the R′ and S′ inputs take on the input values R and S and affect the output of the circuit. The circuit therefore acts as a clock controlled storage element. When the clock is high, a 1 can be stored at the Q output by taking S = 1 and R = 0, and a 0 can be stored by taking R = 1 and S = 0. When the clock goes low, the information (either 1 or 0) stored in the *memory element* is protected from alteration.

3.3.3 D-type flip-flop

A simple D-type flip-flop circuit is shown in Figure 3.10. It is basically a clocked R-S flip-flop with the R-input connected by a NOT gate to the S-input.

TQ 3.8 When D = 1 what will the values R and S be?

We can illustrate the way in which data is clocked or *latched* into this type of storage element, by using a timing diagram as shown in Figure 3.11.

Figure 3.10   D-type flip-flop circuit

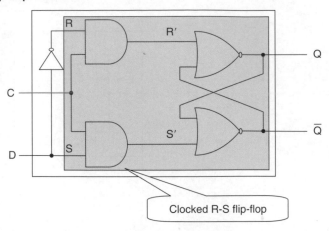

Clocked R-S flip-flop

Figure 3.11   Timing diagram for the D-type flip-flop

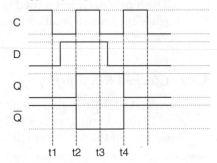

The clock input C is a train of pulses, which change from high-to-low at instants t1 and t3, and from low-to-high at instants t2 and t4. Only when C goes high is the flip-flop able to respond by changing its Q output to that of the D input. For example, despite the fact that D goes high shortly after time t1, it is not until t2, when the clock also goes high, that output Q goes high. When C goes low again at instant t3, the output Q = 1, $\overline{Q}$ = 0 is 'frozen' or *latched* by the flip-flop.

TQ 3.9   If the D input was to change during the period t2 to t3, then what would happen, if anything, to the output?

D-type flip-flops that latch data on the *transition* or edge of the clock rather than on its voltage level, are shown in Figure 3.12. A transition can either occur on the rising, or positive going, edge of the clock when it goes from a low-to-high voltage, or on the negative going edge of the clock, when it goes from a high-to-low voltage. Edge triggered D-type flip-flops can be used for building registers, shift registers and counters.

Figure 3.12   Edge triggered D-type flip-flops

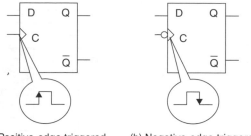

(a) Positive-edge triggered   (b) Negative-edge triggered

3.4   Flip-flop circuits

3.4.1   Simple register

A parallel register is a group of memory elements that can be read from or written to simultaneously. For the circuit shown in Figure 3.13, the pattern of 1s and 0s supplied by the data inputs I0, …, I3 is stored by the D-type memory elements when the write data strobe line is activated.

Once stored, the data can be read in parallel from the B0, …, B3 output lines using the read control line.

TQ 3.10   What logic level would the read line have to be for the B0, …, B3 outputs to reflect the state of the Q outputs?

3.4.2   Shift register

A shift register is a special type of register which accepts and/or transfers information serially. For the circuit shown in Figure 3.14, the information in the form of 1's and 0's is applied to the leftmost flip-flop one digit or bit at a time.

A *shift clock* applies clock pulses simultaneously to all the flip-flops, so that each time the circuit is clocked, the bit present at each D-input is transferred to its Q output. Therefore if the serial data arriving at the leftmost flip-flop happened to be 1100, then after four clock pulses it would have been shifted into the register and be stored as Q3 = 1, Q2 = 1, Q1 = 0 and Q0 = 0. Using a set of AND gates and a read line (not shown), this data could then be read from the register in parallel form, allowing the circuit to perform serial-to-parallel data conversion. Serial-Input-Parallel-Output (SIPO) shift registers are used in serial interface circuits as described in Section 8.2.

3.4.3   Binary up-counter

A counter is a circuit that passes through a sequence of well defined states on each transition of an input clock. Figure 3.15 is an example of an *asynchronous binary counter*, the outputs Q2, Q1, Q0 displaying the sequence

Figure 3.13 4-bit parallel register

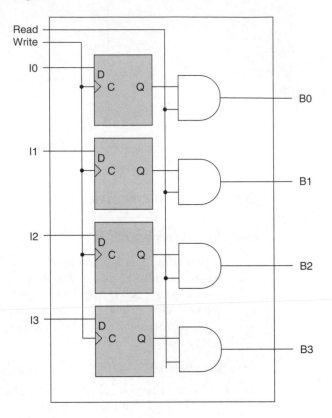

Figure 3.14 4-bit shift register

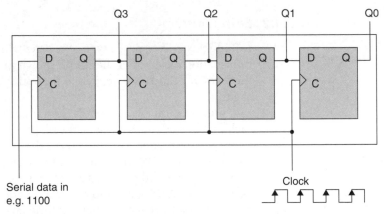

000, 001, 010, 011, . . . after each clock pulse. This is the way we count upwards in the *binary number system* (see Section 2.3).

The circuit uses three negative going edge triggered D-type flip-flops. The leftmost flip-flop or first stage of the counter is connected to the input clock, the other flip-flops being clocked from the output of their adjacent stages. The input to each flip-flop is derived from its $\overline{Q}$ output. The three outputs Q0, Q1 and Q2 are initially reset to zero.

The operation of this counter is best understood by referring to the timing diagram shown in Figure 3.16.

When the first clock transition takes place, the output Q0 changes from 0 to 1, because its D-input comes from its $\overline{Q0}$ output, which is 1. As Q0 changes to 1, $\overline{Q0}$ changes to 0, so that on the second clock transition, Q0 returns to 0 again. The Q0 output is therefore a train of clock pulses having half the frequency of the input clock. In a similar way, the Q1 output is a train of pulses having half the frequency of the Q0 output, which is therefore a quarter of the input clock frequency. The values of Q0, Q1 and Q2 after each transition are recorded in Table 3.2.

After reaching the state Q2 = 1, Q1 = 1, Q0 = 1, any further transitions of the clock will cause this sequence to be repeated.

This form of counter has the disadvantage of introducing delays between successive outputs owing to the signal rippling through the stages. For example, when counting from 011 → 100, the change in the output from the first stage is used to trigger the second stage which in turn triggers the third stage, before the final output becomes stable. For this reason, this type of

Figure 3.15   Asynchronous binary up-counter

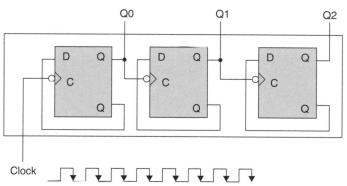

Figure 3.16   Timing diagram for the asynchronous counter

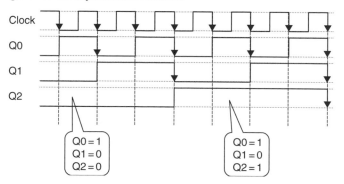

Table 3.2 The output from the binary counter

Clock transition	Q2	Q1	Q0
0	0	0	0
1	0	0	1
2	0	1	0
3	0	1	1
4	1	0	0
5	1	0	1
6	1	1	0
7	1	1	1

Figure 3.17 Tri-state or high-impedance buffer

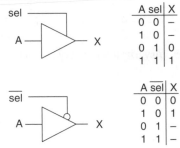

counter is called an *asynchronous* or *ripple-through counter*. Counters that do not suffer from this problem are called *synchronous counters*.

3.4.4 *Tri-state outputs*

The types of devices described above are often connected to the same bus. If they were all to output at the same time then their signals would interfere with each other. The use of the AND gate for controlling read output, as shown in Figure 3.13, causes outputs to go to '0' if the device is not selected for read output. This is itself a valid output value. To overcome this contention problem another type of device is introduced called a *high-impedance buffer*. This will output the value on its input if it is selected, otherwise it will enter a high impedance state, which will mean that nothing will be output. Figure 3.17 shows how this gate is represented.

Figure 3.18 shows how the decoder from Figure 3.5, the register from Figure 3.13 and the high-impedance buffer may be combined to form a part of a memory system. Memory systems are described further in Chapter 6.

Figure 3.18 Simple memory system

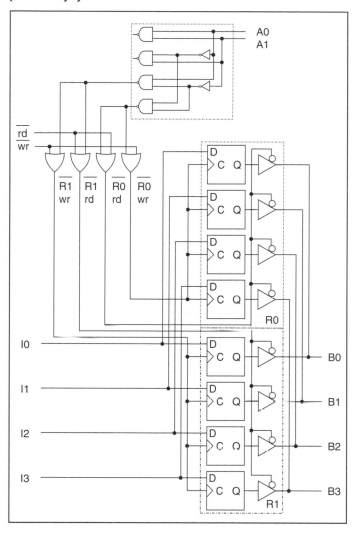

3.5 Summary

Computer chips, however complicated, are made from combinations of a few simple logic gates. These gates may be arranged so that the output is only dependent on the current inputs. Such circuits are termed combinational logic circuits. If the output is dependent upon the current state of the outputs, as well as the inputs, then they are referred to as sequential logic circuits.

Although computer logic is based on only 2 states, the output buffers on many chips use a third state called a high-impedance state. This prevents any output from the gate reaching a shared bus.

Answers to in text questions

TQ 3.1   The output will be at logic 1

TQ 3.2   Both inputs must be at logic 1

TQ 3.3   Because its output is always in the opposite logic state to its input.

TQ 3.4

A	B	S	C
0	0	0	0
0	1	1	0
1	0	1	0
1	1	0	1

TQ 3.5   To add 1 to the least significant bit. (To negate a value, negate all bits then add 1.)

TQ 3.6   If R is taken high, then Q goes low forcing $\overline{Q}$ high. $\overline{Q}$ holds G1 low so that the outputs remain unchanged when R returns to 0. The circuit is now in its original state.

TQ 3.7   Both $R' = 0$ and $S' = 0$

TQ 3.8 $R = 0$ and $S = 1$

TQ 3.9   While the clock is high, the output will follow the D input.

TQ 3.10   The read line would need to be taken 'high', so that if the corresponding Q output was high, the AND gate would signal 1 and if the Q output was 'low', the AND gate would signal 0.

TQ 3.11   Each $\overline{Q}$ output will initially be 1.

EXERCISES

1   Complete the truth tables for the following circuit.

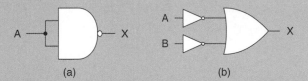

(a)   (b)

In each case suggest another gate that will perform the same logic function.

2   What is the difference between combinational logic and sequential logic?

3   Draw a diagram of an R-S flip-flop.

4   A clocked R-S flip-flop can be built from four NAND gates. Draw a diagram of a suitable circuit.

5   Draw a diagram of an 8-bit SIPO shift register.

6   If the D-type flip-flops in Figure 3.15 were replaced by positive going edge triggered devices, then write down the new output sequence produced by the counter. Assume that the counter is initialised with $Q0 = Q1 = Q2 = 1$.

7   What role does a tristate gate fulfil in a logic device.

8   Draw the logic circuits and truth tables for the following logic expressions

(a) A AND NOT B

(b) A OR (B AND C)

(c) (A AND B) NOR (A AND C)

Central processor unit operation

At the heart of a microcomputer system lies the *Central Processor Unit* (CPU) or *processor*. The processor runs a program by repeatedly fetching and executing instructions from main memory. By using a step-by-step approach, this chapter outlines the way in which this is done using a highly simplified processor. This will provide a foundation for understanding the operation of a real processor in Chapter 5. This chapter and Chapter 5 deal with the principles of *machine code* and *assembly language programming*. Machine code is the native code of the processor while assembly language is a more programmer friendly language that is translated into machine code by a program called an *assembler*. The full treatment of machine code and assembly language programming are found in other texts, some of which are listed in the references at the end of the book. The purpose of this chapter and the next is to explain and demonstrate how the components of a processor work together to carry out tasks.

4.1 CPU details

In Chapter 1 we identified the role of the data, address and control buses for transferring data between the processor and other system components, selecting a memory or I/O device and for synchronising the operation of system components respectively. In Figure 4.1 we see how the system buses relate to internal processor elements. In this simplified CPU architecture only memory read and write control signals are shown.

IP is the *Instruction Pointer*. This is the name used by Intel in their processors, although *Program Counter* is a name commonly used for this register. A *register* is a memory location within the processor. A is the name we have given to a general purpose register within the processor. Such registers are sometimes referred to as *accumulators*.

The *Memory Address Register* (MAR) holds data going on to the address bus. The *Memory Buffer Register* (MBR) holds data going to/from the data bus.

IR is the *Instruction Register*. This holds the instruction currently being executed. The *Arithmetic and Logic Unit* is called ALU for short. The status of the last ALU operation is held in the *Flags register*. The Flags register is often called the *Condition Code Register*.

Figure 4.1 Simple example architecture

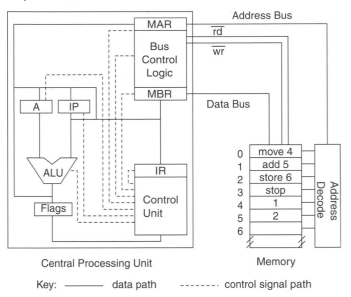

Central Processing Unit   Memory

Key: ———— data path   - - - - - - - control signal path

4.2 Processor–Memory interconnection

A program consists of a series of *instructions* or actions to be carried out by the processor. These actions are performed on data. Instructions and data are stored in primary, or main, memory during program execution. In Figure 4.1, instructions and data occupy various memory locations, each location being identified by a unique *address*.

The code in Figure 4.1 will cause a value to be read, or loaded, from memory location 4 into the accumulator in the CPU. A second value will then be read from memory location 5 and added to the first. Finally the result, currently in the accumulator, will be written back, or stored, in memory location 6.

4.2.1 Fetching instructions

When running a program, the processor fetches instructions by providing an address on the address bus and reading the instruction from the data bus. To carry out this task, the processor uses a number of internal registers.

A register is a small high-speed memory location used for the temporary storage of data or control information. The registers are connected together by an internal data path or *bus*. The flow of data along this bus is managed by the *Control Unit* (CU). To understand the purpose of these registers, we will examine how the first instruction in the program, move 4, is fetched.

Before running a program, the IP must be initialised with the address of the first instruction. This happens to be address 0 for the program shown in Figure 4.1. The *instruction cycle* begins when the address stored in the IP is transferred along the processor's internal data bus into the MAR.

Register Transfer Language (RTL) is a concise way of describing the movement of information through the system. We can represent the operation described in the previous paragraph by the RTL statement:

$$[MAR] \leftarrow [IP]$$

The Register Transfer Language or RTL statement reads as follows:

'the content of'	[ ]
'the instruction pointer register'	IP
'replaces'	$\leftarrow$
'the content of'	[ ]
'the memory address register'	MAR

Figure 4.2 illustrates the operation just described.

The MAR provides an *interface* between the processor's internal bus and the external address bus. Once in the MAR, the instruction address is passed along the address bus to the memory unit. As mentioned in Chapter 1, a bus provides an electrical path to carry information from one unit to another. Having made this transfer, the IP is incremented.

The RTL statement for this operation is:

$$[IP] \leftarrow [IP] + 1$$

TQ 4.1 Describe the meaning of this RTL statement.

The IP now contains $0 + 1 = 1$, which is the address of the next instruction, *add 5*. The IP enables the CPU to keep track of where it is in the program.

As the memory module decodes the address provided on the address bus and locates the *memory cell* containing the instruction, the processor

Figure 4.2 Showing the operation [MAR] ← [IP]

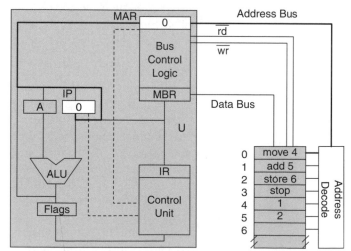

generates a *read signal* on the *control bus* ($\overline{\text{RD}}$). The memory unit responds by placing a copy of the contents of this memory location on the data bus. The item moved is the content of memory address 0, which is the instruction *move 4*.

This instruction is now copied from the data bus and latched in to the MBR. We represent this phase of the instruction cycle by the RTL statement:

$$[\text{MBR}] \leftarrow [\text{M}([\text{MAR}])]$$

which reads:

'the content of the MAR'	[MAR]
'provides an address for'	([MAR])
'the memory module (M)'	M([MAR])
'whose content'	[M([MAR])]
'replaces'	$\leftarrow$
'the contents of the MBR'	[MBR]

TQ 4.2   What is the value of [M(0)]?

This operation is illustrated in Figure 4.3.

The MBR *interfaces* the processor's internal bus to the external data bus. A device that temporarily holds a value as it moves between two other devices is often termed a *buffer*. In this case the MBR acts as a buffer between the CPU registers and the memory module.

Having *buffered* a copy of the instruction into the MBR, the processor now transfers the instruction along its internal data bus into the IR, as shown in Figure 4.4.

Figure 4.3   Showing the operation [MBR] ← [M([MAR])]

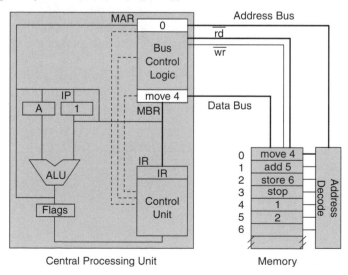

Figure 4.4   Showing move 4 being transferred into the instruction register

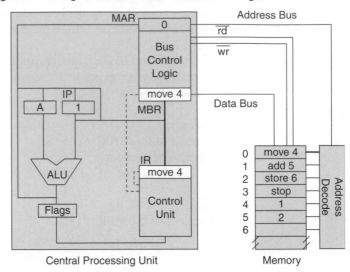

TQ 4.3   Represent this stage of the operation using RTL.

Once in the IR, the instruction is decoded by the *Control Unit* (CU). The CU generates a sequence of control signals from information provided by the instruction's *operation code* (opcode), as shown in Figure 4.5. This phase of the instruction cycle is represented by the RTL statement:

$$CU \leftarrow [IR(\text{opcode})]$$

Control signals are used to initiate events, such as the movement of data between registers. The type and order of events varies from one instruction to another. To generate sequences of such events, a timing reference source or *clock* is used. The clock unit shown in Figure 4.5 provides the CU with this high frequency *clock signal*.

This completes the *fetch* part of the instruction cycle, this phase being the same for all instructions. Following this, the processor enters an *execute* phase, which varies according to the type of operation specified in the instruction. Before we examine the execution phase of *move 4*, we need to describe the *format* of our instructions.

4.2.2   *Instruction format*

Machine instructions, or machine code, formats are dependent upon the architecture of the processor on which they run. As we explained in Section 1.5, machine code, unlike higher-level programs such as C, cannot be transferred from one processor architecture to another. The simple example architecture that we are using in this chapter has a correspondingly simple instruction format. Some of the richness and complexities of machine code are demonstrated in the next chapter where we describe an actual processor.

Figure 4.5   Showing the move 4 instruction being decoded

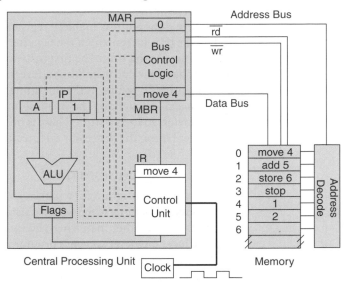

Figure 4.6   Simple instruction format

(1) Machine instructions

Instructions are stored and manipulated by a computer in binary form. For example, the instruction we have symbolically represented as *move 4* might have a binary form 1011001000000100, which we call machine code. Logically, this instruction is composed of two fields, as shown in Figure 4.6(a). These fields are called the *opcode* and the *operand*. The opcode specifies the type of operation the processor is to perform, while the operand specifies the data item to be used. The data item to be used is identified in our simple architecture solely by the *operand address.* The format of the *move 4* instruction is shown in Figure 4.6(b).

The first byte is a binary code for the operation move and specifies that the processor is to move data into its data register. The second byte is the address of the data to be moved, which is address 4.

TQ 4.4   How many different opcodes can we represent with 8 bits?

Although each pattern could be used to represent a different instruction, in practice, some instructions use several *addressing modes*, each mode being identified by a different opcode. We will discuss the addressing modes of a real processor in Section 5.3.

Note that the address in the IP register specifies a 16-bit memory module. When the IP is incremented the next item is not the next bit or the next byte but the next 16-bit unit. The first instruction (move 4) is at address 0. IP initially has the value 0 and thus addresses the 16-bit *move 4* instruction. Incrementing IP results in IP containing the value 1 and thus addresses the 16-bit *add 5* instruction. The smallest unit of memory that can be addressed is often referred to as a *word*. There is no standard size for a word as it is dependent upon the processor architecture.

(2) Assembly language instructions

When writing a program for a particular processor, it is easier to write and understand programs when the instructions are represented symbolically, such as *move 4*, rather than when they are written in machine code. For this reason, most *low-level language* programs are written in *assembly language*.

An assembly language instruction has a *mnemonic* to represent the opcode, such as *move*, and symbols to specify operands or their addresses, such as *4*. If registers are used to specify operands, then these are also included. After writing a program in assembly language, each instruction must be translated into machine code before the program can be loaded into memory and executed by the processor. This is carried out by a program called an *assembler*.

4.2.3 Executing instructions

To support instruction execution, our simple processor uses a register (A) and an ALU, as shown in Figure 4.1. The ALU is a logic block which performs a limited number of arithmetic and logic operations, such as ' $+$ ', ' $-$ ', 'AND', etc. Our ALU operates upon data that has been stored in A or which has been buffered in the MBR. After performing such an operation, the content of A is overwritten with any results produced.

(1) Executing move 4

Having decoded the opcode move as, 'move data from memory into the register A', the CU begins the instruction execution phase by generating control signals to perform the following actions:

$$1.\ \ [MAR] \leftarrow [IR(\text{operand address})]$$

This operation transfers the operand address into the MAR, as shown in Figure 4.7. The CU then performs a memory read operation in the usual way, buffering a copy of the contents of memory address 4 into the MBR:

$$2.\ \ [MBR] \leftarrow [M(4)]\ (\text{This is equivalent to } [MBR] \leftarrow [([MAR])])$$

To complete the execution of this instruction, the CU transfers the operand from the MBR into A:

$$3.\ \ [A] \leftarrow [MBR]$$

These stages are also shown in Figure 4.7.

Figure 4.7 Showing execution of move 4

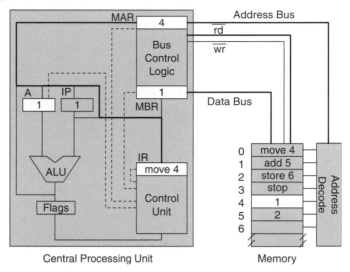

Central Processing Unit   Memory

Having fetched and executed this instruction, the processor begins another instruction cycle. This cycle of fetching and executing instructions is called the *fetch–execute cycle*, and is repeated until the program is terminated in some way. In our simple program, this is accomplished using a special instruction called *stop*.

TQ 4.5   Using RTL, describe the fetch phase of the next instruction cycle.

(2) *Executing add 5*

During decoding, the opcode of the instruction *add*, is interpreted as 'add the contents of a memory address to the data stored in A'. Because the memory address is contained in the operand address, instruction execution begins with the operation:

1. [MAR] ← [IR(operand address)]

This is followed by a memory read operation to fetch the operand:

2. [MBR] ← [M(4)]

The operands to be added are now in A and the MBR, as shown in Figure 4.8. To perform the addition, a control signal from the CU is used to set the ALU into the addition mode. The operands are then transferred into the ALU, which we can represent by:

3. ALU ← [A]; ALU ← [MBR]

It is possible to perform these operations in *parallel* because the operands can move along separate internal data paths. It can be seen from Figure 4.8

Figure 4.8 Showing the parallel operations ALU ← [A] and ALU ← [MBR]

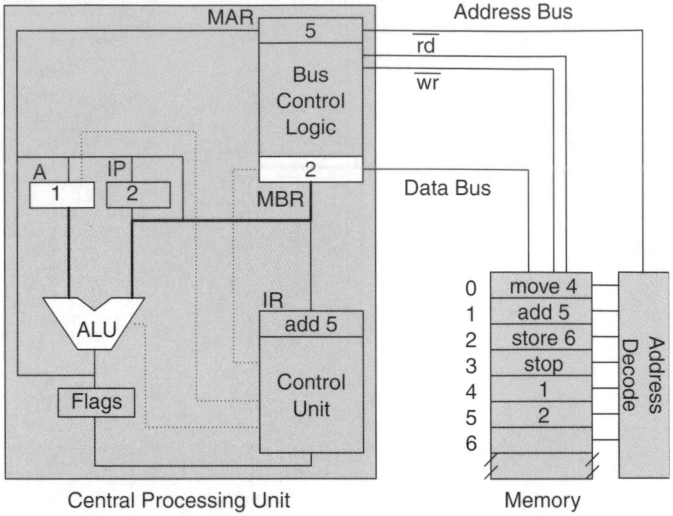

Figure 4.9 Showing the operation [A] ← ALU

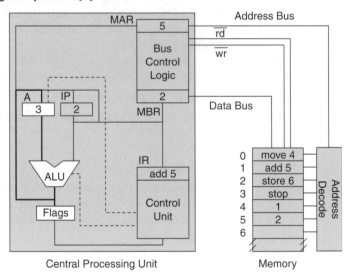

that the circuits connecting the accumulator to the ALU are different to the circuits connecting the MBR to the ALU. It is thus possible to perform both operations at the same time.

Once in the ALU the data is added and the result, $1 + 2 = 3$, is deposited back into the register A, as shown in Figure 4.9. We represent this operation by:

$$4. \quad [A] \leftarrow ALU$$

The processor records information on the outcome of this operation in a *Flags* Register, by setting or clearing certain bits or *flags*. For example, because the result 3 is a non-zero number, the ALU clears (make zero) the zero bit or Z-flag in the Flags register.

TQ 4.6 Another flag is the carry flag. If there is a carry out of the most significant bit of the result then the carry bit will be a one (refer to Sections 2.5 and 3.2.2). If there is no carry out then the carry flag will be zero. How would the carry flag, be affected in this example?

This completes the fetch–execute cycle for the instruction *add 5*. The third instruction in our program, *store 6*, is now fetched in the usual way.

(3) Executing store 6

During decoding, *store 6* is interpreted as, 'store the contents of register A in a memory address 6'. The control unit responds with the following operations:

$$[MAR] \leftarrow [IR(operand\ address)]$$
$$[MBR] \leftarrow [A]$$
$$[M(6)] \leftarrow [MBR]$$

TQ 4.7 What do you think the operation $[M(6)] \leftarrow [MBR]$ represents?

This last operation involves the generation of a write signal on the control bus, as shown in Figure 4.10.

Figure 4.10 Showing a memory write operation

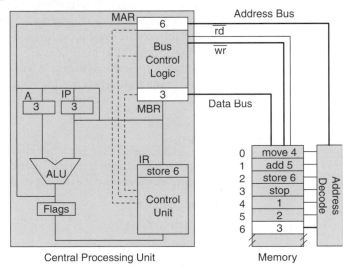

Having completed the execution of instruction *store 6*, the processor fetches and executes the final instruction in the program, *stop*. As mentioned earlier, this instruction halts any further execution of the program.

4.3 Improving performance

When describing microprocessor performance we are primarily concerned with the time it takes the CPU to execute a program. This is the CPU time and is given by:

$$\text{CPU time} = \text{cycles for program (n)} \times \text{clock cycle time (T)}$$
$$= \text{CPI} \times \text{number of instructions (I)} \times \text{T}$$

where CPI is the average number of Clock cycles Per Instruction

The shorter the CPU time, the better the performance (P), which we can express in terms of the instruction execution rate as:

$$P = \frac{1}{\text{CPUtime}} = \frac{1}{\text{CPI} \times \text{I} \times \text{T}}$$

Because $1/T$ = the clock frequency (f), then $P = f/\text{CPI} \times \text{I}$

If f is expressed in MHz and I in millions of instructions, then P is in MIPS (Millions of Instructions Per Second).

TQ 4.8 What is the value of P for a SPARC processor that is clocked at 16.67 MHz, when 1.2 million instructions are executed with a CPI of 1.3?

Because different programs have different mixes of instructions, the value of P varies according to the type of program under test. For this reason, when comparing processor performance, synthetic programs or *benchmarks* are often used. These have a representative mix of the types of instruction used in real programs.

The fetch–execute cycle is performed many millions of times a second. It is therefor important to make it as efficient as possible. A small reduction in the time taken to perform the cycle will generate a large performance gain. There are many techniques used to squeeze as much as possible from a cycle.

4.3.1 *Pipelining*

One approach to improving performance is to divide the fetch–execute cycle into a number of *stages*. An example of this may be to divide the cycle into:

1. instruction fetch;
2. instruction decode;
3. execution stage;
4. write-back.

Figure 4.11 Comparison of clock cycles required to perform pipelined and non-pipelined operations

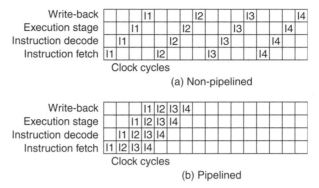

(a) Non-pipelined

(b) Pipelined

It would thus be possible to fetch the first instruction then while it is being decoded to fetch the second instruction. This is an example of a *four-stage instruction pipeline*. Using this simple arrangement, it may be possible to have four instructions in varying states of execution at the same time. A comparison of the execution of four instructions using pipelined and non-pipelined architectures can be seen in Figure 4.11. Each column represents a clock period.

The instruction fetch (IF) stage is used to fetch instructions from memory, or an instruction cache, into the first stage of the pipe. This requires the use of a *fetch unit*, which controls the Program Counter and buses to gain access to memory.

The instruction decode (ID) stage uses the control unit to decode the instruction and identify any source operands. Immediate operands and operands stored in the *register file* are moved into temporary ALU registers during this stage.

The execution (EX) stage is the stage in which the ALU performs operations on the operands stored in its temporary input registers and stores the result in its temporary output register.

The write-back (WB) stage is used to copy back the contents of the ALU's temporary output register to the destination register.

The first instruction (inst 1) enters the pipeline during the first clock cycle and is followed on subsequent cycles by instructions 2, 3, 4 and so on. At the end of each clock cycle, an instruction is latched into the next stage, so that after 4 clock cycles, the first instruction completes. It is at this point that the power of pipelining starts to become apparent, because after the 5th clock cycle, the second instruction completes, after the 6th clock cycle, the third instruction and so on. In other words, after the pipe has been *filled*, one instruction is completed every clock cycle, giving a speedup factor of 4.

TQ 4.9   How did we arrive at a speedup factor of 4?

An important point to note in arriving at this figure is that we have ignored the latency caused by filling up the pipe. This reduces the speedup factor to a value less than four, as the following analysis shows.

If a k-stage pipeline executes (n) instructions using a clock with a cycle time (t), then without instruction overlap, the total time to execute the instructions would be:

$$T_s = nkt$$

If we now allow the instructions to be executed in parallel, by overlapping their stages of execution, then the time taken is:

$$T_p = kt + (n - 1)t$$

where kt is the time for the pipe to fill up to the point where the first instruction completes and $(n - 1)t$ is the time taken for the remaining $(n - 1)$, instructions to execute at a rate of one per cycle. The speedup factor, S, is therefore:

$$S = \frac{nkt}{kt + (n - 1)t} = \frac{nk}{k + n - 1}$$

TQ 4.10 What is the speedup factor for a 4-stage pipeline when n = 50?

This last example shows that the speedup factor approaches the ideal value of 4, with long sequences of sequential instructions. Unfortunately, because of branch and other instructions that alter program flow, the pipeline sometimes becomes filled with instructions that are not needed. In such cases these instructions must be *flushed* from the pipe, so that the pipe can be filled with a new *stream* of instructions from the target address.

As we have seen, filling the pipe produces no throughput and wastes valuable clock cycles. Unless steps are taken to avoid this disruption, the performance advantages of using a pipeline can be severely reduced.

TQ 4.11 The MIPS R4400 and SPARC processors are discussed in Chapter 10. The MIPS R4400 processor uses a deeper 8-stage pipeline than the 4-stage pipeline used by SPARC processors. What disadvantage might there be in doing this?

Pipeline disruption can also be caused by instructions that need more than one clock cycle to execute. Such instructions include load instructions, or instructions that cannot proceed because they depend on the outcome of an earlier instruction that has yet to complete. Under such circumstances the pipeline may be forced to stop or *stall* for one or more clock cycles. The various sources of pipeline disruption are called *hazards*.

(1) Resource hazards

Main memory; caches; buses; register files; and functional units such as the ALU, are examples of some of the *resources* that must be shared by the instructions in a pipelined processor. If two stages need to access a resource at the same time, then the pipeline must stall until the conflict is overcome. This can arise, for example, when a load instruction is being executed, because it needs to make use of the fetch unit also needed by the IF-stage to fetch another instruction into the pipe. Under such circumstances, the IF-stage must be delayed by one or more clock cycles until the operand has been moved into the register file, which effectively increases the average number of clock cycles per instruction.

The problems of resource hazards are generally overcome using hardware duplication. This duplication may be in the form of separate instruction and data caches or dual instruction buffers for multiple instruction fetching.

Worked example

Even with hardware duplication, if the instruction following a load instruction needs to access the operand being loaded, then a delay will occur. By referring to Figure 4.11, explain why this is so.

Solution

After the load instruction is issued (moved from ID- to EX-stage), the following instruction, which is now in the ID stage, cannot be allowed to *read* the operand and move it into temporary ALU registers until the load instruction has finished *writing* the operand into the register file. Figure 4.12 provides an example of a data hazard.

(2) Data hazards

The hazard identified in the previous example is a *read-after-write* hazard, because if the instruction following a load is allowed to read an operand from a register before a write operation has completed, then the program will fail to work properly. There are also two other types of data hazard: *write-after-read,* when an instruction attempts to write to a register before another instruction has finished reading it and *write-after-write,* when an instruction manages to write to a register before an earlier instruction has written to it.

TQ 4.12   Is it possible to have a read-after-read hazard?

Figure 4.12   Data hazard example

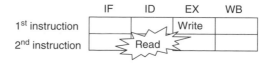

Data hazards can be avoided by using a software approach, that involves the compiler, or by using additional hardware.

The software approach relies on the compiler to identify and avoid data hazards by rearranging the order in which the instructions are executed. This technique is sometimes referred to as *static scheduling*, because the program instructions are rearranged at compile time rather than at run time. As we are considering processor architecture in this book we will not consider this technique any further.

TQ 4.13 Would scheduling the code in this way affect program debugging?

There are various hardware techniques that can be used to deal with data dependencies as they occur in the instruction stream, collectively called *dynamic scheduling*.

Figure 4.13(a) illustrates a read-before-write dependency, which arises when an instruction in the ID-stage attempts to use an operand from the register file, before it has been written back by an instruction currently in its EX-stage. It is not until this latter instruction completes the WB-stage, that valid data becomes available. To avoid stalling the pipeline, some architectures provide an additional data path to allow the operand from an instruction in the EX-stage to be forwarded directly from the ALU's temporary output register to one of its input registers, as shown in Figure 4.13(b). This technique is called *operand forwarding* and requires hardware capable of dynamically detecting the data dependency and switching the output to the appropriate path.

Figure 4.13 **(a) data dependency problem (b) operand forwarding**

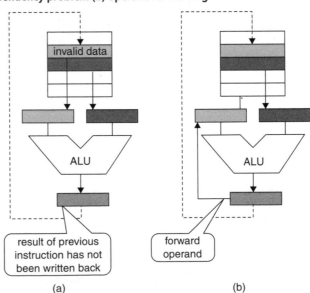

(a)　　　　　　　　　　(b)

Figure 4.14 Simple scoreboarding technique

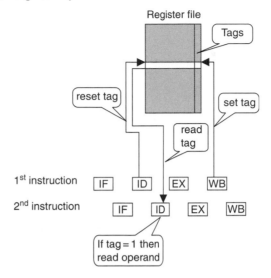

Unfortunately, operand forwarding cannot overcome the problem of load/store instructions, which we described earlier. For short pipelines, load instructions are often dealt with by using a *hardware interlock* that detects the hazard and stalls the pipeline, following the *issue* of a load instruction from the ID-stage to the EX-stage. This remains in force until the load instruction has cleared the pipeline, which creates a delay or *bubble* in the pipe and increases the average number of Clock cycles Per Instruction (CPI). A fairly simple circuit is all that is required to enforce the condition that all instructions following a load must be delayed, when the instruction immediately following it needs to access the operand being loaded.

The problem with *delayed loads* is that all instructions are held up just because one instruction depends on the outcome of the load operation. For pipelines with multiple execution units, it is possible to reduce the effect of this delay through a technique called *scoreboarding*. A simple form of score boarding is illustrated in Figure 4.14.

A 1-bit tag is included in the register file to indicate when a register contains valid data (tag = 1) or when the data is invalid (tag = 0). If an instruction is fetched that will write to a register, then during the ID-stage the tag associated with the register is reset (tag = 0). This indicates to any other instructions wishing to read the register that the value will be changed, and forces these instructions to wait. When the WB-stage is reached and the write instruction updates the register, the tag is automatically set (tag = 1), allowing any stalled instructions to proceed. The Motorola 88010 uses score-boarding to share its register file.

(3) Control hazards

Instructions that alter the Instruction Pointer (IP) and hence the order in which instructions are executed, can also reduce pipeline performance. Such instructions include *branch* instructions, which can be either *conditional* or

Figure 4.15   Effect of conditional branch instruction (i + 2)

Stage

Cycle	IF	ID	EX	WB	
1	i				start up
2	i+1	i			latency
3	i+2	i+1	i		
4	i+3	i+2	i+1	i	i completes
5	i+4	i+3	i+2	i+1	i+1 completes
6	j	i+4	i+3	i+2	i+2 completes
7	j+1	j	i+4	i+3	branch
8	j+2	j+1	j	i+4	penalty
9	j+3	j+2	j+1	j	

branch
taken

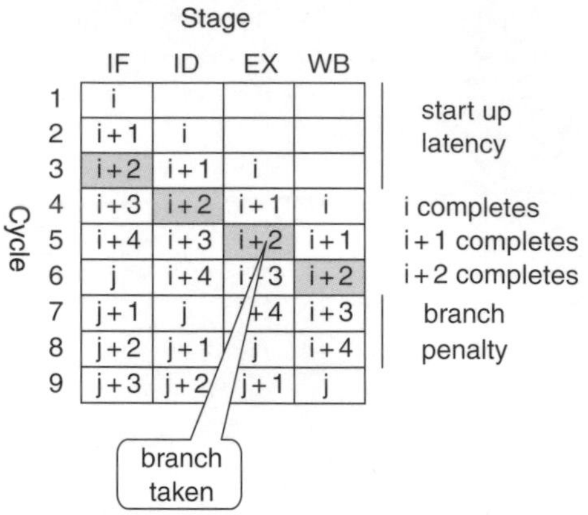

unconditional. Conditional branches generally pose more of a problem, as shown in Figure 4.15.

After the pipe has been filled with the sequential instructions i, (i + 1), (i + 2), ..., etc. and (i + 1) reaches its WB-stage, the conditional branch instruction (i + 2) enters the EX-stage. At this point the outcome as to whether the branch is taken or not is resolved. As we will assume the branch is taken in this case, the instructions (i + 3) and (i + 4) are redundant and must be flushed out of the pipe before the correct instruction sequence j, (j + 1), (j + 2), ..., etc. can proceed. With this particular pipe, two clock cycles are wasted, which we call the *branch penalty*. Of course, if the branch is not taken then no penalty is incurred.

TQ 4.14   Why would you expect an unconditional branch to incur a smaller branch penalty?

Because the probability of a branch instruction is quite high (typically between 10% and 30%), the effect of branch penalties can be very significant, especially if the probability of the branch actually being taken is also high. In fact, if we assume that:

$$P_b = \text{probability that an instruction is a branch}$$
$$P_t = \text{probability that a branch is taken}$$
$$b = \text{branch penalty}$$

$$CPI_{av} = \text{average number of Clock cycles Per Instruction}$$

Then it can be shown that $CPI_{av} = 1 + b \cdot P_b \cdot P_t$ [see exercise 11]

TQ 4.15   If $b = 2, P_b = 20\%$ and $P_t = 65\%$ then what is CPI_{av}?

We can think of the probability $P_b \cdot P_t$ as the effective fraction of the branch penalty incurred by the instructions. If we call this fraction P_e, then the object of any technique used to reduce the performance penalty of a branch instruction is to make $P_e \ll 1$. We will now discuss some of these techniques.

Branch prediction

Branch prediction uses some additional logic to guess the outcome of a branch before it is resolved at the EX-stage. One way in which this can be done is to examine the opcode at the decode stage and to make a presumption on the outcome, such as: 'all Branch on Equal instructions are taken' or 'Branch on Minus instructions are never taken'. The appropriate instructions are then fetched based on these premises, in the hope that they are correct, at least most of the time. Although this form of *static* branch prediction is relatively simple, it cannot be adapted to the particular instruction usage of a given program. With *dynamic* branch prediction however, account of program usage is taken using a small *branch history table*. This table is used to record the outcome of branch instructions that have already been executed and to predict the outcome of these instructions the next time they are executed. This is of special importance with program loops, where a branch might be executed several hundred times before an exit is made. Getting the prediction wrong every time, which could be the case with static prediction, would severely affect performance.

Branch bypassing

By using separate First-In-First-Out (FIFO) instruction buffers, it is possible to fetch both the instruction sequence following a branch and those from the branch target at the same time. This prevents the processor from stalling and allows it to continue processing instructions irrespective of whether the branch is taken. This is illustrated in Figure 4.16.

The buffer containing the unused instruction is merely flushed, the next time a conditional branch is encountered in the instruction stream.

Figure 4.16 Dual-buffer branch bypass

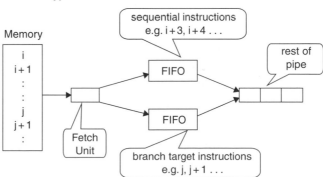

Unfortunately, if two or more conditional branch instructions manage to enter a buffer, then this technique breaks down. This can be overcome by using additional buffers, but this adds to the cost of the implementation.

Delayed branch

This is a software approach and uses static scheduling in the same way as it was used when we considered data dependency. At compile time, a number of delay slots are inserted after the conditional branch instructions, which the compiler tries to fill with instructions that will be executed whether the branch is taken or not. For example, the compiler can determine whether a few instructions that precede the branch can be moved into the delay slots after the branch. In this way, when the branch executes, these instructions are still executed and therefore there is no need to flush the buffer. No operation, *nop*, instructions are used to create the delay slots. The *nop* instruction consumes instruction cycles but has no effect. These instructions are also utilised in the delayed loads described earlier. The *nop* instructions used to create the delay slots cannot always be filled, so a certain percentage of branch penalty can still be expected.

4.3.2 *Cache memory*

Programs exhibit behaviour called *locality of reference*. This refers to the fact that when a program accesses a memory location it will generally be in the same locality as (i.e., physically close to) the last location referenced. The next instruction to be executed is likely to be the one in the next memory location or close to it. The next operand is likely to be in the next memory location or close to it. Cache memory makes use of this behaviour. Cache memory is a very fast form of memory. It needs to be placed very close to the CPU in order to maintain the low access times. There is a limit to how much memory can be placed close enough to the CPU to maintain the required data rate. The inclusion of additional cache memory also increases the cost of the system that may be undesirable in a cost conscious market. The Cache memory is used to hold those instructions and data that are likely to be required in the very near future.

When the next instruction is to be fetched the cache memory is checked first. Most of the time the instruction will be found there. If it is not, then a block of memory is transferred from main memory and loaded into cache. This block will include the currently required instruction and the following block of instructions. These instructions are the ones that are likely to be required next.

It is possible to place instructions and data in different cache memories. This type of architecture is called a *Harvard Architecture*.

There are several places where a cache memory may be located in a system. It is possible to place the memory within the CPU or external to the CPU or to have both. Figure 4.17 shows the architecture of Figure 4.1 amended to support both internal and external cache memory. The internal memory is of

Figure 4.17 Cache memory added to Figure 4.1

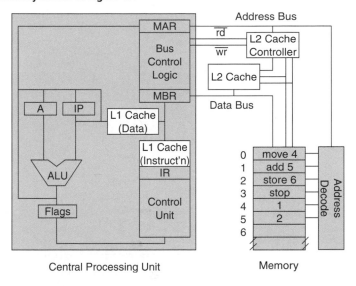

Central Processing Unit   Memory

the Harvard type. The internal cache memory is usually referred to as *level 1 cache*. The cache that is outside the CPU is known as *level 2 cache*.

4.4 The use of microcode

The decoding of instructions in the instruction register was originally carried out by combinational logic circuits. As instruction sets became bigger and more complex so the decode circuits grew in size and complexity. Designing and testing these circuits becomes more and more difficult and error prone.

An alternative approach is to have a processor within the processor to decode and execute instructions.

4.4.1 Hardwired control unit

A hardwired control unit is essentially a logic block, consisting of gates; flip-flops; decoders; and other digital circuits. When an instruction is read into the IR, the bit pattern, in combination with the bit pattern of the *sequence counter*, provides an input to the logic block, as shown in Figure 4.18. The key fields in the instruction always line up with fixed input positions in the logic block; for example, the opcode bits might always line up with input positions 0 to 5. The output bit pattern provides control signals for the data path together with information needed to control the timing signal generated by the sequence counter on the next clock cycle. In this way each instruction causes an appropriate sequence of control signals to be generated. Condition codes (flags) or other information received from the data path can be used to alter the sequence of control signals.

Figure 4.18 Hardwired control unit

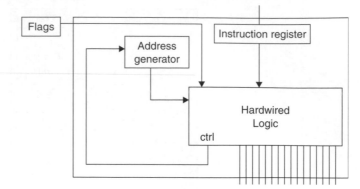

Hardwired control units can only be altered by rearranging the wiring used to connect the various logic components together. This is a time consuming exercise and usually involves re-designing the complete logic block. The main points to be noted about hardwired control units are:

1. They minimise the average number of clock cycles needed per instruction.
2. They occupy a relatively small area (typically 10%) of the CPU chip area.
3. They are less flexible than microprogrammed control units and cannot be easily modified without extensive re-design.
4. They are impractical for use with complex instruction formats.

4.4.2 Microprogrammed control unit

The microarchitecture of our simple processor is illustrated in Figure 4.19(a).

The opcode of the instruction in the instruction register is used to generate the start address of a set of *microinstructions*, or *microprogram*, to be performed to carry out the instruction. Within the control unit, is a special memory module in which there is a routine for performing each opcode. The microinstructions in this memory consist of a bit for each control signal used within the CPU. A microinstruction format to support our simple architecture is shown in Figure 4.19(b).

The 'ctrl' field in the microinstruction provides some basic flow control such as '*branch n*'. The L1 and L0 bits will determine which function the ALU is to perform. The rd and wr bits are used to inform the bus control logic which bus function is to be performed. The remaining bits are used to load a value into a register or to place the content of the register onto the bus. If Bi is set, then the MBR will be loaded from the CPU internal bus, unless there is a signal for the bus control logic indicating the system buses are to be used. If wr is set, then the MBR will be loaded from the internal buses. If rd is set, then the MBR will be loaded from the system buses. The same consideration applies when values are output from the MBR when Bo is set. As the MAR

Figure 4.19 Microarchitecture example

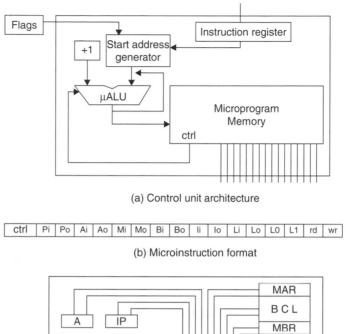

(a) Control unit architecture

ctrl	Pi	Po	Ai	Ao	Mi	Mo	Bi	Bo	Ii	Io	Li	Lo	L0	L1	rd	wr

(b) Microinstruction format

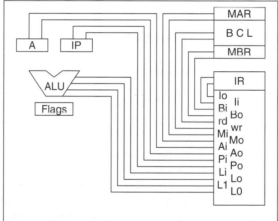

(c) Control signals between the control unit and other CPU components

can only be loaded from the CPU and output onto the address bus the status of rd and wr are not an issue.

The use of *microsubroutines* is a feature included in several microprogrammed control units, because many microprograms require common sequences of microoperations which only need to be included at one place in memory. This reduces the size of the microprogram memory space and helps to reduce the area of silicon occupied by the control unit. One disadvantage in doing this is that some of these microinstructions may perform redundant operations, which adds to the execution time of the instructions.

Hardwired control units are faster than their microprogrammed counterparts. This is because they avoid microprogram memory read operations, which tend to be slower than the basic Boolean operations performed by the hardwired decoder logic, and because they are optimised to take advantage of the regular instruction format.

There are other ways in which a microprogrammed control unit can be constructed, but we shall not consider them in this book. The main points to be noted about a microprogrammed control unit are:

1. They are flexible and allow designers to incorporate new and more powerful instructions as VLSI technology increases the available chip area for the CPU.
2. They allow any design errors discovered during the prototyping stage to be removed.
3. They require several clock cycles to execute each instruction, due to the access time of the microprogram memory.
4. They occupy a large portion of the CPU chip area.

Several microinstructions can usually be executed in a single CPU clock cycle. A control unit may be designed using both microcode and hardwired components to improve performance.

4.5 Summary

Programs are executed by repeatedly fetching instructions from memory into the processor and then executing them. This is called the fetch–execute cycle. Three buses are used to exchange information with the memory module: an Address Bus, a Data Bus and a Control Bus. To organise this flow of instructions, the processor uses a number of special purpose registers including: an Instruction Pointer, an Instruction Register, a Memory Address Register and a Memory Buffer Register.

Instruction decoding is performed by a Control Unit, which generates appropriate control signals in response to the opcode of the instruction. The operand field is used to specify the address of any data required by the instruction. An ALU is used to carry out arithmetic and logic operations on data, temporarily stored in a data register or passed to it from the MBR. A Flag Register is used to record details about the result of the operation by setting and clearing flags.

CPU performance is enhanced through the use of pipelining and caching. A pipeline allows the CPU to overlap the execution of several instructions. Cache memory is a fast memory, which holds the instructions and data that will, it is hoped, be used in the very near future.

Microcode is used instead of, or in addition to, hardwired decode units to reduce development times.

Answers to in text questions

TQ 4.1 The contents of the program counter, plus one, replaces the contents of the program counter.

TQ 4.2   M(0) is the memory location whose address is 0.

   [M(0)] is the contents of memory location 0 or instruction move 4.

TQ 4.3   [IR] ← [MBR]

TQ 4.4   The number of unique bit patterns or opcodes we can represent with 8 bits is 2^8 or 256.

TQ 4.5   [MAR] ← [IP]
   [IP] ← [IP] + 1
   [MBR] ← [M(l)]
   [IR] ← [MBR]
   CU← [IR(opcode)]

TQ 4.6   There would be no carry and therefore the carry flag would be cleared.

TQ 4.7   The RTL statement, [M(6)] ← [MBR], represents a memory write operation, the operand being transferred from the MBR to address 6.

TQ 4.8 $P = \dfrac{16.67}{13 \times 1.2} = 10.69 \text{ MIPs}$

TQ 4.9   If each instruction were completed before the next instruction started, then it would take 4 clock cycles per instruction. With our 4-stage pipeline, this is reduced to 1 clock cycle per instruction, so instructions appear to execute 4 times faster.

TQ 4.10 $S = \dfrac{50 \times 4}{4 + 50 - 1} = 3.8$

TQ 4.11   If the pipe needs to be flushed, then it takes more clock cycles to refill the pipeline.

TQ 4.12   No, changing the order in which the two instructions read a register will not invalidate the operation of the program.

TQ 4.13   Yes, debugging a program by single stepping through the code would be more difficult to follow. In practice, debugging is normally carried out *before* optimising the code.

TQ 4.14   Because it can be detected at the ID-stage which reduces the number of redundant instructions fetched into the pipe.

TQ 4.15 $CPI_{av} = 1 + 2 \times 0.2 \times 0.65 = 1.26$ rather than the ideal value of 1.

EXERCISES

1   State the names and purposes of the following registers: IP, MBR, MAR, Flag.

2   Complete the following RTL description of an instruction fetch cycle:

$$[MAR] \leftarrow [\ ]$$
$$[\ ] \leftarrow [IP] + 1$$
$$[MBR] \leftarrow [M(\ )]$$
$$[\ ] \leftarrow [MBR]$$

3   What is the name of the bit marked Z in the Flags register? How is it affected when a data register is loaded with zero?

4   If an instruction were to modify the contents of the IP register, what affect would this have on the program?

5   For a 16-bit processor with byte addressable memory, the fetch-cycle is modified to include:

$$[PC] \leftarrow [PC] + 2$$

Why is this?

6   What is the difference between a machine code program and an assembly language program? How do we convert an assembly language program into machine code?

7   Describe a typical operation performed by a microinstruction. List the advantages and disadvantages of a microprogrammed control unit compared with a hardwired control unit.

8   An n-stage instruction pipeline can potentially increase the instruction throughput by a factor of n. Why is this seldom the case in practice?

9   Using a suitable example, explain what is meant by data dependency. Describe a dynamic scheduling technique to overcome this.

10 Why do conditional branch instructions tend to reduce the efficiency of an instruction pipeline? Explain what is meant by a delayed branch.

11 Given the following information about a pipeline:

   P_b = probability that an instruction is a branch;
   P_t = probability that a branch is taken;
   b = branch penalty;

then out of n instructions in a pipeline, how many will be

(i) branch instructions?

(ii) non-branch instructions?

(iii) branch instructions which when resolved result in a branch being taken?

(iv) branch instructions which when resolved do not result in a branch being taken?

If it takes $(1 + b)$ clock cycles to execute branch instructions that actually take place and only 1 clock cycle per instruction for the rest, then:

(v) How many clock cycles are needed to execute the n instructions?

(vi) What is the average number of clock cycles per instruction?

CHAPTER

C
H
A
P
T
E
R

5

The Intel 80x86 family of processors

So far in this book we have been looking at computer architecture generally. In this chapter, we will look at how the issues and techniques previously discussed manifest themselves in an actual processor that is commercially available.

The IBM-compatible *Personal Computer* uses a processor that can trace its roots back to 1971. This is equivalent to the middle ages in processor development terms! Over the intervening years the Intel 4004 processor has developed considerably in terms of technology, but the development in terms of architecture has been a case of evolution that has ensured that code designed to run on older versions of the processor will still run on the new processors.

In this chapter we will be looking at the architecture which would be recognisable to a programmer of the Intel 8086 microprocessor. The code examples that will be discussed will run on both the 8086 of the late 1970s and the Pentium 4 processors of the early 2000s. Appendix 4 looks at the development that has taken place in the processor's design over this period.

5.1 The programmers model

5.1.1 *General-purpose registers*

The 8086 has eight 16-bit general-purposes registers. The label and functions applied to these registers are given in Table 5.1. Although they are considered as general-purpose registers and can be used to store any 16-bit value they do have specific purposes for some instructions. These purposes are identified in Table 5.1. The AX register can hold any 16-bit value that may be data, an address or any other type of value but in some cases it will be assumed to hold instruction operands. An example of this is the divide (DIV) instruction. This instruction assumes the dividend will be in the accumulator (AX) and nowhere else. The AX, BX, CX and DX registers can be used as 8-bit registers in addition to being used as 16-bit registers. The 16-bit value can be subdivided into two 8-bit values. If we take AX as an example, then AX can be divided into two 8-bit values

Table 5.1   Intel 8086 general-purpose registers

AX	accumulator for operands and results data
BX	points to data in the DS segment
CX	counter for string and loop operations
DX	I/O pointer
SI	pointer to data in the segment pointed to by the DS register; source pointer for string operations
DI	pointer to data (or destination) in the segment pointed to by the ES register; destination pointer for string operations
SP	stack pointer
BP	pointer to data on the stack

labelled AH and AL. AH is the most significant 8-bits whilst AL is the least significant 8 bits.

5.1.2   Instruction pointer

The instruction pointer (IP) is a 16-bit register that is used to keep track of the next instruction to be executed. This is the only function for which this register can be used.

5.1.3   Segment registers and segment addressing

The 8086 has 16-bit registers. The largest amount of memory you can address with a 16-bit address is 2^{16} or 65536 locations. Each location is a byte, or 8 bits, in size. The 8086 however has a 20-bit address bus to enable it to address 1048576 locations. To enable the 8086 programs to access this entire memory, *segment addressing* is used.

A *segment register* is a 16-bit register that is used to provide the start address of a 65536-byte block (segment) of memory. To form the 20-bit address the least significant 4 bits of the 20-bit address are set to 0 (see Figure 5.1). The four segment registers and their default functions are listed in Table 5.2. The different addressing modes specify a particular segment. Operations on the *stack* will provide *offset* addresses for the *stack segment* (SS). (A stack is a data structure sometimes referred to as last-in-first-out. Data items are added to memory and then removed in reverse order. This type of structure is heavily used by a wide variety of software.) The segments may be in totally separate areas of memory or they may overlap. It is even possible for the four segment registers to hold the same values. In the examples that follow later in this chapter we will assume the segment registers all hold the same value. This simplifies things a little as we do not then need to worry about which

Figure 5.1 Showing relationship between segment register value and segment start address

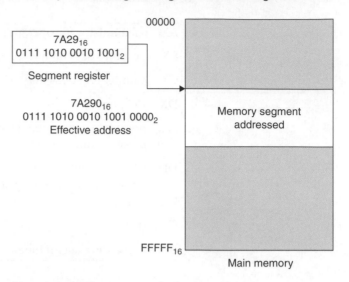

Figure 5.2 Effective address calculation

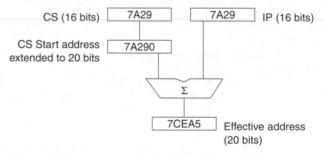

Table 5.2 8086 segment registers

CS	Code Segment start address of segment containing executable code
DS	Data Segment start address of segment containing program data
SS	Stack Segment start address of segment containing a stack data structure
ES	Extra Segment start address of a general segment

segment register a particular addressing mode uses. (This is not an assembly language programming course after all!)

A 16-bit address, which may be held in the IP register, for example, is added to this 20-bit value to form an *effective address* (see Figure 5.2). The IP value will always be assumed to be an offset within the code segment (CS).

Table 5.3 8086 flags

SF	Sign flag	indicates sign of the result of an arithmetic operation
ZF	Zero flag	indicates a zero result of an arithmetic operation
CF	Carry flag	indicates a carry from the high order bit as a result of an arithmetic operation
OF	Overflow flag	Indicates overflow as a result of an arithmetic operation
AF	Auxiliary flag	indicates a carry from bit 3 to bit 4 (from low order nibble to high order nibble) as a result of an arithmetic operation
DF	Direction flag	determines left/right direction for moving or comparing strings
IF	Interrupt flag	process/ignore all external interrupts
TF	Trap	enable single-step mode
PF	Parity flag	indicates the number of 1 bits in the result of an arithmetic operation

5.1.4 *Flag register*

The flag register (FR) is a 16 bit register in the 8086 but only 9 bits are used. The flags used are listed in Table 5.3. The first four flags listed above are those most commonly concerning an assembly language programmer.

Figure 5.3 shows how the components described above are interconnected in a block diagram.

5.2 Instruction types

In the Pentium 4 there are more than 400 different instructions, most of which have a variety of addressing modes (see Section 5.3). The 8086 processor has fewer than 200 instructions and it is this subset of instructions that we will consider in the next few sections. The principle reason for the increase in the number of instructions is the 144 instructions that support the SSE2 technology. (SSE refers to Streaming Single Instruction Stream Multiple Data Stream Extensions. These are instructions designed to support multimedia applications.) There are a number of sources listed under

Figure 5.3   8086 CPU functional block diagram

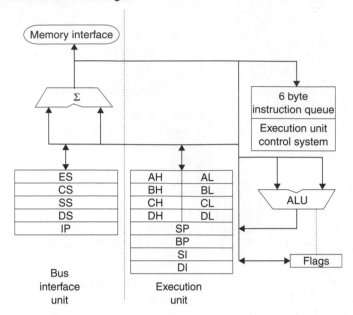

References at the end of this book, which can be accessed for those readers who would like to know more about the instructions available in the Pentium CPU.

The operation of the instructions presented will be described using the Register Transfer Language used in Chapter 4. All values are hexadecimal.

A processor such as the 8086/Pentium needs to offer a variety of instructions. These instructions can be broadly classified as:

5.2.1   *Data movement*

These instructions cause data to be moved to/from registers and memory locations. The data is not altered in any way by the movement.

> MOV AL,3476   value 3476 placed in AL register
> [AL] ← 3476

5.2.2   *Transformation*

These instructions cause the data to be converted from one data type to another. An example of this would be to change a byte data type to a word type.

> CBW   value in AL (8-bit) placed in AX (16-bit)
>   The 8th bit (most significant bit of the least significant byte; underlined in the following examples) is propagated through the most significant byte.
> if [AX] = 1234 then [AX] ← 0034
>   00010010 <u>0</u>0111000$_2$ to 00000000 00111000$_2$

if [AX] = 1291 then [AX] ← FF91
00010010 $\underline{1}$0010001$_2$ to 11111111 10010001$_2$

5.2.3 Data operations

These instructions cause data to be changed. These instructions can be subdivided into:

(1) Logical instructions. These instructions perform operations such as AND, OR and NOT.

> AND AL,BL   AL will hold the result of a logical AND between the values in the AL and BL registers.

(An AND operation is performed between the corresponding bits of each data item.)

if [AL] = 000E and [BL] = 0009 then [AL] ← 0008
(E_{16} = 1110$_2$; 9_{16} = 1001$_2$; 8_{16} = 1000$_2$)

(2) Shift/rotate instructions. The bits in the data location are moved along to the left or right. In the case of the rotate instructions the bit which falls off the end is fed back through the other end (possibly via the carry flag in the flag register).

> ROR AL,1   Bits in AL register will move one place to the right
> if [AL] = 7D then [AL] ← BE
> (0111 1101 becomes 1011 1110)

(3) Arithmetic instructions. These instructions include 'add', 'subtract', 'multiply' and 'divide' operations on integer data types.

> ADD AL,5   Add 5 to the contents of the AL register
> if [AL] = 3C then [AL] ← 41

(4) Status flag instructions. These instructions clear or set flag bits.
> CLC   Clear carry flag
> [CF] ← 0

5.2.4 Floating point instructions

These instructions provide a wide range of operations on floating point data types. In the case of an 80x86 processor this would involve data being passed to an 80x87 floating point unit but an x87 FPU is included within the Pentium CPU. An explanation of how floating point manipulation is handled in these CPUs is covered in Section 5.7.

5.2.5 Flow of control

These instructions allow (un)conditional branching and looping. This includes instructions for calling and returning from subroutines.

> JMP 0100   Next instruction will be at location 0100.
> [IP] ← 0100

5.2.6 *Input/Output operations*

The 80x86 processors have separate memory and I/O address spaces. The I/O instructions cause data to be moved over the I/O buses to devices in the I/O address space. A device that connects the processor to the outside world is called a *port*. To communicate with a port it must be allocated an address known as the *port number*.

> IN AL,3F   Input a byte of data from port 3F.
> [AL] ← [Port(3F)]

5.2.7 *Interrupt instructions*

These instructions may cause a CPU interrupt or respond to an interrupt occurring.

> INT 21   Causes interrupt number 21 to be invoked.
> The service routine for interrupt 21 will be started.
> Each entry in the interrupt table is 4 bytes long
> [IP] ← [(21 * 4)]

The next three sections look at the construction and use of some of the instructions commonly used in assembly language programming. Section 5.7 considers floating point operations in a little more detail.

5.3 Addressing modes

There are a few instructions that operate on a single specific data item or require no data items at all. Examples of this type of instruction are the CLI (clear interrupt flag) and NOP (no operation) instructions. These instructions do not need to specify an *operand*. An operand specifies an item of data on which to perform an operation. Most instructions require one or two operands. The operands are registers, addresses of memory locations or the data items themselves. The operands are generally 8, 16 or 32 bits in length. There are a variety of ways of identifying which operand(s) to use.

(1) Register addressing (or register direct addressing)
   The operands involved in the operation are registers. Figure 5.4 shows an example where the CX and DX registers are used as operands for a subtract operation.

(2) Direct addressing (or memory direct addressing)
   The operand specifies the address of the data item. In Figure 5.5, the second operand is the value 0100 which is the address of the operand to be used. Assemblers will also recognise a variation on this addressing mode known as direct with offset addressing. In this case an offset value is specified with the direct address operand (i.e. ADD AX,[0100] + 2). The assembler will however adjust the direct address operand by adding the offset value to it before translating it using a simple direct address (i.e. ADD AX,[0102]).

Figure 5.4 Example of register addressing

SUB CX,DX
Subtract value in DX register from value in CX register
[CX] ← [CX] – [DX]

Figure 5.5 Example of direct addressing

ADD AX,[0100]
Add the value at address 0100 to the content of AX register
[AX] ← [AX] + [M(0100)]

Figure 5.6 Example of register indirect addressing

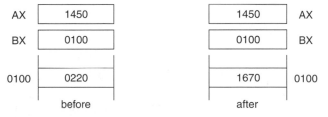

ADD [BX],AX
Add the content of AX to the memory location addressed by BX
[M([BX])] ← [AX] + [M([BX])]

(3) Register indirect addressing
   A register contains the address of the data item. This addressing mode
   can be used with only the BX, BP, SI and DI registers. In the example in
   Figure 5.6 the destination operand uses register indirect addressing. In
   this case the BX register contains the address of the data to be used.

(4) Base address relative addressing (or base-displacement addressing)
   The operand is found by adding an offset to a base value found at the
   address in the BX, SI, DI or BP registers. In Figure 5.7 the SI register
   provides the base address and the data is two locations previous to the
   address given in the SI register.

(5) Immediate addressing
   The operand of the instruction specifies the value to be used.

75

Figure 5.7 Example of base address relative addressing

ADD [SI–2],DX
Add the content of DX to the memory location addressed by SI–2
[M([SI]–2)] ← [DX] + [M([SI]–2)]

Figure 5.8 Examples of immediate addressing

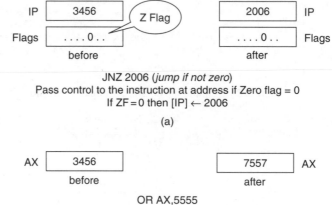

JNZ 2006 (*jump if not zero*)
Pass control to the instruction at address if Zero flag = 0
If ZF = 0 then [IP] ← 2006

(a)

OR AX,5555
Perform an OR operation between the content of AX and the value 5555
[AX] ← [AX] OR 5555
$(3456_{16} = 0011010001010110_2; 5555_{16} = 0101010101010101_2$
$7557_{16} = 0111010101010111_2)$

(b)

In Figure 5.8(a) an example of immediate addressing used by a conditional jump statement is illustrated. Conditional jump instructions can only use this addressing mode. Unconditional jump instructions (JMP) can use any of the addressing modes described in this chapter. The operand provided (2006) is the actual data that will be used. In the case of a jump instruction the operand will be loaded into the IP register.

TQ 5.1 Only one of the operands in the OR AX,5555 instruction illustrated in Figure 5.8(b) uses immediate addressing. Which one uses immediate addressing and what addressing mode does the other use?

Figure 5.9   Example of indexed base register indirect addressing

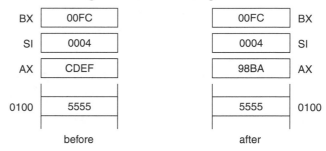

XOR AX,[BX+SI]
Xor the content of AX with the content of the memory location
addressed by summing the content of the BX and SI registers
$[AX] \leftarrow [AX] \text{ xor } [M([BX]+[SI])]$
$(CDEF_{16}=1100110111101111_2; 5555_{16}=0101010101010101_2$
$98BA_{16}=1001100010111010_2)$

Figure 5.10   Example of indexed base register addressing with displacement

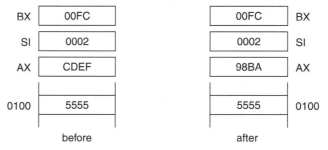

XOR AX,[BX+SI+2]
Xor the content of AX with the content of the memory location
addressed by summing the content of the BX and SI registers and 2
$[AX] \leftarrow [AX] \text{ xor } [M([BX]+[SI]+2)]$

(6) Indexed base register indirect addressing
The address of the data item is determined by adding an index register (SI, DI or BP) to the contents of the BX register. In Figure 5.9, BX is the base register and SI is the index that is added to it.

(7) Indexed base register addressing with displacement
The address of the data item is determined by adding an index register to the contents of the BX register as for the previous addressing mode but now also has a displacement added to the effective address. In Figure 5.10 the displacement is 2.

5.4 Instruction formats

Each instruction needs to specify an operation or *opcode*, and zero, one or two operands.

Figure 5.11 Example of a single byte instruction with no operand

Mnemonic	Opcode
PUSHF	10011100

Figure 5.12 Examples of a single byte instruction including a single operand

Mnemonic	Format	Machine code
PUSH AX	ooooorrr	01010000

(a)

Mnemonic	Format	Machine code
PUSH DS	ooossooo	00011110

(b)

Figure 5.13 Examples of multi-byte instructions including a single operand

Mnemonic	Format	Machine code
PUSH [BX]	ooooooo mm110aaa	11111111 00110111

(a) 2-byte instruction

Mnemonic	Format	Machine code
PUSH [BP + SI − 4]	ooooooo mm110aaa vvvvvvvv	11111111 01110010 11111100

(b) 3-byte instruction

Mnemonic	Format	Machine code
PUSH [DI + 0600]	ooooooo mm110aaa vvvvvvvv vvvvvvvv	11111111 10110101 00000000 00000110

(c) 4-byte instruction

The instruction *PUSHF* (push flags on to the stack) can possibly work only on one operand; the flag register. As there is only a single *stack pointer* (SP register) then the destination does not need to be specifically described. The operands therefor do not need to be specified so an 8-bit opcode is used: 10011100. This is illustrated in Figure 5.11.

Figure 5.12 compares two instructions that fit the opcode and a single parameter into a single byte. Figures 5.12(a) and (b) show two forms of the *PUSH* instruction. Figure 5.12(a) requires a general purpose register and Figure 5.12(b) a segment register as the operand.

The machine code for *PUSH AX* is made up of the opcode 01010 and the operand 000. Each register is represented by a different 3-bit value (see Table 5.4). The format of the machine code for *PUSH DS* is ooossooo. In this case the segment register field (ss) is in the middle of the opcode. In order to specify the DS register the *ss* field must be 11 (see Table 5.4). The opcode is 000ss110.

There is a third form of the push instruction in which the operand specifies the data item using a variety of addressing modes. The instruction still needs a single operand but may take two, three or four bytes. Three examples of this form of the push instruction are shown in Figure 5.13.

The first byte of the instructions in Figure 5.13 contains the opcode (11111111). The second byte specifies the addressing mode used.

Figure 5.13(a) provides an example of base relative addressing using the instruction *PUSH [BX]*. The value of *mm* here will be *00* to indicate no displacement and *aaa* will be *111* to specify base relative addressing (i.e. use the BX register). The machine code for this instruction is *11111111 00110111*. This is thus a 2-byte instruction.

If base relative indexed with a displacement is used such as *PUSH [BP + SI − 4]* then the format of the machine code becomes *11111111 mm110aaa vvvvvvvv*. *mm* will be *01* to indicate that a single signed byte will be used for the displacement. *aaa* will have the value *010* to indicate that the *BP* and *SI* registers are to be used. The resulting code is *11111111 01110010 11111100*. The value −4 is in two's complement notation (see Section 2.4) *11111100*. This form of the push instruction thus requires three bytes.

If indexed addressing with a large displacement (greater than 7F) is to be used as in *PUSH [DI + 0600]* then a 4-byte format is required. *mm* will be 10 to indicate a 2-byte unsigned displacement and *aaa* will be 101 to indicate the DI register is to be used. The resulting machine code is *11111111 10110101 00000000 00000110*. Note that Intel use the *small endian* approach to storing multi-byte values (i.e. least significant byte first) so the value *0600* actually appears in memory as *00 06*.

The push instruction is a relatively simple instruction to look at regards format, as there is only one operand to specify and all the data items addressed are 16-bit values. Many instructions however need to specify two operands and may need to specify 8-bit data items. (We will ignore the problems of 32-bit data items. See the References at the end of the book to investigate this further.)

Let us compare the two instructions *MOV CH,DH* and *MOV DX, [BX + 8]* (see Figure 5.14). *MOV CH,DH* specifies an 8-bit data item being moved from the *DH* register to the *CH* register. The format of this instruction is *oooooodw mmrrraaa* where *oooooo* is *100010*. *d* indicates whether the register specified in the *rrr* field is the source or destination (*1* indicates that *rrr* is the destination). *w* indicates whether 8 or 16 bits are to be transferred (*1* = 16-bits). The *CH* register is represented by the value *101* and *DH* by *110*. So the resulting machine code for this instruction is *10001000 11110101*. A *mm* value of *11* indicates that the *aaa* field specifies a register (*101* or *CH*). A *d* value of *0* indicates that *rrr* (*110* or *DH*) is the source.

The machine code for *MOV DX,[BX+8]* is *10001011 01010111 00001000*. The third byte contains the displacement value of eight. The *d* and *w* bits are both 1 indicating that the *rrr* field refers to the destination register and that a 16-bit data item is to be referenced. *rrr* is *010* which indicates the *DX* register.

Figure 5.14 Examples of multi-operand instructions

Mnemonic	Format	Machine code
MOV CH,DH	oooooodw mmrrraaa	10001000 11110101
MOV DX,[BX+8]	oooooodw mmrrraaa	10001011 01010111
	vvvvvvvv	00001000

Table 5.4   operand codes

	$w = 0$ rrr	$w = 1$ rrr	ss	$m = 0$ aaa	$m = 01; m = 10$ aaa
000	AL	AX	ES	BX + SI	BX + SI + Disp
001	CL	CX	CS	BX + DI	BX + DI + Disp
010	DL	DX	SS	BP + SI	BP + SI + Disp
011	BL	BX	DS	BP + DI	BP + DI + Disp
100	AH	SP		SI	SI + Disp
101	CH	BP		DI	DI + Disp
110	DH	SI		Direct	BP + Disp
111	BH	DI		BX	BX + Disp

Note 1: When aaa specifies BP then the effective address will be within the stack segment (SS used to determine the effective address) otherwise the effective address will be within the data segment (DS used to determine the effective address).

Note 2: If mm = 01 then the displacement is a single signed byte. If mm = 10 then the displacement is an unsigned two byte value.

Note 3: When mm = 1 then aaa values equivalent to rrr.

mm is *01* which indicates a signed byte displacement and an *aaa* value of *111* indicates base relative addressing with a displacement. The range of values for *rrr, ss, mm, aaa* in an 8086 CPU are given in Table 5.4.

5.5 Assembly code examples

We have provided in this section two short pieces of assembler code to illustrate how the basic machine code instructions may be combined to perform a couple of simple operations. It is possible to try these programs yourself and you will not even need to beg, borrow or steal an assembler if you have a PC running windows. MS-DOS had a basic assembler called *debug*, which could be used to assemble and edit small programs. Debug can be accessed from the Windows operating system and details of this utility are in Appendix 2 along with some further examples. (Section 5.7 includes an example of using floating point values.)

(1) Reverse the items in a list

The example code in Figure 5.15 will reverse the 8-bit values in a list. To make things simple all the segment registers hold the same value. This means we will not need to worry about which segment is the default for any of the

Figure 5.15 Code to reverse the items in a list

```
0100   DW 000A                    ;number of items in list
0102   DB 0,1,2,3,4,5,6,7,8,9     ;list
010C   DB 0,0,0,0,0,0,0,0,0,0     ;reserved for reversed list
0116   MOV SI,0                   ;start of original list
0119   MOV DI,[0100]              ;end of reversed list
011D   MOV BX,0102               ;address of original list
0120   MOV BP,[0100]              ;length of first list . . . .
0124   ADD BP,0101               ;. . . add start of first list
0128   MOV AL,[BX+SI]             ;read item from list
012A   MOV [BP+DI],AL            ;write to new one
012C   ADD SI,1                   ;point to next item
012F   SUB DI,1                   ;point to next space
0132   JNZ 0128                   ;repeat if not end of list

after execution

010C   9,8,7,6,5,4,3,2,1,0
```

addressing modes. The values next to each instruction are the memory addresses (actually an offset within the segment). The text which follows the semicolon (;) is comment to give you some idea what the program is doing. The first word defines the number of items in the list (0A hexadecimal or 10 decimal). (DW is an instruction to the assembler rather than a machine instruction. This sort of instruction is called an *assembler directive*. This directive tells the assembler to reserve a word of memory for a data item. DB means reserve a byte of memory. DW and DB are *define word* and *define byte*, respectively.) There then follows the 10 items in the list followed by the 10 locations in which the reversed items will be placed.

Each item will be read into the accumulator (AL) and written to the new list. SI is the index to the original list and DI the index to the new list. BX holds the address of the start of the original list and BP holds the address of the start of the new list. The first four instructions (starting 0116) initialise the registers. The next two instructions read from the first list and write to the second list. The index to the original list is then incremented. The index to the second list is decremented. If the second index has reached zero then the program has finished.

(2) *Find the mean of a list of numbers*

In this example we shall describe a program that will find the mean of a list of numbers. Each number will be an 8-bit value. The divide instruction takes integer data types as its operands and the result will also be integer. The result will be stored as the whole part followed by the remainder each as an 8-bit value. Handling of *real numbers*, numbers with fractional parts, will be discussed in Section 5.7 when we will consider floating point numbers. The program is given in Figure 5.16. As for the previous example we assume all segment registers hold the same value and only the offset within the segment is given.

81

Figure 5.16   Code to find the mean of a list of numbers

```
0100   DW 0008                      ;number of numbers
0102   DB 04,06,12,3A,07,0F,01,11   ;list of numbers
010A   DB 0,0                       ;result and remainder
010C   MOV SI,0                     ;index to list
010F   MOV DI,[0100]                ;index to result
0113   MOV BX,0102                  ;pointer to start of list
0116   MOV AX,0                     ;initialise accumulator (AX)
0119   ADD AL,[BX+SI]               ;add item to AL
011B   ADD SI,1                     ;increment list index
011E   CMP SI,DI                    ;check if at end of list
0120   JNE 0119                     ;add next item if not at end
0122   MOV CX,DI                    ;store no. items in CX
0124   DIV CL                       ;divide AX by no. of items
0126   MOV [BX+DI],AL               ;store quotient. . .
0128   MOV [BX+DI+1],AH             ;. . . And remainder

after execution

010A   0F
010B   06
```

The data is defined first. The first word is the number of data items (eight) followed by the eight data items. (Remember that all the values are in hexadecimal.) This is then followed by two bytes to store the result. The program starts at 010C with two instructions to set up the indexes. SI will act as an index to the list. DI will indicate where the result should be placed. BX is being used to hold the address of the start of the list. The instruction at 0116 initialises all 16 bits of AX though only the lower byte (AL) will be used in the calculation.

The next four instructions make up the loop that will sum the numbers in the list. The current number in the list is added to AL. The SI index is then incremented. If the end of the list is reached SI should equal DI. The CMP instruction at 011E will subtract DI from SI though SI will not be affected; only the flags. If the result is not zero then they are not equal so there will be a jump to the instruction at 0119.

When all the values have been totalled CX is loaded with the number of items in the list. This is so that an 8-bit divisor (CL) can be used. The divide instruction at 0124 is then executed. This will divide the value in AX by the value in CL. In the case of this example, 7E (the result from adding the eight numbers), will be divided by eight. Eight will go F times and this is the value that will appear in AL. The remainder (6) is placed in AH. The final two instructions write the result to memory.

When an 8-bit divisor is used (such as CL) then the dividend will be AX. If we had used CX or DI as the divisor then the dividend would be a 32-bit value created by combining DX and AX. DX being the most significant 16 bits and AX being the least significant. The quotient will be returned in AX with the remainder in DX.

TQ 5.2   Rewrite the code in Figure 5.16 so that it will be able to cope with up to 65535 data items with a combined value less than 65536. (This will require a 16-bit register to hold the result (AX) so 16-bit data items will need to be used. Initialise DX to 0. More advanced programming such as trying to add 8-bit data to a 16-bit register and trying to handle AX/DX as a 32-bit register pair is considered in material listed in the references at the end of this book.)

5.6 Operating modes

There are, as far as a low-level programmer is concerned, three *operating modes* in the Pentium CPU. The operating mode determines which features are accessible.

(1) Real-address mode
Presents to the programmer, the operating environment of the 8086 CPU. The similarity with the 8086 even extends to limiting the memory address space to what can be addressed by a 20-bit address bus. Operand size will also be limited to 16-bit values. This is the mode in which a Pentium processor will power up. The 8086 environment is extended to allow the ability to switch from this mode to either of the other two modes.

(2) Protected mode
This is the *native* mode of the Pentium, allowing segmented or 'flat' linear addressing and a choice of 16- or 32-bit operands. The paging mechanism available in this mode allows access to the 36-bit extended physical addressing capability. Paging is described in Section 9.9. There is a feature called virtual-8086 mode that enables 8086 processes to be executed in a protected multi-tasking environment. Multitasking is described in Section 9.3.

(3) System management mode (SMM)
This mode can be accessed by the operating system to access features such as power management and system security. There is a separate address space reserved for this mode and is addressed in the same manner as the real-address mode.

5.7 Floating point arithmetic

The averaging example in Section 5.6 demonstrates the use of integer division. An integer dividend is divided by an integer divisor resulting in an integer quotient and remainder. Different instructions and registers are required to perform floating point arithmetic. Floating point numbers are the way in which computers represent very large, very small and non-integer values. Appendix 5 explains floating point numbers. In systems based on earlier members of the 80x86 family the floating point arithmetic was actually performed by a totally separate chip – the 8087. The floating point registers and their instructions are now incorporated into the CPU.

There is a stack of eight 80-bit floating point (FP) registers. These registers can be used to process 16-, 32- or 64-bit two's complement format,

Figure 5.17   Floating point example

$$231.25 \times 369.1953125$$

Determining 32-bit Floating point values

$$231.25_{10} = 2^7 + 2^6 + 2^5 + 2^2 + 2^1 + 2^0 + 2^{-2}$$
$$= 11100111.01_2$$
$$= 1.110011101_2 \times 2^7 \qquad \qquad \text{(Biased exponent} = 127 + 7$$
$$= 134_{10}$$
$$= 10000110_2)$$

4	3	6	7	4	0	0	0_{16}
0 100	0011	0 110	0111	0100	0000	0000	0000

Sign | Biased Expo. | Significand

$$369.19531125_{10} = 2^8 + 2^6 + 2^5 + 2^4 + 2^0 + 2^{-3} + 2^{-4} + 2^{-7}$$
$$= 101110001.0011001_2$$
$$= 1.011100010011001_2 \times 2^8 \qquad \qquad \text{(Biased exponent} = 127 + 8$$
$$= 135_{10}$$
$$= 10000111_2)$$

4	3	B	8	9	9	0	0_{16}
0 100	0011	1 011	1000	1001	1001	0000	0000

Sign | Biased Expo. | Significand

$$85376.416015625_{10} =$$
$$2^{16} + 2^{14} + 2^{11} + 2^{10} + 2^8 + 2^7 + 2^{-2} + 2^{-5} + 2^{-7} + 2^{-9}$$
$$= 10100110110000000.011010101_2$$
$$= 1.0100110110000000011010101_2 \times 2^{16}$$
$$\text{(Biased exponent} = 127 + 16$$
$$= 143_{10}$$
$$= 10001111_2)$$

4	7	A	6	C	0	3	5_{16}	
0 100	0111	1 010	0110	1100	0000	0011	0101	01

Sign | Biased Expo. | Significand

$$= 85376.414062125_{10}!$$

32-, 64- or 80-bit FP data or 18 4-bit Binary Coded Decimal (BCD) digits. The floating point formats conform to the IEEE 754 standard described in Appendix 5. The arithmetic is performed in a 67-bit FP ALU and the rounding used can be selected by the programmer. The rounding and exceptions enabled are configured by a code word which will not be discussed any further in this book. There is a set of instructions specifically for manipulating the floating point registers. We will not go through all the instructions but will go through a simple example to give you the idea of how they work.

Figure 5.17 shows how the values that will be used in the code example were determined. The program will multiply 231.25 by 369.1953125. The correct result should be 85376.416015625. In FP format this will be:

$$1.110011101 \times 2^7 \times 1.011100010011001 \times 2^8$$

giving

$$1.0100110110000000011010101 \times 2^{16}$$

Figure 5.18   32-bit floating point code example

```
0100  DB 00,40,67,43              ;231.25
0104  DB 00,99,b8,43              ;369.1953125
0108  DB 00,00,00,00,00,00,00,00  ;Result
0110  FLD DWORD PTR [0100]        ;push 231.25 on to fp stack
0114  FLD DWORD PTR [0104]        ;push 369.1953125 on to stack
0118  FMUL ST,ST(1)               ;multiply two items on top of stack
                                  ;st replaced by result
011A  FST DWORD PTR [0108]        ;Store 32 -bit result in memory

Memory after execution of code

0100  00,40,67,43                 ;231.25
0104  00,99,b8,43                 ;369.195312
0108  35,c0,a6,47                 ;85376.414062125
010C  00,00,00,00                 ;unused
```

The important thing to notice here is that the result of the multiply operation can not be held fully in the 32-bit format. The eight FP registers form a stack so new values are pushed onto the stack and results can be popped off the top. The top item on the stack is referred to by the operand st (or st(0)). The next item will be $st(1)$ down to $st(7)$.

Figure 5.18 provides an example of a program that will multiply the two values explained in Figure 5.17. The values appear to be backwards because Intel processors store values least significant byte first. The values are defined one byte at a time as debug will not allow us to define a 32- or 64-bit value at one go.

The first two instructions push the two operands on to the FP register stack. The FMUL instruction multiplies the first value (st) by the second (st(1)) replacing the value held in the first register. FST takes the value at the top of the stack and writes it to memory. Note that a DWORD PTR specifies the operand as an address to a 32-bit value.

The result shown demonstrates the rounding error when storing the result as a 32-bit FP value. Because the least significant two bits are lost, the result is only 84376.4140625. If we use QWORD PTR instead (Figure 5.19) then the correct result is written to memory.

TQ 5.3   What would be the values used in the code example if the two values to be multiplied were in 64-bit floating point format instead?

In addition to instructions such as FADD, FMUL, FLD and FST, which operate on floating point values; FIADD, FIMUL and FILD will add or multiply st(0) by an integer value or, in the case of FILD, will push an integer on to the stack, that is FIADD WORD PTR [0100] will add a 16-bit integer value to the item at the top of the FP stack.

Primary memory

The memory system of a general-purpose computer is implemented using a number of different storage components. The purpose of this chapter is to describe the organisation of these components and the technologies used to implement them.

6.1 Memory hierarchy

A memory hierarchy has more than one level of storage, each level having a different speed and size. The technologies used to implement the memory components at each level include fast semiconductor technology, for the internal components close to the CPU, and slower magnetic and optical surface technologies, for the external components that are further away. Figure 6.1 illustrates a typical memory hierarchy.

The memory within the computer system, that is the CPU registers, the cache and main memory is categorised as *primary memory*. The remainder of this chapter will concentrate on this memory. *Secondary memory*, such as disks and tapes, will be the subject of the next chapter.

Figure 6.1   A memory hierarchy

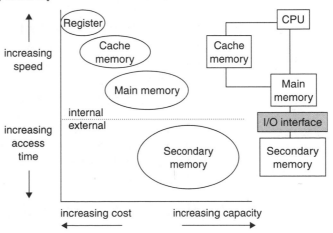

6.2 RAM and cache basics

Processor memory, implemented as a set of high-speed registers, occupies the highest level in the hierarchy. The register set provides only a very limited storage capacity and, as we found in Chapter 5, serves only as a temporary storage area for instructions and operands.

Main memory provides the largest internal storage area that can be directly accessed by the CPU, having a typical storage capacity of between 128 MBytes and 512 MBytes in a PC. There may be more in PCs being used as network servers and in many mainframe computer systems. To reduce cost, main memory is normally implemented using *Dynamic Random Access Memory* (DRAM) chips (see Section 6.3). Because DRAM operates at around one-tenth of the speed of CPU logic, it tends to act as a bottleneck, reducing the rate at which the processor can fetch and execute instructions. To compensate for this, many systems include a small high-speed cache memory.

Cache memory sits between the CPU and main memory and is usually implemented using more expensive *Static Random Access Memory* (SRAM) technology (see Section 6.3). This transparent memory is used for storing frequently used program segments. Each time the CPU requests an instruction or data word, the cache is always checked first. If the information is found in the cache, a 'hit' occurs and the instruction or data word is rapidly retrieved and passed directly to the processor. If the information is not in the cache, a 'miss' takes place and the slower memory is accessed instead. Once the data has been retrieved from main memory after a miss it is placed in cache memory in case it will be required again in the near future.

Memory that is not directly accessible by the CPU is called external memory and includes secondary storage devices such as magnetic disks, tapes and optical storage devices, such as CD-ROMs and DVDs. These devices, which must be accessed through input–output (I/O) interface circuits, are the slowest components in the memory hierarchy. They provide a high-capacity storage area for programs and data not immediately required by the processor.

TQ 6.1   Contrast the cost, in pence per KByte, of storing information in primary and secondary memory, given the following data: 256 MByte DRAM costs £70 and a 40 GByte hard disk costs £80.

A memory hierarchy is therefore used because slow-speed memory is cheaper than high-speed memory and because only currently executing program segments need to be held in internal memory.

6.3 Semiconductor memory chips

The basic element of a memory chip is the memory cell, which can store a single binary digit. These cells are often grouped together to form words, each cell in the group sharing a common address. *Random Access Memory* (RAM) cells can be read from and written to, while *Read Only Memory* (ROM) cells are either read from only or, in the case of *Programmable ROM* (PROM), read mostly. In the early days of the modern computer system, the main memory was called *core memory*. The reason for this was because each memory cell was a tiny ferrite toroid (ring) or core. The data was represented by the magnetic state carried by the core. A characteristic of this type of memory is that it will hold the magnetic state even when the power is removed from the computer. Magnetic core memories were then superseded by memory systems built from microelectronics (such as that in Figure 3.18) and they used an electrical charge to represent the data. This type of memory requires the continued presence of an electricity supply to maintain the data. Once the electricity is removed the data is lost. The former type of memory is known as *non-volatile* memory while the latter is *volatile*. ROM memory is an example of non-volatile microelectronic memory but more on that later.

6.3.1 *Random Access Memory (RAM)*

There are two basic types of semiconductor RAM: *Static* RAM (SRAM) and *Dynamic* RAM (DRAM). The internal organisation of a typical SRAM memory chip is shown in Figure 6.2.

The cells are arranged in a matrix with rows and columns. An address supplied on the address line A_0, ..., A_9 is used to select a particular row, each cell in the row being connected to a separate column line. The cells are arranged in 8s which we call *byte organised*. The column lines are used to transfer data bytes between the addressed rows and the data lines D_0, ..., D_7, which connect the chip to the data bus.

Figure 6.2   1024 $\times$ 8-bit static RAM chip organisation

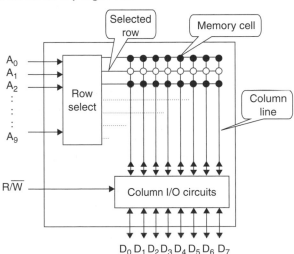

Figure 6.3 1024 × 8-bit SRAM chip

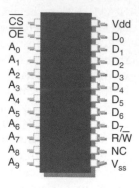

TQ 6.2 How many rows can the 10 address lines A_0, ..., A_9 select?

Reading and writing data is controlled by the read–write ($R/\overline{W}$) control line, which is connected to the column I/O circuit. A read operation is selected by taking this line high, and a write operation is selected by taking the line low. This latter state is indicated by the bar over the W.

SRAM cells store data by using cross-coupled *transistor* circuits acting as R-S flip-flops (see Section 3.3). (A transistor is a sort of microelectronic switch. It is the basic building block of logic gates.) Because these cells require four or six transistors per cell, SRAM chips can store fewer bits per mm² of silicon than DRAM. They are also more expensive in terms of the costs per bit of storage space. The main advantage of SRAM over DRAM is its shorter access time. A typical SRAM chip is shown in Figure 6.3.

The chip select pin, $\overline{CS}$, is used to select the chip for read or write access, and the output enable pin, $\overline{OE}$, is used during a read operation, to gate data from the memory array to the output data pins D_0, ..., D_7. The pins labelled V_{dd} and V_{ss} are for supplying power to the chip.

TQ 6.3 What does the bar over the chip select pin indicate?

DRAMs store information using one transistor per memory cell and currently provide the most compact and low-cost form of semiconductor memory. Each storage element is basically a *capacitor* (a device for storing charge), with a transistor being used to enable reading and writing. When a '1' is stored, the charge on the capacitor immediately begins to leak away. To maintain the charge, a special *refresh circuit* is used, which periodically renews the charge on all cells about once every 16 ms. DRAM cells are usually organised into a square matrix, with separate decoders for the rows and columns, as shown in Figure 6.4. To read data from a DRAM memory cell a particular memory row is selected by the row select circuit. A particular

Figure 6.4   16384 × 1-bit DRAM organisation

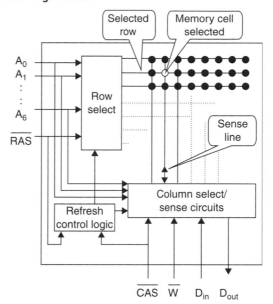

cell in the row is selected by the column select circuit. The sense circuit then determines whether a charge is present in the selected cell. The read operation from a DRAM memory cell is destructive and alters the charge state of the cell, the sense circuit is responsible for restoring this state immediately after a read operation, either by adding charge or by removing it. This causes a time delay between successive requests to read a DRAM cell, which is called the cycle time.

To read a particular cell, the row address is provided on A_0, ..., A_6 and latched into the row select decoder by a *row address strobe* ($\overline{RAS}$). This is followed by the column address, which is latched into the column select decoder by a *column address strobe* ($\overline{CAS}$). After a short delay, the data bit appears at D_{out}.

Data is written into a selected cell by applying the data to D_{in} and by asserting the write control signal $\overline{W}$, just before the column address is latched with the $\overline{CAS}$ strobe. Periodic refreshing is then carried out using an internal address generator and an external timing circuit. The timing circuit applies pulses to the address generator using the $\overline{RAS}$ and $\overline{CAS}$ strobes, which refreshes the memory chip a row at a time.

Figure 6.5 shows a typical *bit organised* DRAM chip. Because each chip only stores one bit, an 8-bit word, for example, would be stored using eight chips. Until recently a set of memory chips were placed on a small board called a *Single In-line Memory Module* (SIMM). PCs available today generally provide this form of memory on *Dual In-line Memory Modules* (DIMMs). These modules combine several chips on a small circuit board that is plugged into a retaining socket on the motherboard.

Figure 6.5 (a) 16384 × 1-bit DRAM chip (b) DIMM

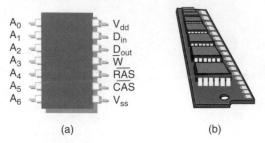

(a)

(b)

Figure 6.6 16K × 8-bit ultraviolet EPROM

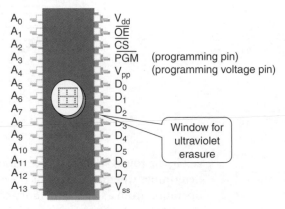

6.3.2 Read Only Memory (ROM)

ROMs are normally used for programs and data tables that must be resident within the computer when power is first applied. ROMs fall into two classes: fixed and programmable.

Fixed or mask-programmable ROMs have bit patterns that are set into the chip's memory matrix during manufacture. Using an appropriate photographic mask, transistors are created at selected junctions between row and column lines. Mask-programmable ROMs are expensive to produce in small quantities and are therefore only used for large scale production.

The term Programmable ROMs (PROMs) is normally used to describe a read only memory in which cells contain *fusible links* between the row and column lines. These links can be broken or 'blown' by passing a suitable current through selected cells, to form the required bit patterns. Because the fused links can not be restored, PROMs can only be programmed once.

Erasable Programmable ROMs (EPROMs) can be programmed, erased and then reprogrammed several times. For this reason EPROMs are sometimes referred to as *read mostly* memory. One form of EPROM is the ultraviolet erasable ROM. This uses a special type of transistor that works in a similar way to the fused links. Their advantage over PROMs is that the transistors can be 'cleared' by exposing the cells to ultraviolet light through a small window in the top of the chip. This normally takes about 20 ms. An EPROM, organised as 16K × 8bit, is illustrated in Figure 6.6.

Electrically Erasable Programmable ROMs (EEPROMs) are like UV-erasable EPROMs except that they can be programmed and erased electrically, which allows them to be updated in situ. They are more flexible than EPROMs and allow individual bytes to be addressed and altered separately. Unfortunately, write operations take significantly more time than read operations.

6.3.3 *Semiconductor device characteristics*

As processor speeds increase, it becomes necessary to feed the CPU with data and instructions at greater rates. Memory technology has struggled to keep up with the performance required by the latest processors. This has resulted in a number of incompatible memory devices. Before looking at a few of these, it is first necessary to explain how a processor may be used with different memory technologies. A processor, such as an Intel P4, has a single interface designed to communicate with the devices that will provide it with data and instructions. There are, however, many different devices designed to communicate in different ways. Different computer systems, particularly PC computer systems, will use only a specific set of these devices. It would be very wasteful and expensive if the processor were designed to communicate with all possible devices, instead it is built with a single interface known as the *front side bus* (FSB). The FSB enables the processor to communicate with a special chip, or chips, referred to as the system *chip set*. This chip set will then determine which device types the system will support. The chip set, for example, will determine which one of the memory types discussed later in this section the system will support. At the time of writing, these chipsets come in pairs and are typically referred to as the north bridge and south bridge. Figure 6.7 illustrates how they fit within the computer system.

Figure 6.7   PC chip set

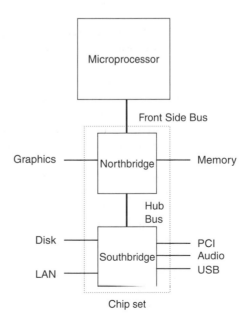

The north bridge component is responsible for collecting together the data from the different components in the system and passing it on to the processor. It deals directly with the high performance components, specifically the memory and graphics systems. The lower performance components, such as the disk, network, on-board audio, external interfaces such as the universal serial bus (USB) and peripheral component interface (PCI) devices are handled by the south bridge. The specific specification and functionality of a particular set of chips vary between systems. The same processors can be used with each chip set as the FSB is common. The FSB of Intel and AMD processors is different so there are separate chip sets for each processor family.

We will now describe the basic characteristics of three types of memory used in PC systems.

(1) Synchronous Dynamic RAM (SD-RAM)

Synchronous DRAM is so called because its operations are synchronised with the clock speed of the processor (see Section 6.4.2). The memory is provided on small boards called *dual in-line memory modules* (DIMMS) to make it easy to install. These modules provide a 64-bit interface and are generally rated at 66, 100 or 133 MHz. A 133 MHz module (usually labelled as PC133 memory) will be able to provide 133 million 64-bit words to the north bridge each second. This corresponds to a data rate of 133×8 million bytes each second (1064 MBytes per second or 1.064 GBytes per second).

(2) Double Data Rate RAM (DDR-RAM)

In order to achieve data rates greater than that provided by PC133, a technique is used which can divide the clock pulse into two and thus double the effective clock rate. DDR-RAM also comes on DIMMs with a 64-bit interface but at effective clock rates of 200, 266 and 333 MHz. The data rates offered are thus 1600, 2128 and 2664 MBytes per second, respectively. These memory modules are usually sold under the label of PC1600, PC2100 and PC2700.

The AMD processors use a 200 or 266 MHz FSB that is divided by two to give a 100 or 133 MHz clock for the DDR-RAM. These processors are therefore generally matched with PC1600 or PC2100 memory. Although a data rate of 2.7 GBytes per second greatly improves on the 1.064 GBytes per second of the SD-RAM, it is still insufficient to fully support the P4 chips. The P4 has a FSB of 100 MHz which uses quadrupling technology to provide an effective clock rate of 400 MHz. This means that the P4 FSB supports a data rate of 3.2 GBytes per second. There are developments to produce a 400 MHz version of the memory modules which would be capable of supplying the required data rate. There are however P4 chips now being produced which have a 533 MHz data clock (4.264 GBytes per second) that requires the DDR-RAM camp to continue to play catch-up. Another approach being considered is to offer a 128-bit interface. Coupled with a 400 MHz clock, such an interface would provide a data rate of 6.4 GBytes per second.

Figure 6.8   Simplified RD-RAM module

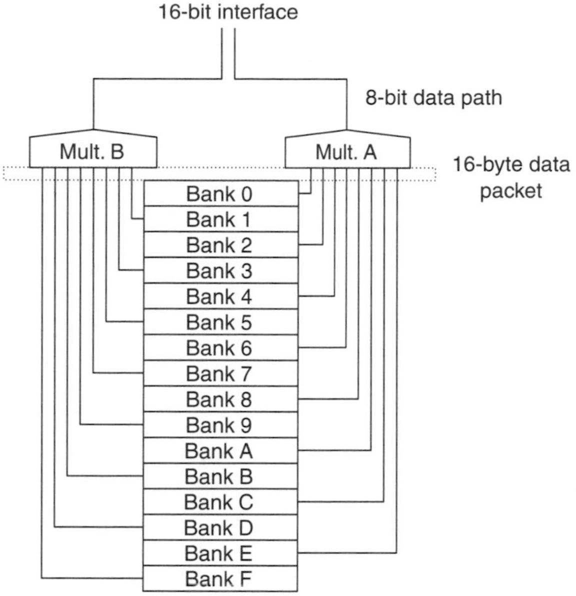

(3)   Rambus Dynamic RAM (RD-RAM)

To provide data and instructions at an appropriate rate to its P4 processors, Intel recommended the use of RD-Memory. This is a departure from the SD-RAM type of memory followed for the development of DDR-RAM. RD-RAM uses a 16-bit interface on rambus in-line memory modules (RIMMs) at clock speeds of 600, 712 or 800 MHz (PC600, PC700 and PC800 modules). The resulting data rates are thus 1200, 1424 and 1600 MBytes per second. These modules are used in pairs giving a top data rate of 3.2 GBytes per second.

Although the use of RD-RAM is the obvious choice for P4 based systems, the memory module costs are significantly greater than for DDR-RAM. The result is that the P4 systems with RD-RAM are not as popular as AMD based systems with DDR-RAM. To enable the P4 systems to be more price competitive, chip set manufacturers provided chip sets which enable the P4 to be used with PC2700 DDR-RAM. The P4-533 MHz processors will be significantly hampered by the use of PC2700 memory and PC1066 RD-RAM (4.2 GBytes per second) is becoming available to support the faster P4 chips. This may mean that the more expensive RD-RAM becomes more popular with the faster P4 chips being used to their full potential (until the 128-bit 400 MHz DDR-RAM becomes available?). One other thing to note about RD-RAM is that the speed comparisons above are for bursts of data. If data is being read from memory serially then RD-RAM will perform close to the data rate figures stated above as it uses a pipelining technology (see Section 4.3.1).

Figure 6.8 illustrates a simplified representation of a RD-RAM module, concentrating on the data output side. Consecutive memory items are placed

Figure 6.9   Simple address decoding scheme

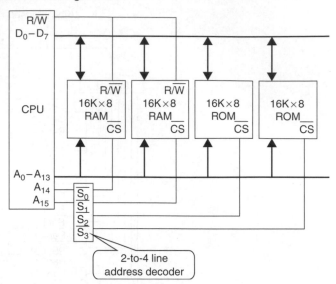

in different memory blocks. This enables 16 consecutive data items to be retrieved from the DRAM simultaneously. These data items are called a *package*. These items are placed on two data paths which feed a high speed multiplexor. The multiplexor will place each of the eight bytes on the two data paths on the data bus in turn.

The latency involved in RD-RAM (the time to fetch a data package from DRAM and present it to the multiplexors) is relatively high compared to DDR-RAM. The difference in performance between PC2700 and PC800 memory reduces if the applications being run have a more random pattern to memory access.

6.4   Data and address buses

6.4.1   *Address decoding*

A computer memory system usually contains several RAM and ROM chips connected to the processor by a system bus, as shown in Figure 6.9. Reading or writing to memory is carried out by using the low order address lines to select a location within a chip and the upper address lines to select the chip itself, through the chip select pin, $\overline{CS}$. Only when selected, is a chip electrically connected to the data bus.

In Figure 6.9 the lower fourteen address lines $A_0 - A_{13}$ are used to select one of the 16 KB locations within a chip, and the two upper address lines A_{14}, A_{15} are decoded to select one of the four chips. You will notice that the R/$\overline{W}$ control line is only connected to the RAM chips, as the ROMs can only be read when selected.

Worked example   A truth table for the 2-to-4 line decoder (see Section 3.2.3) is given below: Which chip will be selected by the address $C000_{16}$?

A_{15}	A_{14}	$\overline{S}_0$	$\overline{S}_1$	$\overline{S}_2$	$\overline{S}_3$
0	0	0	1	1	1
0	1	1	0	1	1
1	0	1	1	0	1
1	1	1	1	1	0

Solution $C000_{16} = 1100\ 0000\ 0000\ 0000_2$ With both A_{15} and A_{14} high the decoder would cause the output $\overline{S}_3$ to go low and activate the ROM chip on the far right of Figure 6.7.

By decoding the upper address lines in this way, the 2^{16} (64K) memory address space, accessible by the CPU, is mapped into four 16K regions, as shown in Figure 6.10.

In addition to RAM and ROM chips, interface chips that control I/O operations, can also form part of the main memory address space. Memory-mapped I/O is discussed in Chapter 8.

6.4.2 Bus timing

To co-ordinate the transfer of data between the processor and memory, some form of timing must be used. With a *synchronous bus*, a master clock provides the timing reference source, which can be read by all devices connected to the bus. The clock transmits a regular sequence of 1s and 0s, called *clock cycles*. A timing diagram specifies when various bus events should

Figure 6.10   Memory map corresponding to Figure 6.9

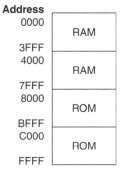

Address	
0000	RAM
3FFF	
4000	RAM
7FFF	
8000	ROM
BFFF	
C000	ROM
FFFF	

Figure 6.11   Timing diagram for a synchronous bus

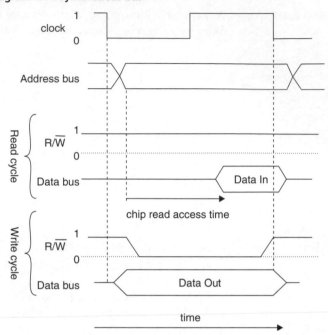

take place relative to this clock. For the simplified SRAM timing diagram shown in Figure 6.11, a read or write operation begins when the clock makes a 1 to 0 transition. Shortly after this transition the CPU puts an address on the address bus, the address bus being represented by two parallel lines, which are crossed at those instants when the address changes.

During a read cycle, the R/$\overline{\text{W}}$ line is held at logic 1 and data is read from the data bus into the CPU, towards the end of the clock cycle. Before the CPU reads this data, the memory chip must provide stable data on the bus.

During a write cycle, the CPU puts data on the data bus and signals a write operation by taking the R/$\overline{\text{W}}$ line low. Towards the end of the cycle, the CPU restores the R/$\overline{\text{W}}$ line to logic 1, latching the data into the memory chip.

TQ 6.4   Given the following timing data, what is the largest acceptable read access time for the memory chips connected to this bus?
clock cycle time = 500 ns
valid address occurs 200 ns after start of bus cycle
data read from bus 50 ns before end of bus cycle

When there are memory chips with different access times, the clock must be selected to allow the slowest component to participate in data transfer. Each read or write operation is then completed in a time called the *memory cycle* time, which in our example is the time for one clock cycle.

DRAM timing is more complicated than SRAM timing, because of the way in which the row and column addresses are set up and because the cycle time is longer than the access time.

6.5 Cache memory

As we mentioned earlier, a semiconductor cache memory is a small (to reduce cost) high-speed memory that acts as a buffer between the CPU and the main memory. The cache alleviates the bottleneck caused by the difference in speed between the CPU and main memory, by taking advantage of a property of program behaviour called the *principle of locality*.

6.5.1 Principle of locality

Because of the nature of programs and the way data is structured, it is found that during execution, memory references do not take place randomly, but are localised. For example, programs tend to reuse data and instructions that have recently been used (*temporal locality*) and instructions and data referenced close together in time, also to be close together in memory (*spatial locality*). We can appreciate how this locality arises by referring back to the simple program to reverse the items in a list, which we discussed in the last chapter (see Section 5.5.1).

This program used a loop to process each character in the string. When the loop was entered, the instructions forming the body of the loop were reused over and over again until the end of the string was reached. While this portion of the program was being executed, memory references were clustered into two regions: one just above address 0128, where the loop instructions were stored and the other near address 0102, where the string was stored.

Cache memory systems exploit this general property of program behaviour and enhance system performance by maintaining the currently active portions of a program in the high-speed cache. How these regions are identified will now be discussed.

6.5.2 Principle of cache operation

A semiconductor cache contains a limited number of *slots* or *lines* for storing *blocks* of main memory. Each block is typically four to sixteen words. During program execution, instead of reading instructions or data words directly from main memory, the CPU first searches for them in the cache. If the word is found, a 'hit' is signalled and the word is transferred from cache to the CPU, as shown in Figure 6.12(a).

If the word is missing from the cache, it is fetched from main memory, the cache being updated with the block containing the word as shown in Figure 6.12(b). Because of spatial locality, this increases the probability of finding, at least in the short term, subsequent words in the cache.

A measure of cache performance is the *hit ratio* (h), which is the fraction of all memory references that are satisfied by the cache and which avoid the

Figure 6.12   (a) A cache 'hit' (b) A cache 'miss'

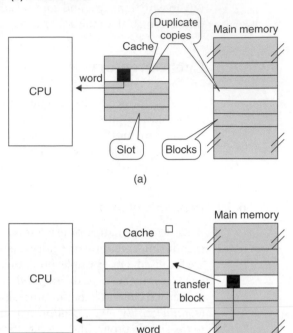

(a)

(b)

need to access main memory. If the access time for the cache and main memory are t_c and t_m, respectively, then the average time t_{ave} to access a word, is given by:

$$t_{ave} = ht_c + (1 - h)t_m$$

Notice that if all memory references are in the cache (h = 1), the average access time is reduced to that of the cache, while if there is no cache present, (h = 0), then the access time is equal to that of main memory.

TQ 6.5   If tc = 3 ns, tm = 12 ns and h = 0.9, then by how much is the system speeded up by using this cache memory?

A cache memory must be organised in such a way as to allow fast and efficient word searching. To do this, blocks of memory must be mapped into cache locations using some form of mapping function. We will now consider how this can be done.

6.5.3   *Associative cache*

With an associative cache, blocks of main memory are mapped into cache slots and marked with a block number or *tag*, as shown in Figure 6.13(a).

Figure 6.13 **(a) Associative cache organisation (b) A cache search**

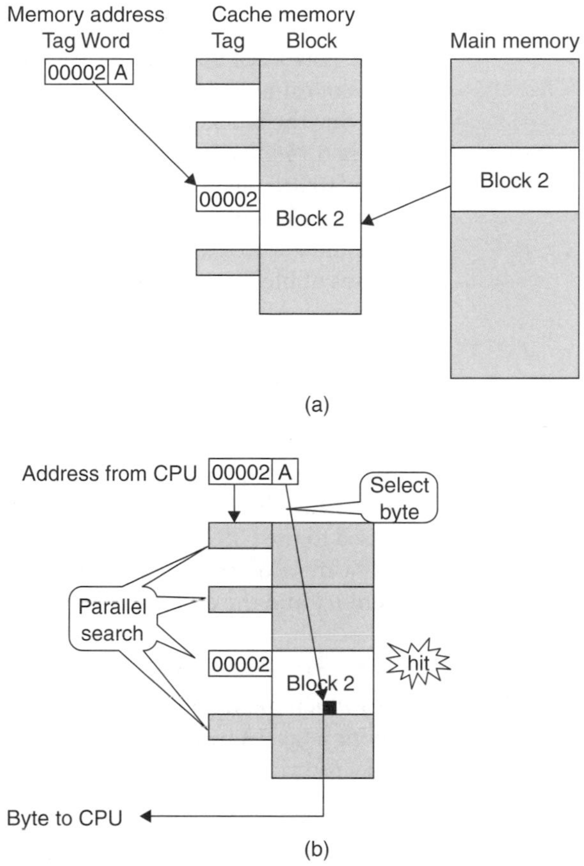

(a)

(b)

The tag is determined by the upper portion of the memory address, called the *tag field*, which, in this example, is the upper 20 bits of the 24-bit address. The lower four bits or *word field* determines the position within the block.

During a cache search, the tag field of the address generated by the CPU is simultaneously compared with the tags stored in the cache, as shown in Figure 6.13(b). If the tag field matches a tag in the cache, a 'hit' occurs and the byte selected by the word field is transferred to the CPU. If a 'miss' occurs, the byte is fetched from main memory and the 16-byte memory block containing the requested byte is inserted into a spare cache slot. This data transfer adds to the time penalty of a cache miss.

Parallel searching is carried out using special electronic circuits built into the cache. These circuits are complex and add to its cost. To reduce this cost, alternative cache organisations are often used, which employ ordinary random access memory.

TQ 6.6   How would the byte value 7A at address $FE802_{16}$ be stored in the cache?

6.5.4 *Direct-mapped cache*

With a directly mapped cache organisation, the problem of searching the cache is avoided by assigning each memory block to just one cache slot. The slot number of a block can be derived from its memory address, allowing the block to be retrieved from the cache by simply indexing into it. Figure 6.14 illustrates how this mapping scheme works for a cache having 4096 (1000_{16}) slots and 16 bytes per slot.

The 24-bit memory address is divided up into three fields: a tag field, a slot field and a word field. The 8-bit tag field divides main memory into 256 groups of blocks, each block being assigned a slot number given by the 12-bit slot fields. Although no more than one block from the same set can occupy a given cache slot, blocks from different slots can. To identify the group to which a block belongs, its tag must be stored along with it.

When accessing the cache, as shown in Figure 6.15, the slot field of the address generated by the CPU is used to index the cache. The stored tags are then compared with the tag field of the CPU address. If they match, a 'hit' occurs and the word field is used to select the appropriate byte, which is then passed to the CPU.

If a 'miss' occurs, the full CPU address is used to fetch the byte from main memory and the cache line is filled with the block containing the byte.

TQ 6.7   Into which main memory locations would a block stored in slot 0FF and having a tag 5A be moved, if the block had to be swapped out of the cache to make room for another?

Figure 6.14   Direct-mapped cache

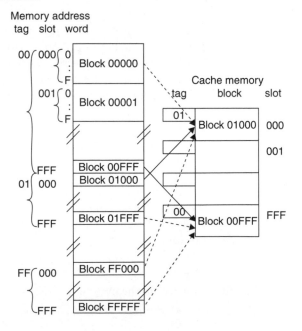

Figure 6.15 Accessing a direct-mapped cache

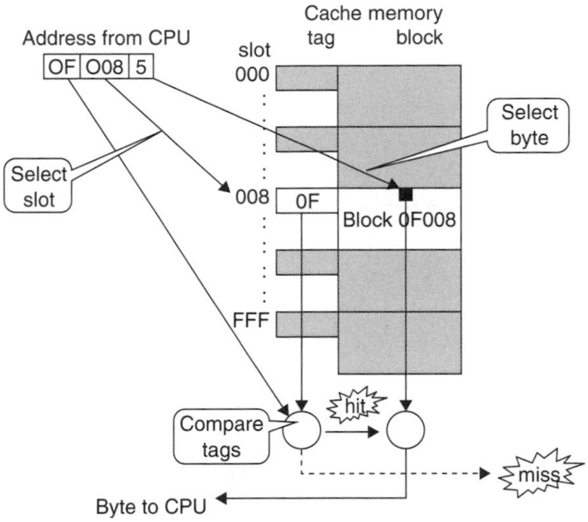

The main problem with direct mapping is that blocks *share* specific cache slots and only one of these blocks can be in the cache at any one time. If a program frequently accesses two blocks that map into the same slot, then blocks must repeatedly be swapped in and out of the cache, severely degrading its performance. One solution to this problem is to organise the cache so that more than one block can occupy the same slot. This is called set-associative mapping.

6.5.5 *Set-associative cache*

A set associative cache can store a number of tag-block pairs in each cache line, the number of pairs forming a set. A two-way cache organisation, is shown in Figure 6.16.

Each main memory block is mapped into one of the 2^{12} sets according to the set-field of its 24-bit memory address. Thus the 16-byte block between 09$\underline{0080}$ and 09$\overline{008}$F maps into set 8, as does the block between 0F$\overline{0080}$ and 0F$\underline{008}$F, each block occupying a separate slot and being identified by a unique tag.

When the cache is accessed by the CPU, the set field is used as an index into the cache in the same way as the slot field was used with the direct-mapping scheme. Having identified the set, both tags are compared simultaneously with the tag field of the address. If a 'hit' occurs, the byte selected by the word field is passed to the CPU, otherwise the byte is fetched from main memory and a new block is transferred into the set.

When a 'miss' occurs and the set is full, it becomes necessary to replace one of the blocks in the cache set with a new block. A popular form of *replacement algorithm* is the *least recently used* (LRU), which as its name suggests, replaces the block that has been least recently accessed by the CPU. To determine which block this applies to, an extra bit is included with each cache entry, which is modified each time the CPU accesses that set. Another replacement policy is *first-in-first-out* (FIFO), which replaces the block that has been in the set the longest.

Figure 6.16 **Two-way set-associative cache organisation**

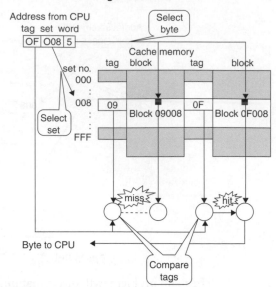

6.5.6 *Cache coherency*

An important issue of cache design is how to deal with writes. If the cache is only used for storing instructions (*instruction cache*), then this is not a problem because instructions are only read. If on the other hand, the cache is used for storing data (*data cache*) or data and instructions (*unified cache*), then reading, modifying and writing data back into the cache can create a situation where the data stored in the cache is inconsistent with that in main memory. To maintain data consistency or *cache coherence*, some form of *write policy* must be adopted.

One of the simplest policies to implement is *write-through*, which maintains consistency by following a cache write operation with a write to main memory. One disadvantage in doing this is that the CPU has to wait for the write operation to complete and this can severely degrade performance when there are multiple writes to the same block.

An alternative and widely used policy is *write-back*, where instead of immediately writing the block back to main memory, a status bit is used to mark the cache line as modified or *dirty*. Only when it becomes necessary to replace the modified block, is it copied back to main memory. This allows the CPU to write and read at the same speed and reduces the wait or *stall time*. Unfortunately, if there are special I/O controllers in the system, that can move data to/from main memory without the intervention of the CPU, such as DMA controllers (see Section 8.4.3), then maintaining consistency in this way can be a problem.

6.6 Summary

Computer memory is organised into a hierarchy of different layers, because fast memory technology is more expensive than the slower memory technology. The ingenuity of memory module suppliers is being tested by the processor manufacturers as they strive to keep up with the ever increasing demands for data and instructions at higher speeds. A small high-speed cache memory allows the internal memory to 'appear' as high speed memory, by storing a limited number of recently used memory blocks, that by the locality principle, are likely to be used again. Three mapping schemes are used for storing blocks in a cache: associative, direct and set-associative.

Answers to in text questions

TQ 6.1   Primary storage: $7000/256.1024 = 4.8$ pence per KByte

Secondary storage: $8000/40.1024.1024 = 0.0002$ pence per KByte

The cost of storing information in primary memory is therefor 2400 times more expensive than secondary memory.

TQ 6.2 2^{10} or 1024

TQ 6.3   The bar over the chip select pin indicates that the chip is selected by taking the pin low, in the same way as the bar over W on the read/write line indicated that the line was taken low for a write operation.

TQ 6.4   Maximum read access time for the chip $= 500 - 200 - 50 = 250$ ns

TQ 6.5 $t_{av} = 0.9 \times 3 + 0.1 \times 12 = 3.9$ ns

Without a cache memory (h = 0) and $t_{av} = t_m = 12$ ns

Therefore the speedup factor is $12/3.9 = 3.08$

TQ 6.6   The tag is FE080 and the word field indicates that the byte occupies position 2 in the block, therefor the cache line entry would appear as:

FE080 bb bb 7A bb bb bb bb bb bb bb bb bb bb bb bb bb [bb indicate bytes]

TQ 6.7   Address $5A0FF0_{16}$ to $5A0FFF_{16}$

EXERCISES

1   If a static RAM chip is organised as 2048×8-bit, then
   a) How many bits are stored?
   b) How many address pins will it have?

2   Explain why a PC800 memory module would result in a better performing P4-400 MHz system than a PC2700 module and why it

would not be possible to replace a PC2700 memory module with a PC800 module.

3 List the relative advantages and disadvantages of the three cache mapping schemes described in this chapter.

4 What is the difference between *write-through* and *write-back* when describing a cache coherence policy?

5 The access time of a cache memory is 4 ns and that of main memory is 15 ns. It is estimated that 85% of a program's memory requests are for reads and 15% for writes. If the hit ratio is 0.95, and a write-through policy is used, what is the average access time for this system?

6 A four-way set-associative cache uses a least recently used (LRU) replacement algorithm. To support this, each block in the set has two bits that are used for counting when the block was last used. The counter work as follows:

When 'miss' occurs, the block whose counter has reached zero is replaced by the newly referenced block. On being entered in the cache, the counter of this new block is initialised to 3, while all other blocks in the set have their counters decremented by 1.

When a 'hit' occurs, the counter of the block containing the referenced word is reset to 3. Before this is done, any block whose counter is greater than that of the referenced block is decremented by 1, while all other counters are left unchanged.

If the cache currently has the four blocks A, B, C, D in a set, with block counters equal to 0, 1, 2 and 3 respectively, then after the following sequence of blocks have been referenced: E, B, E, D, A, E, which blocks will be in the set and what will their counter values be? (see Figure 6.17).

Figure 6.17

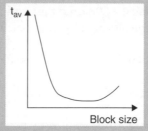

7 The expression $t_{av} = ht_c + (1 - h)t_m$ for the average access time of a cache does not take into account the time required to transfer a block of words into the cache. Measurements show that t_{av} varies with block size as shown below.

How do you account for this?

Secondary memory

In Chapter 6 we looked at the RAM, Random Access Memory, that is very closely attached to the processor chip. The big problem with this memory is that when the power is switched off, the stored data is lost. In every computer system, it is necessary to be able to store data and programs even when the power to the computer system is turned off. The devices that provide this facility are called secondary memory or backing storage and this chapter looks at a number of these devices. The two main technologies used for secondary storage devices are magnetic surface and optical technology.

7.1 Magnetic surface technology

Dynamic magnetic storage systems record data by inducing tiny magnetized spots called *dipoles* on to a moving magnetic surface. To read or write data, the surface is moved past a read/write head, as shown in Figure 7.1(a). Data is

Figure 7.1 Magnetic surface recording

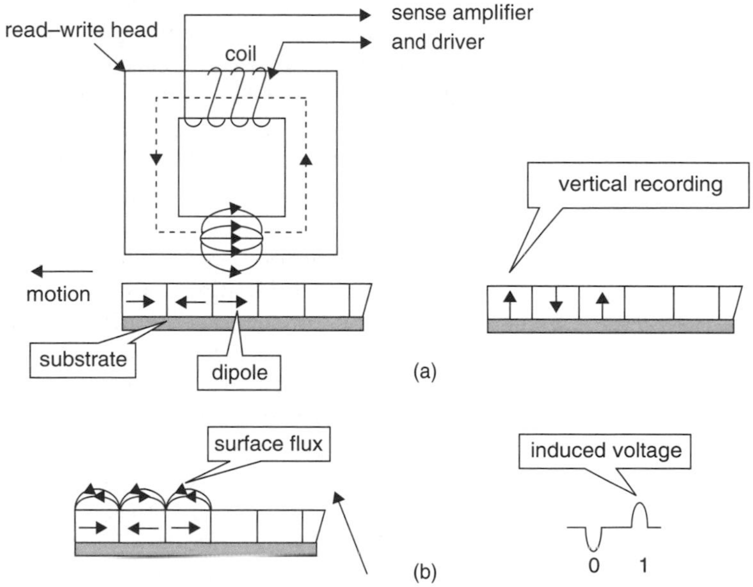

written on to the surface by driving a current through the head coil windings. The direction of the current determines the orientation of the dipole and hence whether a binary '1' or '0' is stored. With *horizontal recording*, the dipoles lie along the direction of motion of the surface, whilst with *vertical recording*, they are oriented in a perpendicular direction. During a read operation, the surface magnetic field generated by a dipole Figure 7.1(b) induces a voltage signal across the coil, the polarity being dependent upon the direction of the magnetic field. After passing through the sense amplifier, the signal is fed into an electronic circuit where it is processed and the encoded data extracted.

7.2 Magnetic disk storage

7.2.1 *Hard disks*

A widely used form of secondary storage is the *hard disk*, shown in Figure 7.2(a). Data is magnetically recorded on to circular *tracks* using a small read–write head, which floats about 2.5 microns above the surface of the rotating disk. A micron is a millionth of a metre. Because of the very close proximity of the head to the disk surface, any dust or dirt on the disk is liable to cause the head to crash into the disk surface and damage it. A particle of cigarette smoke looks like a rock on the surface of a disk. For this reason, hard disks are assembled under clean-room conditions and then sealed, so that they cannot be removed. The closeness of the head to the disk surface also makes hard disk drives vulnerable to mechanical shock when they are operating, so they should be treated with care. The head is attached to an actuator arm, which allows it to be stepped radially across the surface from one track to another and also enables the head to be moved to a safe position when the drive is not running. Tracks are divided up into *sectors*, each sector being used to store a block of data.

With a multiple-disk system, as shown in Figure 7.2(b), separate read–write heads are used for each surface. The heads are mounted on to a single actuator arm, which moves them to the same track numbers on each surface. Each set of corresponding tracks is referred to as a *cylinder*. The disk (platter), spindle motor and head actuator are usually contained in a sealed chamber called the *hard disk assembly* (HDA). The HDA is controlled by a *disk controller*, which specifies the track and sector numbers together with the type of operation (read or write) to be performed.

Reading from and writing to the disk take place in serial fashion. During a read operation, the controller transfers one or more blocks of data from the disk into a temporary storage area, called a *sector buffer*, a block being typically 512 bytes. During a write operation, the contents of the buffer are transferred serially to the specified track and sector. To assist the controller in these operations each sector contains in addition to data, an address (track, head, sector), synchronisation bytes and error checking information.

To access a particular sector, the head must first be stepped to the appropriate track and time allowed for the appropriate sector to pass underneath it. The time taken to do this is called the *access time* and clearly

Figure 7.2   Magnetic disk storage

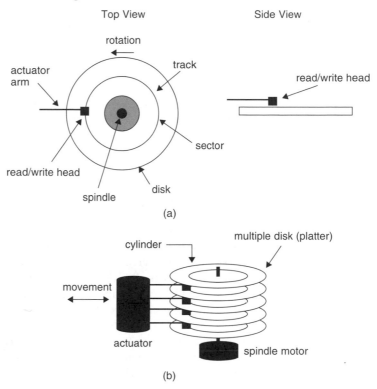

(a)

(b)

depends upon the positions of the head, track and sector when the operation begins. When describing disk access times, an average value is normally used, based on the average time taken to step to a track (*seek time*) plus the time taken for a sector to reach the head (*rotational latency*). The average rotational latency is normally assumed to be the time taken for half a revolution of the disk.

TQ 7.1   If a disk rotates at 7200 rpm, what is the average rotational latency? If the access time is 6.5 ms, what is the average seek time?

The trend was to build hard drives with between two and 10 platters and offer storage capacities of between about 2 and 20 GBytes. However, if you open up a recently manufactured hard disk, it is likely to have just two platters with what looks like four heads although the label on the drive case will probably state that the drive has 16 heads. This is made possible because of the exceptionally high quality of the magnetic surfaces and head manufacture that can now be achieved with the head assembly for each surface operating as four virtual heads. The separation between the tracks is much smaller as are the heads themselves. The four virtual heads on each of the four surfaces enable 16 tracks to be read without movement of the head

111

actuator arm, thus having the same characteristics as an eight platter disk system but in a much smaller physical enclosure. Disk capacities of 80 to 150 GBytes are now common and cheap.

Access times vary from between about 2 and 20 ms with current rotational speeds being 5400 or 7200 rpm. The rate at which the drive and controller can send data to the system (data transfer rate) can be close on 10 Mbps.

With continued advances in read/write head technology, magnetic surface quality and more efficient encoding schemes, even higher capacity, physically smaller and faster magnetic disk storage systems are likely to become available.

7.2.2 RAID systems

There are two major problems with hard disks. First, if the hard disk in your machine crashes, all data and programs are lost and so some form of backup is necessary and second, if a disk capacity of more than say 150 Gbytes is required it will be rather expensive. RAID (Redundant Array of Independent Disks) helps to overcome these problems.

In simple terms, RAID uses two or more cheap hard disks to provide a backup and increased capacity. There are a number of different ways in which the disks can be configured but there are six accepted ways, called levels, that are defined. Each level has benefits and drawbacks and is designed to provide solutions to specific needs. RAID operates by using a technique known as striping, which means that each disk is divided into a number of smaller storage areas known as stripes. A stripe can be any size between 512 Bytes (a sector) up to several MBytes. The various levels of RAID use these stripes and the multiple disks in different ways.

(1) RAID 0

Here a number of disks are connected together to make one large disk. However, data is not written on one disk until it is full then onto the next disk and so on but rather the first stripe on disk 1 is written to then stripe 1 on disk 2 is used then stripe 1 on disk 3 and so on. Thus if a file is to be stored, file blocks are written across all disks using the stripes. As the hard disk controllers are able to carry out concurrent reading and writing to each disk, the parallel writing activity speeds up the writing process. The same increase in performance applies also to reading from the disk system. At the same time a disk system with a higher capacity is realised. RAID 0 does not provide any fault handling capacity because if one disk fails, the whole disk system fails. Figure 7.3 shows the basic idea of RAID 0.

Figure 7.3   RAID 0 basics

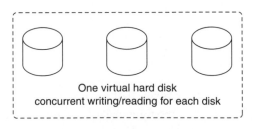

One virtual hard disk
concurrent writing/reading for each disk

(2) *RAID 1*

This involves the use of pairs of striped disks where the data is written to both disks in the pair at once. If one disk controller is used for both disks in each pair, the process is called *mirroring* and if a separate disk controller is used for each disk in the pair, it is called *duplexing*. RAID 1 has the total capacity of just one of the disks in each pair but it is a highly reliable system and the down time, if one of the disks crashes and duplexing is being used, can be almost zero. This can be a good RAID system to have if a high reliability, constantly available server computer is needed for a network.

(3) *RAID 2*

The data is striped across two or more disks and one or more extra disks are used to hold error correcting code for the stored data. This means that if one of the disks crashes, the data that was held on that disk can be regenerated using the appropriate error correcting code held on another disk. RAID 2 systems are expensive, mainly because of the amount of error correcting code that has to be stored, and are very rarely used.

(4) *RAID 3*

This is based on RAID 0 in that data is striped across a number of disks then an extra disk is used to hold parity information. RAID 3 uses small stripes and has a problem if large records (bigger than the stripe size) are being stored. The problem is that to read a record means reads of several disks which cuts out concurrent I/O. However, the data transfer rate is high as data can be streamed from several disks in parallel. Parity information is much less bulky than error correcting code but does not give such good error detection. RAID 3 gives increased performance, a virtual large disk and a measure of fault tolerance via the parity data held on the extra disk. Figure 7.4 shows a RAID 3 configuration.

Figure 7.4   RAID 3 configuration

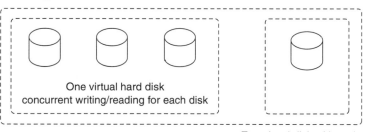

One virtual hard disk
concurrent writing/reading for each disk

Extra hard disk with parity
information for virtual hard disk

Figure 7.5   RAID 4 with striped parity disks

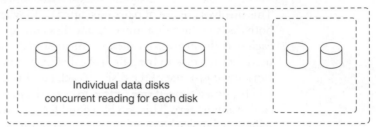

Individual data disks
concurrent reading for each disk

Extra hard disks with parity
information for individual data disks

(5) *RAID 4*

Uses an extra disk to hold parity information for a number of disks just like
RAID 3 but the stripes on the data disks are much larger than RAID 3, which
overcomes the problem of long records having to span disk drives. This
means reads can be done concurrently but because each write must update
the parity disk, writes cannot be carried out concurrently. A variation, which
overcomes this problem to a certain extent, uses multiple striped disks to
hold the parity information. This makes storage utilisation sense only if a
large number of data disks are being used. The individual data disks have
their own controllers and effectively operate on their own. The advantage of
this system is that a disk failure does not pull down the whole disk system.
Figure 7.5 shows how RAID 4 could be implemented.

(6) *RAID 5*

The data is striped across the group of disks. Parity information is also
striped across the group of disks in such a way that parity for one disk is held
on another disk. This means that if one disk fails, its data can be regenerated
from the parity information held on the other disk. The amount of parity
data that is required is obviously less than the data itself but is still
considerable in volume. Raid 5 provides a reasonably cheap increase in
capacity, increased performance and good fault tolerance.
In practice, the most common forms of RAID are 0, 1 and 5.

(7) *Proprietary RAID systems*

There are a number of vendors who supply their own variety of RAID systems.
These often use a mixture of the levels detailed above and are normally
intended for use in network servers that require very high degrees of reliability.

7.2.3   Floppy disks

Floppy disks, which are removable storage devices, have undergone a
considerable amount of development since their introduction over 20 years
ago. The introduction of the $5^{1}/_{4}$ inch disk in early PCs was hailed as a great

Figure 7.6   Floppy disk drive construction

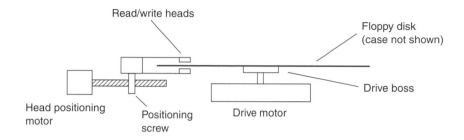

advance. The idea is exactly the same as for a hard disk except that the magnetic surface is a magnetizable coating on a flexible disk of plastic, housed in a plastic sleeve. The early popular $5^1/_4$ inch disk could hold 360 KBytes of data, 180 KBytes on each side. Each side had 20 tracks split into 18 sectors with a sector holding 512 bytes of data. This was enhanced to a quad density double sided format which could hold 1.2 MBytes. Very soon after the introduction of the 1.2 MByte floppy disk came the $3^1/_2$ inch 720 KByte floppy disk in the hard plastic case with which we are all familiar today. The storage has been increased first to 1.44 MBytes and then to 2.88 MBytes. The capacity of these disks has not been increased further because of the restrictions of compatibility placed upon floppy disk drives in that a drive should be able to read all three formats. The floppy disk drive, see Figure 7.6, has a read/write head for each side of the disk. $3^1/_2$ inch floppy disk cases have a write protect shutter, on the bottom right hand side, which can be opened to prevent the disk being overwritten. Disks with 1.44 and 2.88 MByte capability have a second opening on the bottom left hand side which can be detected by the disk drive.

7.2.4   *Magnetic tape systems*

Very early PCs used an ordinary cassette audio tape for exchangeable storage following on from the tradition of their mainframe cousins who used large reel magnetic tape storage. The introduction of the floppy disk initially eliminated the use of magnetic tape storage for PCs but it was soon realised that with PC hard disk sizes of 10–20 MBytes needing to be backed up for security reasons, the magnetic tape cassette, regained its importance. High quality tape drives were produced, which could use high quality audio tapes and then these were superseded by special data cartridge drives that used DAT (Digital Audio Tapes).

Tape drives for PCs can hold up to 130 GBytes of data with a data transfer rate of up to 50 Mbps and so they are still relevant today. They are easily added to a system to provide automatic backup of vital data. The big problem with magnetic tape systems is that the data is stored serially which means that data cannot be accessed randomly. The big advantage is the very low cost per bit for storage.

7.2.5 *Exchangeable disk drives*

Mention was made in Section 7.2.3 that floppy disk drive technology had not allowed floppy disk storage capacity to go above 2.88 MBytes. However, the technology for producing magnetizable surfaces has progressed dramatically. This fact has been exploited in devices such as zip drives. The exchangeable disk used in a zip drive is very much like a $3^1/_2$ inch floppy disk but it is capable of holding up to 750 MBytes of data with a data transfer rate of up to 64 Mbps. The zip drive itself is a precision version of the standard floppy disk drive, which can handle the greater track and bit densities demanded by the storage capacity of the zip disk.

7.2.6 *Portable hard drives*

Before leaving this section on magnetic storage devices, it is worth mentioning the work that has been put into the development of hard disk drives for portable computers. The main problem to be overcome here is to make the hard disk drives rugged enough to be able to withstand the rough handling that these computers can be subjected to. As explained earlier, the disk heads fly very close to the surface of a running disk and mechanical shock can cause the heads to crash into the surface of the disk. A number of modifications have been incorporated into the construction of hard disk drives for portable computers which makes them less susceptible to shock damage but brings the penalty of a higher price. A new use for these rugged hard disk drives is to provide a high capacity exchangeable storage facility for standard PCs. Capacities up to 80 GBytes are readily available. The ways in which these devices are connected to the PC are covered in the next chapter, which deals with input and output.

7.3 Optical disk storage systems

Dynamic optical storage systems store data as a series of variable length *bumps*, made along a spiral track in the surface of a hard disk. To read the data, light is focused onto the disk using a low-power semiconductor laser and the variation in intensity of the reflected light caused when light reflects from a bump, rather than the land area between the bumps, is used to detect the encoded data. The mechanism required to enable an optical storage device to be read is shown in Figure 7.7.

The requirement is to be able to focus a beam of light onto the surface of the disk and take the reflected light beam and redirect it to a light detector rather than back to the light source. The optical physics behind this activity is quite complex and the detail is beyond this book. However, here is a very

Figure 7.7   Schematic of mechanism for reading an optical storage device

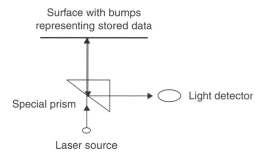

much simplified explanation. The light beam from the laser is sent through a special prism that affects a characteristic of light known as *polarisation*. The effect is that the reflected light beam from the disk bumps passes back to the prism but rather than passing straight through the prism, the beam is bent and it emerges out of the side of the prism where it is focused onto a light detector. As mentioned above, the track containing the bumps is a spiral, which starts near the centre of the disk and spirals towards the outside edge of the disk. So another important part of the disk reading mechanism is the tracking device, which keeps the laser beam focused onto the spiral as the disk rotates. A facility must also be provided that ensures that the rate at which the data is read from the disk is constant as the further towards the outside of the disk the part of the spiral is, the faster is the linear speed, if the rotational speed of the disk is kept constant.

7.3.1   CD-ROM

A CD-ROM is a compact disk read-only memory. The disks are mass produced by stamping pits into a polycarbonate substrate using special nickel-plated master disks. The substrate is then coated with a thin reflective layer and finally protected from scratching by lacquering. The pits that are stamped into the disk produce bumps on the other side of the disk and this is the side that is illuminated by the laser. To give some idea of the dimensions involved, the track is about 0.5 microns wide, a minimum bump length is about 0.8 microns and has a height of 0.125 microns and the track separation is 1.6 microns. The track can be up to 5 Km long.

Although master disks are expensive to manufacture and test, each master is capable of stamping out up to 10000 disks, making CD-ROM storage cost effective for large production runs. Once manufactured, the pattern of bumps in the surface of a CD-ROM cannot be altered.

To read the disk, a sophisticated optical system, based on Figure 7.7, is used. The light source is a low-power laser diode and the light detector is a photo-diode. When a bump passes over the spot of laser light, the light tends to be scattered, reducing the intensity of the reflected beam. In contrast, when the land between the bumps passes over the spot of laser light, there is no scattering and hence a much higher reflectivity. Therefore, as the disk rotates, the light reaching the spot detector is modulated according to the pattern of bumps made in the disk substrate. The signal that this generates can then be processed to extract the encoded data.

Data is stored along the spiral track in *sectors*, where sectors are counted from the centre outwards. Each sector contains 3234 bytes, 882 bytes being used as an *Error Detection Code/Error Correction Code* (EDC/ECC) and also to provide control information. The remaining 2352 bytes are defined according to various *colour book* standards. The CD-ROM Mode 1 *yellow book standard*, allows 2048 of these bytes to be used for data, the remaining bytes being used for synchronisation, header and as an additional EDC/ECC. The 4-byte header contains the address of the sector in minutes:seconds:blocks measured from the beginning of the track.

The storage capacity of a 120 mm disk is quoted as 650 MBytes although not all of this is available for user data as a small amount of storage is required for disk administration. The average random access time depends on the rotational speed of the disk. The basic standard provides a rotational speed that gives a data transfer rate of 150 Kbps. Computer CD drive speeds are specified as multiples of this basic speed so a X16 (pronounced times sixteen) CD drive delivers a transfer rate of approximately 2.4 Mbps and a X48 CD drive has a transfer rate of approximately 7.2 Mbps. Because of the error correction system, the unrecoverable error rate is as low as 1 in 10^{12} bits.

When comparing optical with magnetic surface storage, there are a number of advantages. The storage density, see DVDs later, can be higher than that of a magnetic disk. The effect of mechanical shock cannot damage the disk, as can be the case with hard disk drives. The optical system of a CD drive is typically 1 mm above the surface of the disk and so debris, in the form of dust, is no real problem. This allows optical disks to be removed from the drive when not in use or when data needs to be exchanged. Finally, because of the error detection/correction codes used with optical disks, less stringent quality requirements are needed during their manufacture than are needed for hard disks, making them more economical to produce.

7.3.2 *WORM devices*

Write-Once-Read-Mostly (WORM) optical storage devices, allow users to archive data by storing it on an initially blank optical disk. A popular WORM disk is the Compact Disk-Recordable (CD-R), which has a reflective layer that can be permanently altered and used to store data.

The CD-R drives contain two semiconductor lasers, one for writing and the other for reading data. The laser used for writing has a typical power rating of 30 mW, which means that it can heat the surface of the disk to form holes, create bubbles or otherwise alter the reflectivity of the film deposited on it. The laser used for reading has a lower power rating and therefore cannot alter the recorded data. It operates in the same way as the laser diode we described for the CD-ROM.

Early CD-R disks used a magneto-optical process which involved the incorporation of a magneto-optic layer on the disk surface. In these systems, the higher power laser heated a spot on the spiral track and at the same time a magnetic field was applied to the spot. This double action changed the reflectivity of the spot and so two different reflectivities could be achieved thus allowing zeros and ones to be recorded. The reading process used the lower power laser in the same way as is done with a CD.

The CD-R disks that use magneto-optical layers are now obsolete as they have been superceded by CD-R disks that use a photo-sensitive dye layer, which is normally reflective, instead of the magneto-optical layer. These disks are much cheaper to manufacture and the recording process is much simpler as only laser light is needed. Again two lasers are used, a low power source for reading and a higher power source which when focussed onto a spot of the dye, destroys the reflectivity of the spot. The destruction of the reflectivity is a one way process and so CD-R disks can only be written to once. As far as light is concerned, a disk can be made which has the same effect as if it had actual lands and bumps. The disks so produced can be read by a standard CD drive and their storage capacity is the same as a standard CD. Typically, writing speeds are about one-third of reading speeds. A word of warning though, these disks can be damaged if exposed to very strong sunlight.

7.3.3 CD-RW devices

Write-Read-Erase-Memory (WREM) optical storage devices are disks that look identical to a CD-R but they have a heat-sensitive layer, that is sensitive to different heat levels, deposited on a polycarbonate substrate. Heated by a laser to one heat level produces a very reflective spot on the heat sensitive layer when it cools and heated to another higher level produces a very dull spot when it cools. The changes are reversible and so the disk can be rewritten when required. CD-RW disk drives have a laser that can be set to three different power levels. First, there is a low-power level used for reading the disk. Second, there is a level that is able to make the heat-sensitive layer reflective, which is called the erase setting. Third, there is the write power level which is used to produce the non-reflective spots. Reading these disks uses the same type of mechanism as for a normal CD but some older type CD drives have difficulty in reading them. CD-RW disks have the same storage capacity as normal CDs and similar read and write speeds.

7.3.4 DVD for data storage

Digital Versatile Disks are now being used in computer systems and most new PCs are fitted with DVD drives. The DVD disc is the same size as a CD disk but due to the reduced track width and the spacing between turns of the spiral and the reduced pit/bump length, the storage capacity is much increased. A further increase in capacity is obtained because DVD disks can be multi-layer and double sided. Figure 7.8 shows a cross section of a DVD-ROM.

A double sided, double layer DVD is manufactured by producing a stamped polycarbonate disk, similar to the process used for CDs, for the four layers. The backs of the two inner layer disks are coated with a dense reflective coating and the backs of the outer layer disks are coated with a semi-transparent reflective gold mist. All disks are now coated with a lacquer and placed together in the order shown in Figure 7.8. The disks are now pressed together and subjected to infrared heating to fuse them together.

Figure 7.8   Cross section of a double sided double layer DVD

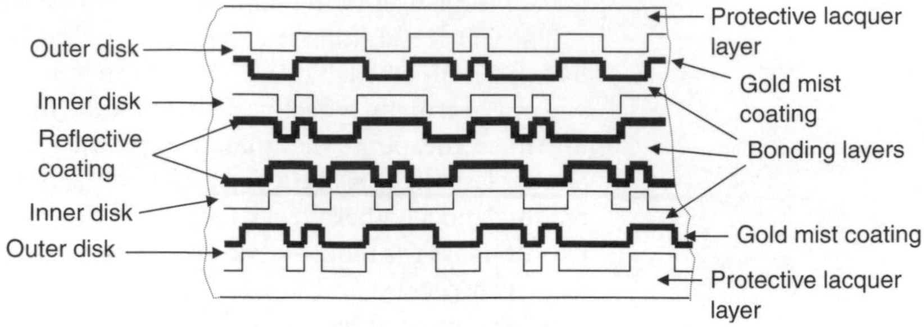

Table 7.1   Typical CD and DVD dimensions

	CD	DVD single sided single layer	DVD double sided double layer
Data storage			
capacity	650 MBytes	4.4 GBytes	15.9 GBytes
Length of track	5 Km	12 Km	48 Km
Size of bumps			
height	0.125 microns	0.120 microns	0.120 microns
minimum length	0.83 microns	0.4 microns	0.44 microns
Track width	0.5 microns	0.32 microns	0.32 microns
Track separation	1.6 microns	0.7 microns	0.7 microns

To read the disk, the laser can be focused onto the inner layer, through the semi-transparent layer, or focused onto the semi-transparent layer to get data from the outer layer.

Table 7.1 gives a comparison between typical CD and DVD dimensions. The bump dimensions for the multi-layer DVDs need to be slightly larger than for the single-sided version to give reliable reading. The capacity of a DVD is greater than would be expected from purely smaller dimensions compared with a CD. The extra capacity is because the error correction system used is more efficient and needs less data than a CD, hence the overhead is less and more space is available for actual data and slightly more of the disk surface is used. In the case of multi-layer DVDs, the inner layer track starts in the centre of the disk and the outer layer track starts on the outside of the disk. This provides for an uninterrupted flow of information when reading from the end of the inner track to the start of the outer track as the laser tracking system does not have to reset to the centre.

7.3.5 DVD WORM and WREM devices

At the time of writing this book, recordable and erasable-writable DVD disks in single layer, single-sided format are just being introduced. The technology is similar to that used for the respective CD disks. Currently, the price of the drives is about five times the price of CD drives. Types available are DVD−R, DVD−RW and slightly improved versions known as DVD+R and DVD+RW.

7.4 Summary

Magnetic surface technology is used for implementing hard disks, floppy disks, exchangeable disk and tape storage devices. Ruggedised hard disk systems are used in portable computers and also for exchangeable storage up to 80 GBytes. Large-scale hard disk storage is often implemented as RAID systems which also provides automated backup. Optical technology is used for implementing CD-ROMs, WORM and WREM devices at the cheap end of the exchangeable disk storage range but DVD disks, although somewhat more expensive, are growing in popularity because of their high storage capacity.

Answers to in text questions

TQ 7.1 Each revolution takes 1/120 seconds.
On average, a sector will be half a revolution away from the head, so the rotational latency will be 1/240 or 4 ms.
With an access time of 6.5 ms, the seek time will be 6.5 − 4 = 2.5 ms.

EXERCISES

1 The following specification refers to a hard disk drive:

number of heads 16

number of cylinders 30800

rotational speed 7200 rpm

sectors per track 63

bytes per sector 512

(a) What is the storage capacity of the system in MBytes?

(b) What is the maximum data transfer rate in Mbps?

2 The label attached to a hard disk drive says that it has 24 heads 27000 cylinders and 63 sectors per track. Each sector can store 512 bytes of data. When the disk drive is opened up, it is found to have two platters.

(a) Explain how a two platter disk system can have 24 heads.

(b) Calculate the storage capacity of the system in GBytes.

3   A 74 minute CD-ROM is read at 4500 sectors per minute.

   (a)   How many sectors are there on the disk?

   (b)   If each 3234 byte sector contains 2048 bytes of data, what is the storage capacity of this disk from the user's point of view?

   (c)   What purpose do the other bytes serve?

4   Calculate the number of 1.44 Mbyte floppy disks that would be required to store the data on a full 650 MByte CD-ROM.

5   Draw up a table to compare the maximum running times of videos that can be stored on DVDs that are

   (a)   single sided, single layer

   (b)   double sided, single layer

   (c)   double sided, double layer

6   Optical disks and exchangeable magnetic disk systems enable users to exchange data and make back-up copies. Describe the relative merits of each type of storage medium and indicate the type of application for which they are most suited.

Input–Output

Input–Output (I/O) is a term used to describe the transfer of information between a computer's main memory and the various I/O devices attached to it, often called *peripheral devices*. Peripheral devices are generally slower than the CPU and frequently require special control signals and data formats. To match these characteristics with those of the CPU and its internal memory, interface circuits are used. This chapter describes the basic principles of PC interfacing and the methods used for scheduling data transfer and gives coverage of the basic principles of some common peripheral devices.

8.1 PC buses

Earlier chapters have looked at the data, control and address buses, which enable the processor, main memory and control unit to inter-communicate at high speed. The I/O devices, connected to the PC, need to obtain data from, and send data to, the main memory. Over the past two to three years, processor manufacturers have produced processors with higher and higher operating speeds and this has lead to problems with connecting to the other components that are on the motherboard. The processor manufacturers have solved these problems by producing their own special chip sets. The result of this is a great variety of individual architectures that solve the problems in different ways. Figure 8.1 is our attempt to show the general idea, without resorting to a specific manufacturer's detail design. The processor is connected to a very high-speed bridge, which we have called the Processor Bridge. This provides high-speed access to the main memory via multiple data paths. The first level cache is part of the processor chip and is not shown separately. The need to have a fast graphics capability means that the video controller is also connected to the processor bridge. The bridge that we have called the Peripheral Bridge, acts as a multiple interface unit to serial and parallel ports and a Peripheral Component Interconnect (PCI) bus and an Industry Standard Architecture (ISA) bus. The ISA bus is an old standard and ISA sockets are rarely provided in currently produced machines. The PCI bus has the same number of parallel data wires as the processor and operates at a speed in excess of 500 Mbps. The PCI bus supplies the disk controller and a number of specialised interface chips associated with networked devices and allows a number of sockets to be placed on the motherboard into which PCI compliant cards can be plugged. The ISA bus

Figure 8.1   A generalised PC I/O bus system

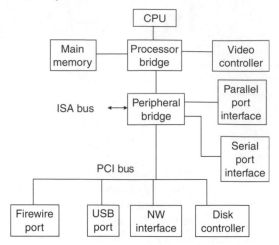

Figure 8.2   (a) Parallel (b) Serial I/O

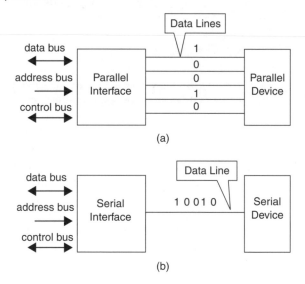

allows more sockets to be placed on the motherboard into which ISA compliant cards can be plugged.

8.2 Types of interface

Although there are many different types of interface, one important characteristic that distinguishes them is whether they support *parallel* or *serial* data transfer. A *parallel interface* transfers several bits together using a separate data line for each bit, as shown in Figure 8.2(a), while a *serial interface* transfers the data bits one at a time over a single data line, as shown in Figure 8.2(b).

Parallel interfaces tend to be used for locally connected high-speed devices, while slower or remotely connected devices are connected by a serial interface.

At a minimum, an interface circuit contains at least a one-word buffer register called an I/O *port*. The CPU can address this register and receive or send data by reading/writing to it. The interface handles any necessary data transformations and timing/control that the CPU would otherwise have to carry out itself.

Most microprocessor manufacturers provide several parallel and serial *peripheral support chips* for interfacing I/O devices to their systems. These support chips are usually *programmable*, allowing them to be modified under program control to match the characteristics of different I/O devices. They can range from relatively simple or 'dumb' circuits that provide just a few basic ports, to more 'intelligent' chips such as disk controllers, capable of moving blocks of data to and from memory, without any intervention by the CPU.

8.2.1 *Parallel I/O*

A simplified block diagram of a parallel I/O interface is shown in Figure 8.3. The unit has three registers: a *data register*, a *control register* and a *status register*, which the CPU can access over the system bus. The *external data bus* is a collection of parallel data lines, which can be configured as input or output by writing a suitable bit pattern into the *control register*. Once configured, data is transferred to or from this bus by writing/reading the data register or *port*, which acts as a *buffer* between the system bus and the *external data bus*. The *status register* is used to record or flag events, such as device ready and data available. By inspecting this register, the CPU can decide when to send or receive data.

(1) Handshaking

The external data bus must be capable of supporting data transfer with a wide range of different peripheral devices. Because the speeds of these devices are usually unknown, *control* or *handshake signals* are provided to synchronise the bus activities of the interface with those of the I/O device.

Figure 8.3 Parallel I/O interface

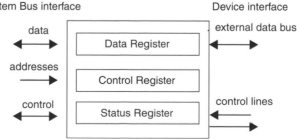

Figure 8.4 Data transfer using handshaking

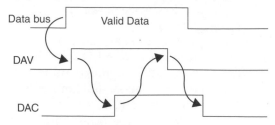

Figure 8.4 illustrates how *handshaking* is used to transfer data from an output port to a printer. This particular *handshake protocol* uses two control lines, labelled Data Available (DAV) and Data Accepted (DAC). Each control signal is *asserted* by taking its line voltage high (e.g. 5 V) and *negated* by taking its line voltage low (e.g. 0 V).

The handshake is initiated by the interface, which puts data on the data bus and asserts DAV to indicate that new data is available. When the printer detects this signal, it reads the data from the bus and acknowledges its reception by asserting DAC. In response, the interface negates DAV and removes the data from the bus. After processing the data, the printer negates DAC to complete the handshake and to indicate that it is now ready for the next character.

Most I/O interfaces allow the control lines to be programmed to suit the needs of a particular device. For example, they can be programmed to provide a *pulsed* handshake or to change an assertion from *active-high* to *active-low*.

(2) *The parallel port*

The most common peripheral device connected to the parallel port is the printer. Other devices such as scanners and external hard disk drives can also be connected to the parallel port although the current trend is to connect such devices via the USB port (see later). The physical connection to the parallel port is by means of a 25-pin, DB-25, socket normally fixed to the rear of the processor box. The original specification for the socket allocated pins 2 through 9 for the output of data and pins 1 and 10 through 17 for control signals. Pins 18 through 25 are either not used or connected together and connected to the case to provide a ground. This specification was satisfactory for printers, where the data is going in one direction, but was not appropriate for external hard disk drives that need to have read and write capability. The current specification for the port allows pins 2 through 9 to operate with data flowing in either direction in what is called *half-duplex* mode. The standard for this is IEEE 1284.

8.2.2 *Serial I/O*

As we mentioned earlier, serial data transfer involves passing data bits one at a time or in *bit-serial form*, over a single data line. Because computers and peripheral devices normally process data in parallel, a serial I/O interface

Figure 8.5 Basic principles of serial transmission

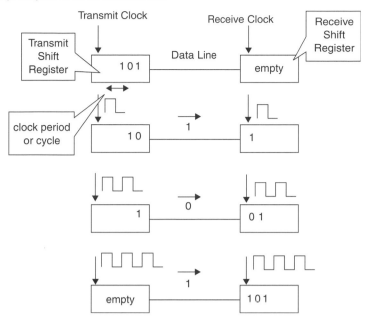

must be capable of converting data from *parallel-to-serial* form when transmitting and from *serial-to-parallel* form when receiving. The conversion is performed by *shift registers*, as we discussed in Section 3.4.2. Figure 8.5 illustrates how a 3-bit data word could be transmitted and received using a pair of shift registers.

After parallel loading of the transmit shift register, the data bits are shifted one after the other on to the data line by the transmit clock. The bits are represented by voltages, such as +12 V for '0' and −12 volts for '1'. At the receiver, the bits are sampled and shifted into the register on each cycle of the receive clock.

To recover the transmitted data correctly, the receiver needs to know when to begin sampling the voltage signal and must then keep its clock in step with the transmit clock, at least for the duration of each transmission. We will now discuss how this can be done.

(1) *Asynchronous serial transmission*

With asynchronous transmission, data is transmitted as a series of characters, each character being encapsulated in a *frame*, as shown in Figure 8.6. A character frame begins with a start bit and is terminated by one or more stop bits, each character occupying between 5 and 8 bits. The frame also includes an optional *parity bit*, which is used for error detection.

The receiver detects the arrival of each frame by its start bit, which takes the voltage on the line from its idle or logic 1 state, to its logic 0 state. This forces the receiver to reset its clock and begin sampling the data signal at the centre of each bit period. Sampling and shifting continues until a specified number of bits have been received. After checking for the parity and stop bit(s), the

Figure 8.6   Format of a typical asynchronous character frame

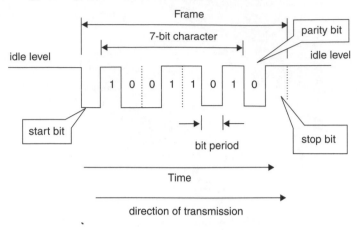

Figure 8.7   Sampling the signal

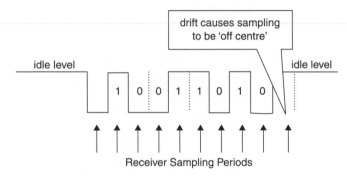

receiver transfers the character into its data register. Flags are then set in the receiver's status register to indicate that the data register is full and to report any error conditions.

TQ 8.1   If we transmitted 100 characters using the frame format shown in Figure 8.6, then how many error detection and control bits would we need to send?

Because the receive clock runs independently of the transmit clock, it is possible for a *drift* or change in its frequency to cause the data signal to be sampled 'off centre', as illustrated in Figure 8.7.

To reduce the possibility of sampling error, the receiver clock is often arranged to run at 16 or 64 times the bit rate of the received data. By doing this, a small change in the frequency of the receiver clock will still allow the data to be sampled close to the centre of each bit period.

The speed at which serial data can be transmitted depends upon the frequency at which the voltage signal can change from one level to another. A term often used when describing serial data transmission is the signalling or *baud rate*. The baud rate is the number of signal transitions that can take place in one second. When, as in Figure 8.6, a transition represents a change from binary 1 to binary 0, or binary 0 to binary 1, the baud rate is the same as the number of bits transmitted per second or *data rate*.

TQ 8.2   How many characters would we transmit in one second, if our transmission system was operating at 1200 baud?

(2) Error detection

Due to the presence of electrical *noise*, there is always a possibility that some of the data bits might become changed or corrupted during transmission. One simple *error detecting* technique is to embed an additional *parity* bit within the transmitted frame before it is sent. If *even parity* is used, the parity bit plus the number of 1s in the character must be an even number, and if odd parity is used, the number of 1s must be an odd number.

TQ 8.3   What form of parity is being used in Figure 8.6?

If on receipt of the frame, a parity error is detected, then the receiver would flag the event in its status register. This could be used to cause the communication software to take some action, such as requesting a re-transmission.

TQ 8.4   If the character plus parity bit in Figure 8.6 is received as 01011010, with the first two bits in error, will the error be detected?

Parity checking is effective only when there are a small number of bits and when the probability of a bit error is low.

(3) Synchronous serial transmission

With *synchronous* transmission, the transmitter and receiver are synchronised to a shared clock and data is transmitted in blocks rather than as individual characters. Figure 8.8 shows a typical bit-oriented synchronous transmission frame.

Each frame contains an arbitrary number of data bits, together with a few extra bits for address, control and frame checking. The frame checking bits are called a *Frame Check Sum* (FCS). The entire bit stream is enclosed by *flag*

Figure 8.8   Synchronous transmission frame (bit-oriented)

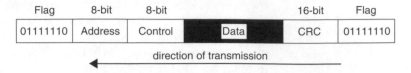

Flag	8-bit	8-bit			16-bit	Flag
01111110	Address	Control	Data		CRC	01111110

direction of transmission ◄—————————————

bytes, to indicate the start and end of a frame. The flags use a special bit pattern that is prevented from occurring in the data by inserting extra 0-bits at the transmitter and deleting them at the receiver. This is called *zero-bit insertion* or *bit stuffing*. To keep the transmitter and receiver synchronised, timing information is encoded into the bit stream. At the receiver, a clock extraction circuit recovers this information and uses it to provide a clock signal for sampling the data line. Between frames, synchronisation is maintained by transmitting a continuous stream of idle flags. Because of the reduced amount of control information in each frame, synchronous transmission is more efficient than asynchronous transmission and is used for high-speed data transmission.

(4)   *The serial port*

In early PCs this was the most common way to connect all external devices other than the printer. The serial port, often called a communications or COM port normally had two physical 9- or 25-pin sockets fixed to the back of the processor box labelled COM1 and COM2. The original intention was to use the serial port to connect to a MODEM and the pin usage, as shown in Table 8.1, reflects this.

The meanings of the pin functions are as follows:

Carrier Detect is used to indicate if the modem is connected to a live telephone line.

Receive Data is the data input line from the modem.

Transmit Data is the data output line to the modem.

Data Terminal Ready informs the modem that the computer wishes to engage in I/O.

Signal Ground is a common return path for signals.

Data Set Ready is a signal from the modem indicating that it is ready to communicate.

Request to Send is where the computer asks the modem if it is OK to send it data.

Clear to Send is a response from the modem saying that it is OK for the computer to send it data.

Ring Indicator is for the modem to tell the computer that the other end is ringing.

With different pins used for input and output, half-duplex communication is provided. The control signals, although intended for a MODEM, can be used by any device connected to the port to provide *flow control*. Flow control is the mechanism that allows different speed devices to interoperate successfully.

Table 8.1 Serial port connector pin usage

9-Pin connector		25-pin connector	
Pin	Function	Pin	Function
1	Carrier Detect	1	Not used
2	Receive Data	2	Transmit Data
3	Transmit Data	3	Receive Data
4	Data Terminal Ready	4	Request to Send
5	Signal Ground	5	Clear to Send
6	Data Set Ready	6	Data Set Ready
7	Request to Send	7	Signal Ground
8	Clear to Send	8	Carrier Detect
9	Ring Indicator	9 to 19	Not used
		20	Data Terminal Ready
		21	Not used
		22	Ring Indicator
		23 to 25	Not used

Consider the case where a PC, which is a fast producer of data, wishes to send data to a slower peripheral device, such as a printer. The PC is continuously sending a Request to Send signal and listening for a Clear to Send signal. If a Clear to Send signal is received, the PC sends data at the same time checking the Clear to Send signal. Should the Clear to Send signal cease, the PC stops sending data until the Clear to Send signal is again received.

(5) Device drivers

There are many different types of computers and even more different types of peripheral devices. How is it that almost any computer can work with almost any peripheral device via the ports described above? The answer is that the interconnection is made possible by means of a *Device Driver*. A device driver is a software program that converts data and control signals produced by a computer into the correct form of data and control signals expected by the particular peripheral device that the driver has been written for. When a peripheral device is purchased, a floppy disk or a CD-ROM is supplied that has device drivers for all the popular operating systems and computers with which the peripheral device is likely to be used. Before a new peripheral device can be used, the appropriate device driver must be loaded onto the hard disk. Most operating systems in use today are able to sense the devices connected to the ports and initiate the device drivers, which in turn

Figure 8.9   Memory-mapped I/O

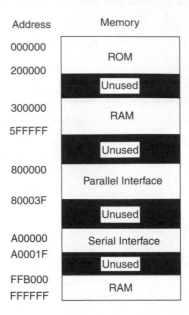

configure the ports, to which the peripheral devices are connected, to operate in the appropriate manner.

8.3 I/O addressing

There are two methods of addressing an I/O interface: *isolated* I/O and *memory-mapped* I/O. With isolated I/O, special instructions such as IN and OUT are used to access a separate I/O address space. This scheme is used by the Intel 80x86 family of processors. One advantage of using special instructions is that they can be arranged to be *privileged* and only available under a certain operating system mode of operation, see Section 9.1, so that all I/O operations are confined to the operating system.

The second method assigns portions of the main address space to the registers of each interface, as shown in Figure 8.9. As an example, the data and status registers of a parallel interface might be memory-mapped to hexadecimal addresses 800000 and 800002. These registers can then be accessed using ordinary memory reference instructions. The main disadvantage in doing this is that the address space available for expanding RAM or ROM is reduced. This is usually quite acceptable for general-purpose computer systems with a relatively small I/O requirement and is the method used by the Motorola 68000 processor.

8.4 Modes of I/O transfer

There are three basic ways of managing or scheduling the transfer of data between memory and an I/O device: *programmed* I/O, *interrupt-controlled*

Figure 8.10   Polling loop flow chart

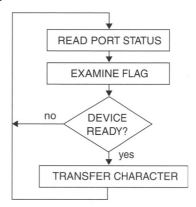

I/O and *Direct Memory Access* (DMA). The extent to which the CPU is actively involved in the transfer depends upon the 'intelligence' of the interface and the particular mode of transfer adopted.

8.4.1   Programmed I/O

We begin our discussion by considering polled or programmed I/O. With programmed I/O, the processor is totally in control of all aspects of the operation. Each data transfer is carried out by executing a polling loop, as illustrated by the flow chart in Figure 8.10.

In this example, the processor schedules the transfer of data to a printer, by first reading the ports status register to see if the printer is able to accept another character. If on examination of this register the 'ready' flag indicates that the printer is busy, the processor loops back and reads the status register again; otherwise, it transfers a character into the data register. Each time data is written to the register, the interface resets the 'ready' flag and the processor resumes polling on the next character.

The disadvantage with programmed I/O is that the process of checking status bits can waste a lot of otherwise useful processing time, particularly with slow peripheral devices like printers. Even with a relatively fast printer, a processor capable of executing a million instructions per second will often poll a status register about 1000 times before sending a character. Keeping the processor tied up in a polling loop makes poor use of its processing power.

8.4.2   Interrupt-driven I/O

A more efficient strategy, called *interrupt-driven* I/O, lets the device signal to the processor when it needs servicing. This frees the processor for much of the time and allows it to continue with more useful tasks, such as running other user programs or managing the system's resources.

(1)   Interrupts

Virtually all processors have one or more *interrupt request* pins for detecting and recording the arrival of interrupt requests. When an interface or other

Figure 8.11   Interrupt and possible acknowledgement

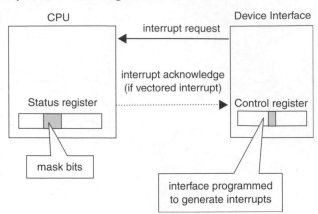

circuit signals an interrupt, as illustrated in Figure 8.11, the processor records the request as pending. Towards the end of each instruction cycle, the processor examines any requests and determines whether to accept and process them, or whether to ignore them and continue executing its current program. The decision depends upon the setting of *interrupt mask* bit(s) in the processor's status register.

When an interrupt is accepted, the processor passes control to an *interrupt handler* or *service routine or device driver*, which performs a task, such as sending a character to a printer. Before control is passed to the service routine, the processor preserves the contents of its Instruction Pointer (IP) and Flags Register (FR), by *pushing* them on to a special area of memory called the *stack*. It also sets the mask bits in the Flags Register to match the *priority level* of the interrupt request, before loading the Instruction Pointer with the start address of the service routine.

For *autovectored* interrupt handling, the start address is found by generating a vector number, the number being related to the priority level indicated by the interrupt request pins. This is used to extract the start address or vector from a table of *exception vectors*, which are stored in some fixed memory location. Exceptions are deviations from the normal activity of the processor.

If *vectored* interrupt handling is used, then after receiving the interrupt, the processor sends an *interrupt acknowledgement* signal (shown by a dashed line in Figure 8.11). The device responds by putting a vector number on the data bus, which the processor reads and uses to index the exception table.

After loading the PC with the address of the service routine, the exception handling program is executed until an *Interrupt Return* (IRET) instruction is encountered. This instruction *pulls* or *pops* the FR and IP from the stack and passes control back to the interrupted program.

TQ 8.5   In what ways do interrupts differ from subroutine calls?

Figure 8.12   Use of priority encoder to handle multiple interrupts

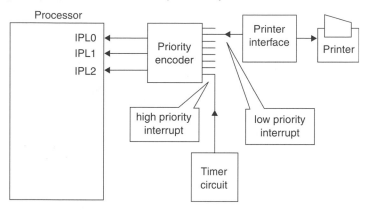

(2)   *Prioritised interrupts*

When interrupts are generated by a number of different devices, a priority scheme must be used to decide which interrupt should be handled first and whether one interrupt can interrupt another. Assume that a processor has three pins for requesting interrupts: IPL0, IPL1 and IPL2. Normally the pins are held high, a request being made by pulling one or more of the pins low. The priority of the request ranges from level 7 (highest) to level 0 (lowest). A level 7, or *non-maskable* interrupt is generated by taking all three pins low, whilst a level 1 interrupt is generated by asserting IPL0. To arbitrate between simultaneous requests, an interrupt *priority encoder* is usually used, as illustrated in Figure 8.12.

In this illustration, because the system timer interrupt is of a higher priority level than the printer interrupt, then if both devices generate interrupts simultaneously, the priority encoder will forward only the timer interrupt to the processor.

When the processor processes an interrupt, it sets an interrupt mask to the same priority level as the interrupt. Any further interrupts are then ignored, unless they have a higher priority than the one being serviced.

It is possible to extend the number of interrupting devices beyond seven by connecting more than one device to the same interrupt line. In such cases, when an interrupt is received, the service routine must identify which of the devices, connected to the interrupt line, is the source of the request. This is done by examining the status registers of each device in turn to find which device has its *interrupt flag* set. Once found, the service routine selects the appropriate handler.

8.4.3   *Direct Memory Access*

One disadvantage of interrupt-driven I/O is that all data transfers involve moving data to and from the processor's registers. Added to this, there is the overhead caused by preserving and retrieving the IP, FR and any other registers used by the service routine. For rapid data transfer this can be too slow and an alternative strategy, called *Direct Memory Access* (DMA), must be used.

Figure 8.13 Concept of disk/DMA controller configuration

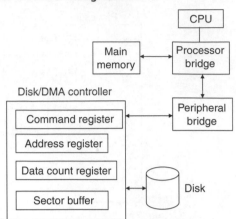

Many device controllers, particularly those used for block devices, support DMA. An example of such a device is a disk controller, which transfers blocks of bytes directly between a hard or floppy disk and main memory, as illustrated in Figure 8.13.

In Section 7.2, we described how magnetic disks were divided into tracks and sectors, each sector being used to store a block of data. To read a sector, the CPU first loads the controller's *address register* with the memory address of the data buffer to be used and the controller's *data count register* with the number of bytes to be read. A few bytes are then written into the *command register* to specify the track, sector numbers and the mode of transfer to be used ('read' in this case). The controller responds by stepping the read/write head to the appropriate track and reading the serial bit stream from the specified sector into its *sector buffer register*. After reading the block and checking for any errors, the DMA controller copies the buffer into memory, using information provided by the address and data count registers. The controller does this by first gaining control of the system bus through a series of handshakes with the CPU. As *bus master*, the controller now has full control of the buses and begins writing the bytes one after the other into the address specified in the address register. After each byte is written, the data count register is decremented and the address register incremented. This continues until the data count register reaches zero, at which point, the controller relinquishes control of the buses and hands it back to the CPU. Normally after doing this, the controller generates an interrupt, to inform the CPU that it is ready to be initialised for a further transfer.

The mode of operation we have just described is called *burst transfer mode*. Although this is the fastest mode of I/O transfer, it forces the CPU to idle for the duration of the transfer, which is acceptable only on simple systems. For most systems, it is more efficient for the DMA controller to just slow the CPU down by 'stealing' bus cycles. This method of operation is called *cycle stealing mode*.

In cycle stealing mode, just before the CPU begins a bus cycle, it is suspended, and a single word is transferred by the DMA controller. After regaining control, the CPU then completes the bus cycle, for example, by fetching an instruction or reading an operand. It should be noted that suspending the CPU in this way is not the same as interrupting it, as no register preservation needs to be carried out. The overall effect of this mode of transfer is to cause the CPU to slow down, rather than forcing it to temporarily halt.

Even with a DMA controller, there is still a need for CPU intervention after each block is transferred. To reduce CPU involvement, particularly when an operation requires several blocks to be transferred, a more specialised controller or *I/O processor* is used. I/O processors or *channel controllers* can execute a series of I/O instructions in the form of an *I/O program* that is stored either in controller memory or in a fixed area of main memory. The I/O instructions include details of the number and size of blocks to be transferred, which blocks need to be read and written and the transfer addresses involved. Normally this program is set up by the operating system.

8.5 I/O buses

The parallel and serial port sockets are two ways in which devices can be connected to a PC. There are a number of other ways that make use of I/O buses. We will consider a number of these, starting with using sockets inside the processor box and then looking at two more that use external sockets.

On the motherboard of most PCs are a number of sockets into which optional printed circuit boards may be plugged. These are often referred to as expansion slots. There are two distinctly different types of socket and each conforms to a standard. Older machines have Industry Standard Architecture (ISA) slots and more recent machines have Peripheral Component Interconnect (PCI) slots. Some motherboards have two or three of each.

8.5.1 ISA bus

This is a slow bus that works at 16 MBytes per second and uses a large 98-pin socket. In the early days of PCs, many different ISA plug-in cards were produced. These included network interface cards, modem cards, real time clock cards (needed before a real time clock was part of the motherboard), sound and video cards for providing the connection to external loud speakers and the monitor, plug-in hard disks and interface cards to external modems, hard disks and games joysticks. Some plug-in boards will have internal connectors to which internal devices may be connected while others will have connectors that can be accessed from outside the processor box to enable external devices to be connected. At a time when the clock speed of processors was 25 MHz, the ISA bus speed was more than adequate. The ISA standard has undergone a number of upgrades in terms of speed and data path width. The original ISA had a data path 8 bits wide, which was then increased to 16 bits then to 32 bits to keep up with the increase in the word size of processors. The data rates were increased from 16 to 32 (Extended ISA, EISA) to 100 and finally to 132 MBytes per second (Video Electronics Standards Association Local Bus, VL-Bus). Two ISA slots may be found on some current motherboards thus providing an extended life for old ISA cards.

8.5.2 PCI bus

This is a high-speed bus that uses a relatively small 120-pin socket of which 47 are used. The idea is the same as for ISA in that plug-in printed circuit boards are plugged into the sockets. PCI gives direct access to main memory, data transfer rates up to 1 GBytes per second with a data path width of 64 bits and considerable independence of operation without the need to use the CPU. All current expansion cards use PCI bus sockets but the computer industry is already working towards a higher performance replacement.

8.5.3 *Integrated Drive Electronics bus*

If you look inside any PC processor box, you will see a number of flat multi-core cables known as ribbon cables. The widest one, which is connected to the hard disk, is the Integrated Drive Electronics (IDE) cable and forms the IDE bus. The IDE bus is the most common way in which storage devices are connected to the PC internal bus. The IDE specification is designed for those storage devices where the controller is an integral part of the disk drive and provides a standard interface for all manufacturers of disk drives. The controller is the printed circuit board that is mounted on the disk drive. The printed circuit board provides an electronic interface to the head and sector layout of the disk drive.

The IDE ribbon cable consists of 40 separate wires and has three connectors on it, one at each end and the third connector, two-thirds of the way along the cable. The connectors that are closest to each other are connected to disk drives and the other end connector is plugged into a special connector on the motherboard. The motherboard connector is fed from the peripheral bridge via an on board chip. When two disks are connected to the same cable, one is defined as a master and the other a slave. The master is connected to the end connector and the slave to the intermediate connector. The disks are normally configured to be a master or a slave by setting jumpers on the disk drive circuit board.

Like most aspects of computers, IDE has been enhanced over the years. These enhancements have enabled increases in data transfer rates and disk storage sizes to be handled and connection to CD-ROM and DVD drives, floppy disk drives and internal magnetic tape back-up devices. Extended IDE (EIDE) increased the data transfer rate from 4 to 16 Mbps with the capability to handle disk sizes over 100 GBytes and Ultra-IDE has a data transfer rate of over 33 Mbps and using an 80-core ribbon cable, a transfer rate of over 66 Mbps can be achieved.

Some motherboards have two IDE channels, so providing the facility to connect up to four disk drives. When using multiple disk drives, IDE provides a facility to set which is the master and which are the slave devices. This facility is known as *cable select* (CS) and it requires the jumpers on the drives to be set to CS and special IDE cables to be used. What makes the cables special is that only one ribbon cable has pin 28 connected to one of the drives. The drive receiving a signal on its pin 28 becomes the master, the others default to being slaves.

The IDE ribbon cable connected to floppy disk drives has fewer cores than the hard disk cable and is connected to a special connector on the motherboard.

TQ 8.6   If a PC has a hard disk and a CD-ROM drive, which should be the master device?

8.5.4   Universal Serial Bus

(1)   USB concepts

Almost all new PCs will have at least two Universal Serial Bus (USB) connectors on their back panel. These connectors and their associated cables and hubs are the means by which any device can be connected to the computer. Printers, scanners, mice, keyboards and external storage devices are amongst the multitude of peripheral devices that are being produced that have USB connectability. Simply plugging into the USB port enables up to 127 devices to be connected with each being able to operate at up to 6 Mbps. The maximum bandwidth of the system is 12 Mbps so no more than one device can operate at 6 Mbps at any one time. Any device connected to the USB port is detected by the operating system and its driver is loaded automatically. USB devices are *hot pluggable* which means that they can be connected and disconnected at any time without upsetting other connected devices.

USB uses two types of connector, an 'A' type which is rather flat and plugs into the computer and a 'B' type which is nearly square and plugs into the peripheral device. Some peripheral devices have a fixed lead with an 'A' type connector on the end for plugging into the computer.

The USB hub provides a convenient way of connecting more than two peripheral devices to a computer. The hub, which can have four or eight ports, is connected to one of the computer's USB ports and allows four or eight devices to be connected. Hubs can be connected to hubs, as shown in Figure 8.14, until the maximum of 127 devices is reached.

The USB cable consists of a twisted pair for carrying data and two further wires that provide a 5-V, 500 mA supply for driving small peripheral devices such as a mouse or a games joystick. The four wires are covered by a shielding braid and an outer cover of PVC. Individual USB cables cannot be more than five metres long and any connected device must not have more than 30 metres of cable between it and the computer.

Hubs can be *unpowered* or *powered*. Unpowered hubs are suitable for connecting devices that have their own power supply and powered hubs can be used to provide additional power to that supplied by the computer via the USB cable.

(2)   USB operation

When the computer is switched on, the USB system assigns an address to all devices connected to the USB ports. Any device subsequently connected to

Figure 8.14   A typical USB configuration using hubs

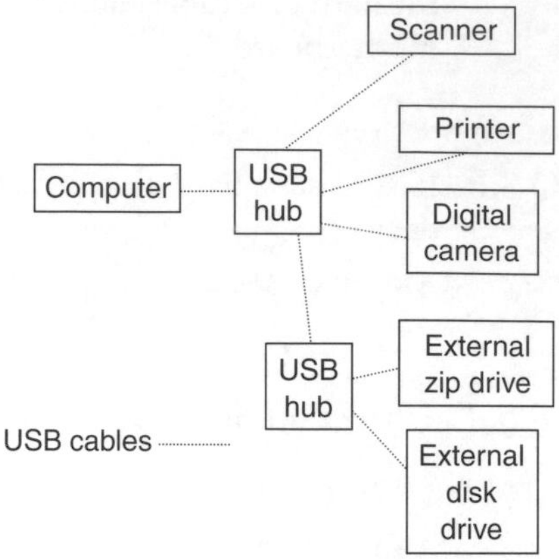

the USB cable is also assigned an address. Each device is interrogated to find out what type of data transfer is required. The possibilities are interrupt, bulk and isochronous. Interrupt is for devices that send very little data on an occasional basis, such as a keyboard. Bulk is for devices that receive or send data in large blocks such as a printer. The block is up to 64 bytes long and error checking is done to ensure correct transmission. Isochronous is for devices that require a stream of data that must be sent in real time. A loud speaker is a device that requires this type of transmission. Isochronous transmission has no error checking. Devices that use interrupt and isochronous transmission are given priority over devices that require bulk transmission in an attempt to share the available bandwidth and provide the type of service the connected device requires.

The bus is also used by the computer to send control information to devices and receive responses from devices. This traffic has the highest priority.

8.5.5   *Firewire*

Firewire, also known as the IEEE 1394 High Performance Serial Bus, is like USB in that it provides a facility to connect peripheral devices to a computer. The devices are connected in a string, called daisy chaining, to a Firewire port, which has a special IEEE 1394 connector. Firewire does not use hubs. The 1394 connector is not as flat as a USB type 'A' connector and has six pins rather than four. Firewire is actually older than USB and was designed to allow fast streamed or isochronous transfer of data between devices such as digital video cameras and computers. Firewire provides a hot pluggable connection with the operating system sensing devices connected to the firewire cable. When the computer is switched on, the devices are sensed and allocated a unique number in a similar fashion to USB. With Firewire, devices can send data to each other without involving the computer. Up to 63 devices can be interconnected using a single Firewire system with data transfer rates of up to 400 Mbps being possible. Firewire uses a cable that has

Figure 8.15 **An example of a Firewire system**

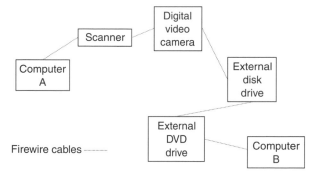

two twisted pairs of data cables and a pair of power providing cables that can provide power to non-powered Firewire devices. Individual Firewire cables can be up to 4.5 metres long and when used in daisy chain fashion, the total length can be up to 72 metres. Firewire is a little more expensive to implement when compared with USB, which is one of the reasons that USB is the more popular. Figure 8.15 shows an example of a Firewire system.

8.5.6 *Small Computer System Interface*

Small Computer System Interface (SCSI), pronounced Skuzzy, is a high-speed parallel interface primarily intended for connecting multiple hard disk drives to high performance computer workstations or high-end servers. The motherboard can have a SCSI controller card plugged into a PCI socket or a SCSI capability may be provided as part of the motherboard. In either case, a multiway socket is provided on the outside of the processor box and an internal connection for a ribbon cable for connecting to internal devices.

The big problem with SCSI is that there are a number of variations which use different cable sizes, different connectors, different bus widths, different data transfer rates, different bus speeds and either a maximum of seven or 15 devices that can be connected.

Internal devices have a single SCSI connection and are connected to the SCSI ribbon cable, which has a connector at each end and one or more connectors along its length. One end of the cable connects to the motherboard if an integrated controller is provided or to the controller card if a plug-in card is used and the devices are connected to the sockets on the ribbon cable making sure that the end connector on the cable is used. Connecting to the end connector provides what is known as electrical termination, which prevents electrical signal reflections from occurring.

External devices have two SCSI connectors on them, enabling the devices to be connected in a daisy chain. The end of the external SCSI bus must be terminated to prevent signal reflections. Some devices provide automatic termination if only one of their connectors is used and if one such device is to be connected it should be connected as the last device in the chain. If no such device is being connected, then a special terminator must be plugged into the unused connector of the last device in the chain.

Table 8.2   Some varieties of SCSI

SCSI variety	Bus speed (MHz)	Data transfer rate (MBytes per second)	Max number of connected devices	Bus width (bits)
Sync SCSI	5	4	7	8
Async SCSI	5	5	7	8
Wide SCSI	5	10	15	16
Fast SCSI	10	10	7	8
Fast Wide SCSI	10	20	15	16
Ultra SCSI	20	20	7	8
Ultra2 SCSI	40	40	7	8
Ultra3 SCSI	40	160	15	16

SCSI devices must be allocated a unique identifier in order that they can be addressed. This identifier can be hardware set or with some versions of SCSI, the controller can allocate the identifier by setting software switches in the connected devices.

Mention was made above to the fact that there are a number of varieties of SCSI. Table 8.2 shows some of the variations that are in use.

8.6   I/O devices

There are many different types of peripheral devices that can be connected to a PC. This section covers the basic principles of a few of the most common. The way in which a particular peripheral device is physically connected to the PC depends to a certain extent on the device and there may also be a choice from several options. Typical methods of connection will be discussed with the description of the peripheral device.

8.6.1   Input devices

These include keyboards, mice, games joysticks, scanners, cameras, optical mark readers, magnetic readers and bar code readers.

(1)   Keyboards

A keyboard consists of a matrix of switches. When a key is pressed, the CPU needs to be interrupted and given a binary code to inform it which key or

Figure 8.16   Section of a keyboard switch matrix

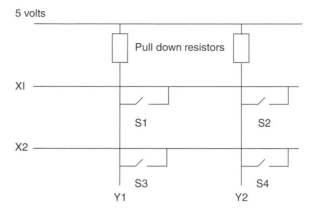

5 volts

Pull down resistors

XI

S1   S2

X2

S3   S4

Y1   Y2

Table 8.3   Signal values for a four key matrix

S1 closed	Y1 = zero when X1 = zero
S2 closed	Y2 = zero when X1 = zero
S3 closed	Y1 = zero when X2 = zero
S4 closed	Y2 = zero when X2 = zero

keys have been pressed. We have covered the interrupt aspect earlier in this chapter so we will consider only how which key has been pressed is determined and sent to the CPU. The keyboard contains a complex microchip which continuously scans all the switches, several times a second, looking for one or a combination of switches that have been pressed. Remember that shift, Ctrl and Alt keys being pressed in conjunction with another key means a different code to that produced by pressing a single key. When a key press is detected, the keyboard chip sends an interrupt signal to the serial port to which it is connected, followed by an appropriate binary code in serial format. The code is loaded into the port buffer ready for the CPU to read. The key scanning then continues.

Figure 8.16 shows a small section of the key matrix. With the switches open, the pull-up resistors make the Y lines 5 V. These lines are monitored by the keyboard processor. The X lines are normally connected to a 5-V supply but in turn are taken to zero volts by a scanning supply. If no switches are closed, the Y line voltages remain at 5 V. However, if say switch 2 is closed, as X1 is taken to zero volts by the scanning supply, line Y2 will be pulled to zero volts. Combining the scanning signal and the voltages on the Y lines tells the keyboard processor which keys have been pressed. Table 8.3 shows the combinations for the four keys.

Keyboards are most commonly connected to a special socket on the back of the processor box, which is in turn connected to the serial port. However, there is a growing tendency to use an optical connection, similar to that used in TV remote controls, or even a radio connection. This gives greater freedom in positioning the keyboard. In both cases, a computer end receiver is connected to the keyboard socket and the keyboard is fitted with a battery to supply the keyboard electronics and the optical or radio transmitter.

(2)   Mice and games joysticks

The mouse is the device that has undoubtedly had the greatest impact on PC use. It is used as a pointing and selection device and for many applications is the sole means of input to the computer. There are many varieties of mice, but the most common consists of a small plastic case, which has two or three switches on top and a ball on the bottom. The ball is rotated by moving the mouse over a flat surface and in doing this, a pointer or cursor symbol displayed on the monitor screen can be positioned. Clicking the mouse switches with the cursor over symbols and other parts of the screen display, triggers software action.

The construction of the mouse is very simple. The switches are normal micro switches and the ball presses on two shafts mounted at right angles. The shafts are connected to position detecting devices, which can be either electrical or optical and the movements are encoded and sent to the computer in serial mode. Movement of the mouse generates an interrupt and the movement information is sent to the serial port buffer where the CPU can process it into cursor movement on the screen.

Mice are connected to the computer by means of a cable plugged into a special socket on the back of the processor box. As with keyboards, mice are now available with optical and radio connection to the computer.

A tracker ball is like an upside down mouse with a larger ball. The ball is mounted in a plastic block and is moved using the fingers. The switches are mounted close to the ball and are used in the same way as those on a mouse. Tracker balls are often found as a built-in feature on portable computers. Games joysticks are similar in operation to a mouse except instead of a ball driving the position detecting devices by means of two shafts, a joystick is mechanically coupled to the position detecting devices. The head of the joystick is often fitted with a switch that is used to trigger actions in the game being played. Again the connection to the computer is serial and can be via cable, optical or radio links. Some PCs have a special games port or socket, which is internally connected, to the serial port.

(3)   Scanners

A scanner in its simplest form consists of a flat glass plate on which a picture or page of text is laid face down and is illuminated by a strong light. Under the plate is an optical sensing device mounted on a carriage, which moves from side to side, and at the same time the carriage is moved from the top of the picture or page to the bottom. The sensing device can make over ten thousand side-to-side scans in the length of the page. The sensing device is looking for changes in tone and colour and is encoding these changes to form what is known as a *bit map*. The bit map is then stored as a file. The bit map file produced when a text document is scanned can be further processed to produce a word processor type document, which can be further processed. This process is sometimes called Optical Character Recognition (OCR). The file produced from a scanned picture can also be processed and edited using graphics software.

In reality, although the top to bottom scanning is normally accomplished by moving the carriage from top to bottom, the side-to-side scan makes use of a line of optical sensors that are optically scanned across the page. The greater the number of sensors and the smaller the vertical distance moved for each horizontal scan, the better the definition and quality of the scanned image. Typical scanners produce the equivalent of 1200 dots per inch (dpi) horizontally and 2400 dpi vertically with 48-bit colour depth. Scanners can be connected to the parallel port but the USB bus is becoming the preferred method of connection.

Scanners are relatively slow devices taking between 30 sec to scan and produce a black and white A4 size image bit map to 1.5 minutes for a full colour image bit map.

The bar code reader and the hand held scanner are two other types of scanners worthy of mention. The bar code reader is used to read the striped bar codes that are printed on many of the goods we buy. It consists of a beam of low-power laser light that is scanned across the bar code. The light reflected from the spaces between the bars is detected and converted into a code. The code is used to identify the product. The Universal Product Code (UPC) is an international standard for bar coded products. The hand held scanner consists of a line of sensors mounted on a bar that is contained in a plastic case. The sensors are just behind a window and behind the sensors is a light source. The scanner is moved by hand down the image to be scanned. The scanning process is not very accurate and these devices are only used when a portable scanner is needed. For a fully portable application, the scanner is often connected to a palm top or personal organiser type of computer.

(4) *Magnetic input devices*

Credit cards, railway tickets and personal identity cards have magnetic stripes onto which data can be stored. The data can be read and even written by swiping the card through a reader/writer. The mode of operation is identical to that used for magnetic tape with the exception that the codes often contain error checking facilities as the manual swipe process can be rather erratic.

The read/write devices are normally connected to the serial port or USB bus.

Magnetic Ink Character Recognition (MICR) is a technique used on cheques and some other banking documents. The characters use a standard font and are printed using ink that contains iron oxide. The iron oxide can be magnetised and the magnetic patterns read to detect the individual characters. The benefit of MICR is that people as well as computers can read the characters.

TQ 8.7   What is the effect on a credit card if a strong magnet is wiped over the magnetic stripe?

TQ 8.8   What is the effect on a cheque if a strong magnet is wiped over the MICR characters?

8.6.2 *Output devices*

There are many different types of output devices and a whole book could be written covering these alone. We will look at the basic principles of a few of the most common.

(1) *Monitors*

These include cathode ray tube (CRT) based devices, which operate like a standard TV screen and liquid crystal systems that are used on laptop computers. Almost all computers are now equipped with colour monitors and this description covers colour and not monochrome devices.

A schematic of a CRT is shown in Figure 8.17. In the base of the tube are three electron guns that produce a stream of electrons that are projected towards the face of the tube. The inside face of the tube is coated with groups of three different phosphor spots and these collectively are called a pixel. The resolution of the screen is determined by the number of pixels on the screen. There are a number of standards the most common of which is super video graphics array (SVGA), which has a range from 800 horizontal by 600 vertical pixels (800 $\times$ 600) to 1600 $\times$ 1200. Each spot in the set of three glows with a different colour when hit by a stream of electrons. The colours

Figure 8.17   Schematic of a CRT

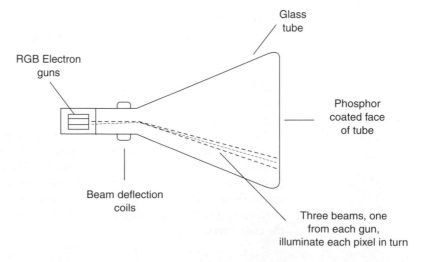

are red, blue and green. The apparent colour of a pixel is a mixture of these three colours with the colour being produced by varying the intensity of the three electron beams. The actual number of different colours that can be produced depends on the graphics card that is being used to drive the display and the number of bits used to code the colour of the pixel. Many graphics cards are capable of being set to different standards. Two common standards are 16 and 256 colours, which use four and eight bits respectively. A third standard, using 24 bits, makes provision for 16 million colour shades and gives what is known as *true colour*.

The groups of spots are sequentially scanned using a method known as *raster scan*. The scan starts at the top left hand pixel and progresses across the top to the right hand end. The beams are now moved to the next row of pixels and these are scanned left to right. The scanning proceeds to the bottom of the screen covering all rows. Because the afterglow of the pixel phosphors is quite short (afterglow is the residual glow after the electron beams have left the pixel) a refresh scan rate of at least 60 times a second is needed to prevent the eye seeing the scanning taking place.

CRT based monitors are available in different sizes with the size being specified by the diagonal dimension across the viewing area of the screen with 15, 17 and 22 inch screens being the most popular sizes. CRTs are bulky and heavy and the cases they are housed in take up a great deal of desk space.

(2) *Liquid crystal displays*

The physics of these devices is complex and outside the scope of this book so we provide only a simplified description. LCDs are light and very flat and absorb very little power, which makes them ideal for laptop computers especially when powered by a battery. The display is bright but does not have such a wide viewing angle as a CRT. As far as the video card is concerned, the LCD looks and behaves like a CRT.

An LCD consists of two transparent plates, the size of the display, with a liquid crystal substance sandwiched and sealed between them. There is a matrix of vertical and horizontal control wires between the liquid crystal and the rear plate that control the pixels and a matrix of colour filters just behind the front plate. Behind the rear plate is illumination, normally provided by a cold cathode light source. Figure 8.18 shows a simplified cross section of a LCD.

Figure 8.18 Simplified cross section of a liquid crystal display

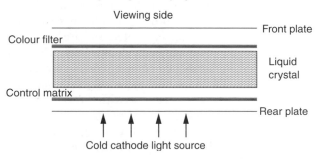

There are two types of control systems used inside the LCD, passive and active. Passive control uses an electric field set up at the pixel by applying a voltage to the appropriate vertical and horizontal control wires. Active control uses a *thin film transistor* at each pixel. The drive current needs of the transistors are much lower than that required by passive control and the display is much sharper and brighter.

LCDs are more expensive than CRT based displays but can be built much larger than is possible with a single CRT. Active controlled devices are more expensive than passive controlled devices.

In spite of their higher cost, LCDs are becoming increasingly popular as desktop computer monitors because they take up very little desk space and reduce the very low radiation risk that is associated with CRTs to zero.

(3) *Printers*

These can be grouped into impact printers, where a print head produces an image on the page by means of an ink impregnated ribbon in much the same way as was used in old-fashioned typewriters, and non-impact printers where the image is thrown or sprayed onto the page. The quality of the print is measured in dots per inch with 600 dpi giving a reasonable image.

Current impact printers almost all use a dot matrix print head. The print head itself consists of between seven to 24 electromagnetically driven needles arranged in a vertical line. The head is moved across the page such that each character is formed from between five to 48 columns. For each column, the appropriate needles are pushed against an inked ribbon, which marks the paper. The normal mode of operation, known as draft mode, prints quickly and produces a reasonable quality of text. Higher quality printing can be obtained by moving the head over the paper in smaller increments horizontally and by moving the head vertically by a small amount so as to produce overlapping dots. The effect of this is to increase the dpi and hence the quality of the printed image. Dot matrix printers are normally used for printing text and are suitable for use with multi-part paper. The technique is also used in small printers that are used to produce tickets and cash till receipts. Dot matrix printers can be used to produce graphical images but the quality is rather low as is the printing speed when used for this purpose.

The most common non-impact printers are ink jet and laser printers. Ink jet printer technology has evolved considerably over the years to a point where they are very cheap to produce and achieve a very high quality of both monochrome and colour printing for text and graphics. Colour prints of photographs, taken with a digital camera, look almost as good as those taken using photographic film. Laser printers can handle much larger volumes than ink jet printers and are the favourite for large offices that have bulk printing needs. Colour laser printers are available but their initial cost is high as are their running costs in terms of consumables.

A monochrome ink jet printer has a black ink cartridge, which holds the ink, and integral with this is the print head. A colour printer has a cartridge that holds cyan, magenta and yellow inks in separate chambers of an ink cartridge and three integral print heads, one for each colour ink. Figure 8.19 shows a simplified diagram of the print head part of an ink jet printer.

Figure 8.19 Simplified diagram of an ink jet printer print head

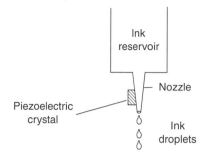

Figure 8.20 Schematic of a laser printer

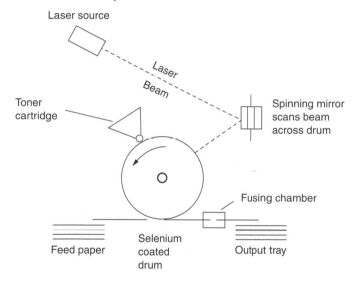

The ink is ejected from a small nozzle in the print head towards the paper in the form of a droplet thus forming a dot. Droplet ejection can be achieved in two ways. Method one is to boil the ink by means of a heater in the base of the nozzle, the resulting expanding bubble forces a droplet of ink out of the nozzle. Method two works by flicking a droplet from the end of the nozzle by vibrating the nozzle at a high frequency using a piezoelectric crystal. The cartridge containing the print head is mounted on a carriage that moves across the page which is to receive the printing and the page is moved in the vertical direction using friction rollers so that the whole page can be covered. The character and image forming process is identical to the dot matrix printer but using sprayed on dots rather than impact created dots.

The laser printer is a derivative of the office photocopier and Figure 8.20 is a schematic that illustrates the essential parts.

The laser printer has also undergone a developmental process that has had a major impact in reducing their price but they are still more expensive than ink jet printers. They have a minor drawback in that they need to go through a warm up period, which means that they take some time to produce a single copy. However, they are relatively fast for producing multiple copies. They are quiet in operation and produce good quality printing at a price per copy that is lower than an ink jet printer.

The following is a basic description of how a laser printer works. The rotating drum has a coating of selenium which has the property that normally it is an electrical insulator but when exposed to light it becomes a conductor of electricity. The coating on the drum is initially given an overall electrical charge. The laser beam is then scanned across the width of the drum while it is rotating, being deflected by the spinning mirror. Where a spot of laser light falls on the drum, the selenium is turned into its conducting state and the charge leaks away at the spot. The intensity of the laser beam is altered by the bit map of the image that is to be printed on the page of paper. At the end of the scan revolution of the drum, the selenium coating has a charge image identical to the bit map of the image. Toner is now applied to the drum where it sticks to the discharged spots. A sheet of paper is now pressed against the rotating drum and the toner is transferred to the paper. The paper with the toner on it is now heated by fuser rollers, which melts the toner onto the paper.

All the printers discussed above have complex electronics including storage as part of the printer, which means that the computer only needs to send the characters or the bit map to be printed and the printer does the rest.

(3) *Sound output*

Early PCs had a small internal loudspeaker that was used to provide the user with audible warning beeps. Lately, with the introduction of computer games and the growing use of computers in learning situations and the ability to play video films supplied on DVDs on the computer, the need for quality sound reproduction in stereo or even 'surround sound' has arisen. The poor quality internal speaker was first replaced with two speakers sometimes mounted inside the monitor cabinet, one on each side of the display or in separate cabinets that could be positioned each side of the user to provide stereo listening. The trend now is to provide high-quality amplifiers as part of a plug-in sound card, with the amplifiers powering Hi-Fi speakers in specially designed cabinets. As an alternative, the low-level digital sound signals are fed to self-powered speakers, again contained in special cabinets, with the audio power amplifiers being contained in the cabinets. Ever more complex sound cards are being produced that handle between four and eight channel surround sound that is available on the latest types of home entertainment DVD disks. These require four to eight separate speaker cabinets that can be placed in the appropriate positions to create the surround sound environment. Computers are now the main tool for editing video films and software packages are available that enable animated graphics to be produced. Firewire connected video cameras provide the raw material for the graphic designers to use and a Musical Instrument Digital Interface (MIDI) enables music to be added. The finished audio/video product is then saved on recordable DVD disks.

8.7 Summary

A peripheral device is connected to a computer system through an interface. The type of interface required depends upon whether the device supports parallel or serial data transmission. Programmable interfaces contain addressable registers for storing data, reporting status information and controlling the way in which the interface operates. Register addresses can be arranged as part of the main memory address space (memory-mapped) or as part of a separate I/O address space (isolated-I/O).

Peripherals located more than a few metres away from the computer use serial data transmission and require a serial interface, such as USB or Firewire. Serial data can be transmitted on a character-by-character basis, using asynchronous transmission, or in blocks, using synchronous transmission. Asynchronous transmission is slower and less efficient than synchronous transmission.

Three scheduling strategies are used to control data transfer between peripheral devices and memory: programmed I/O, interrupt-driven I/O and Direct Memory Access (DMA). Programmed I/O is simple but inefficient in terms of processor usage. Interrupt-controlled I/O is usually more efficient but is too slow for very fast I/O, such as reading or writing blocks of data from a disk. DMA offers the fastest form of I/O, using a controller to transfer data directly between main memory and the I/O device. DMA can be used in burst transfer mode or cycle stealing mode. Cycle stealing mode is preferred in high performance systems, as it slows the CPU down rather than causing it to stop for the duration of the transfer. To reduce the intervention of the CPU even further, some systems use more intelligent I/O processors or channel controllers.

USB is becoming the most common method of connecting devices to computers as it is cheap and easy to use. Most peripheral devices are now available with a USB connection.

High-end workstations and servers that have multiple hard disks use a SCSI bus to connect the disks to the system but care must be taken as there are several versions of SCSI and they are not compatible. With the lowering of prices for flat liquid crystal type displays, many new desktop computers are using this type of display in preference to the older CRT type of display.

Ink jet printers are the most common office and home printer where small quantities are the norm. They produce good quality and cheap colour printout. For the larger quantities of printout where speed is important, laser printers are used. Colour laser printers are available but they are expensive to purchase and relatively expensive to run. Dot matrix impact printers are still widely used when multi-part pre-printed paper is being used.

Answers to in text questions

TQ 8.1   The bit pattern stored would be 11111111 and therefor the port would be configured as an 8-bit output port.

TQ 8.2   For each character we need to send one start bit, one stop bit and a parity bit. Therefor to send 100 characters, we need to transmit 300 extra bits.

TQ 8.3   Because the bit rate is the same as the baud rate, then 1200 bits per second (bps) can be transmitted. Each character frame contains 10 bits, therefore the character data rate is 120 characters per second (cps).

TQ 8.4   The total number of 1s in the character plus parity bit is 4. Therefore even parity is being used.

TQ 8.5   With a 2-bit error, the received data still has even parity and therefore the error will pass undetected.

TQ 8.6   Subroutine calls take place when an instruction is executed, whereas Interrupts are caused by a signal.
　　　　Subroutine calls cause only the IP to be pushed on to the stack, while Interrupts preserve both the IP and FR. Subroutines end with a RTN instruction whereas Interrupt service routines end with an IRET instruction.

TQ 8.7   The stored data would be destroyed as the magnet would corrupt the stored bits.

TQ 8.8   There would be no effect as the characters receive their magnetisation when they are read.

EXERCISES

1   By referring to Figure 8.7, draw a diagram of an asynchronous character frame when the ASCII character, 'A', is being transmitted. Assume that even parity is used and that the frame is terminated by a single stop bit.

2   Interrupt service routines can use any of the processor's registers, not just the PC and SR. Why does the processor therefor only preserve these two registers automatically, leaving the task of preserving any other registers to the interrupt service routine?

3   A keyboard interface is polled 10 times a second, to ensure that all keystrokes entered by the user are captured. If the polling routine occupies 50 clock cycles and the processor is driven by a 100 MHz clock, then what percentage of processing time is wasted by this operation?

4 Why is polling unacceptable for handling disk transfers?

5 The Motorola MC68000 processor has no dedicated bus or specialised instructions to support I/O and relies entirely on memory-mapped I/O for transferring data to/from peripheral devices. Discuss the disadvantages of this strategy compared with that used by Intel processors.

6 Why is DMA and not interrupt-driven I/O used for handling hard disk data transfers?

7 A DMA controller can operate in burst transfer mode or cycle stealing mode. How do these modes differ and why is the latter mode usually preferred?

8 Most mice have two buttons but some have three buttons and others have a wheel. What is the purpose of this third button and the wheel?

9 Using several of the popular computing magazines as sources of information, produce a table to show connection options for as many peripheral devices as you can find. List the peripheral devices as rows and serial, parallel, USB and Firewire as the column headings. Put a tick in the appropriate cell to indicate an offered option.

10 This is a practical exercise. Investigate laser printer page printing times. How do the actual times compare with the times specified in the advertising material? Account for any differences.

11 Some monitors have a touch sensitive screen. Find out what is meant by a touch sensitive screen and suggest a suitable application for such a screen.

12 Write a short report that gives details of the range of sound output systems that are available for a PC. Include in the report comments to indicate the types of application for which a particular sound system might be suitable.

Operating systems

An *operating system* is a collection of system processes that manage the resources of a computer and control the running of user programs. The purpose of this chapter is to describe various hardware features that are used to support a typical microcomputer operating system.

9.1 Overview

Microcomputer operating system software is normally supplied on a CD and then copied onto the computer's hard disk. When a computer is switched on, the CPU executes a *bootstrap* program, part of which must be held in ROM. This program loads the *kernel* (principally responsible for process management) and other frequently needed portions of the operating system into main memory and sets it running by altering the instruction pointer, as illustrated in Figure 9.1.

The operating system then sets about creating various tables, lists and other data structures needed to manage the resources of the system. Resources include memory, I/O devices, files, buffers and the CPU itself. It also sets up vectors in the exception vector table (see Section 8.4.2), so that it can provide services to the user. It is then ready to accept commands through a GUI or some other form of user interface.

Figure 9.1 Physical resources managed by the operating system

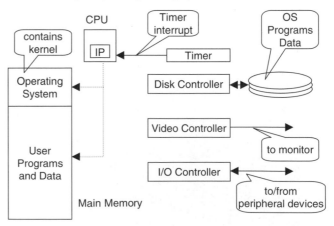

The operating system manages all the resources of the system and so needs access to all the instructions offered by the machine code of the processor. User programs need to be denied access to certain instructions, particularly those affecting input, output and interrupts. If user programs were allowed access to these instructions they would be able to circumvent the controls imposed by the operating system. The processor mode that allows access to all the instructions is often referred to as *supervisor mode*. The processor mode that limits the instructions available is often referred to as *user mode*. Protected mode, in the 80286 and later processors, does not allow any operations on the interrupt flag or use of the IN and OUT instructions. Real mode allows access to all instructions. The Windows operating system runs in real mode while application programs run in protected mode. To execute a user program, the operating system first loads it into main memory and then switches from supervisor mode to user mode. The operating system will switch the processor to user mode before initiating the execution of a user program. The operating system hands control of the CPU to the user program by setting the instruction pointer (IP) to the address of its entry point instruction. The user program then runs until either a *system call (trap)* or hardware *interrupt* returns control back to a part of the operating system kernel called the *interrupt handler*. Traps and interrupts are examples of *exceptions*, which as we mentioned in Chapter 8, are events that alter the normal execution of a program. The interrupt handler is responsible for determining the cause of the exception and for initiating an appropriate service routine.

9.2 Power-on self-test (POST) and system boot-up

When a computer is powered-up, there needs to be some code for it to run. In a PC system this code is stored in a ROM called the *Basic Input Output System* or *BIOS*. The principle function of any such code is to load the operating system. The program performing such a function is known as the *bootstrap loader*. The following explanation gives some of the details of the BIOS actions that must be performed before loading the operating system into the memory of an 80x86 processor-based system. The 80x86 processor, on being powered-up or reset, will clear its registers, set the CS register to F000 and IP register to FFF0 (abbreviated to F000:FFF0). The address F000:FFF0 is a location within the BIOS ROM, which contains the address of the POST code. The actual code varies from one BIOS manufacturer to another but will generally involve testing the processor, CMOS, keyboard, timer, RAM, video and DMA controller. As the video device may not be working at this stage, errors are reported via the speaker. The meaning of the *beep* codes will generally be found in the manual for the motherboard.

In the case of an 80x86 system, on successful completion of the POST, an interrupt 19_{16} is invoked. The interrupt handler for interrupt 19_{16} is the bootstrap loader that will load the operating system loader program from the first sector of the boot disk. The loader program will then be run to load the operating system.

Figure 9.2   CPU time divided between user programs

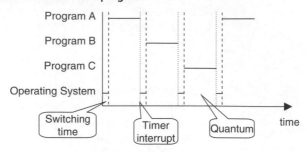

9.3   Multiprogramming/multitasking

Many modern operating systems have the ability to give the impression that they can execute several programs at once, even though there is often only one CPU or processor in the system. This is called *multiprogramming* or *multitasking*. By periodically interrupting the processor, each program is given control of the processor for a short time interval or *quantum*. Figure 9.2 indicates how this process works.

Switching between programs is triggered by a hardware device called an *interval timer*, which generates a *time-out interrupt* after a predetermined period of time has elapsed. Each time-out invokes the interrupt handler, which saves the *context* of the processor before handing over control to a *dispatcher* or *low-level scheduler*. The context includes the IP, stack pointer (SP), status register (SR or flags) and other processor registers that might be overwritten by other programs. The dispatcher then searches a list of potentially runnable programs using a *scheduling algorithm* to select a suitable program to run next. It then restores the context of the processor to that which existed when the selected program was last halted and sets it off running again.

To look deeper into the inner workings of an operating system, we need to introduce the concept of a process.

9.4   The process concept

A process, which can be a *user process* or *system process*, consists of an executable program, the data associated with it and an *execution context*. The execution context includes the processor context we have just described, together with other information, such as a process identifier (PID), a priority level and a process state.

There are three basic process states: *Ready, Running* and *Blocked*, which we have represented by circles in the state transition diagram shown in Figure 9.3.

When a user process is in the Running state, the processor is executing its program code. If a timer interrupt occurs, the process is moved into the Ready state and another process is selected from a list of Ready processes and

Figure 9.3 State transition diagram

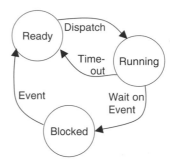

Figure 9.4 Structure of a typical PCB

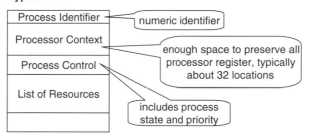

moved into the Running state. If a process in the Running state requests an operating system service for which it must wait, such as an I/O request, the process is moved into the Blocked state. The process remains in this state until the event on which it is waiting, such as the arrival of an interrupt from a DMA controller, has taken place. The operating system then moves the process back to the Ready state.

While one process is blocked, awaiting the completion of an I/O transfer, the operating system is free to reschedule another process. This allows the operating system to make efficient use of the computer's limited resources.

TQ 9.1   How does DMA assist in improving efficiency?

9.5 Process management

When a user initiates the running of a program, a process is created to represent its state of execution. One way that an operating system may do this is by loading the program code and data into memory and creating a data structure called a *Process Control Block* (PCB), which it uses for management purposes. The structure of a typical PCB is given in Figure 9.4.

Figure 9.5 Process queue structures

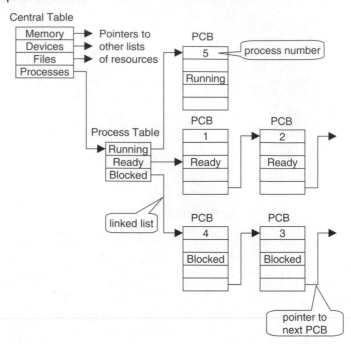

Each PCB has storage space for an identifier; the processor context; process control information and a list of any resources 'owned' by it, such as files and I/O devices. The process control information includes details of the state and priority level of the process, together with information needed for managing memory and inter-process communication.

Before a new process can be scheduled, its PCB must be initialised and added to a list or queue of other Ready processes. This is done by setting the IP entry of the processor context to the start address of the program code and the SP entry to the top of the memory area allocated for its stack. The process control information entries are initialised to various default values, which includes setting the process state to Ready. Figure 9.5 illustrates a typical process queue structure.

The operating system uses a *central table* to provide access to all the lists and data structures it uses to manage the system. Among its table of pointers is a pointer to a *process table*. The process table has three further pointers: one to the currently running process; another to a list of Ready processes and a third to a list of Blocked processes. The first PCB in a linked list is said to be at the 'head' of the list. As processes make transitions between states, their PCBs are updated and moved from one list to another. Only the operating system is allowed to access these data structures to prevent malicious or accidental damage by user programs. Most operating systems enforce this by running user processes in user mode and system processes in kernel or supervisor mode, as we mentioned earlier. We shall see later, that memory management hardware can be used to prevent any attempt by a process in user mode from accessing an area of memory allocated to the operating system.

TQ 9.2 If a time-out occurred and process 1 was chosen to run next, then what changes would be needed to the lists shown in Figure 9.5?

TQ 9.3 Sometimes a very low priority process is added to the list of Ready processes that is always able to run. Why is this?

9.6 Process scheduling

There are several different scheduling algorithms that can be used by the dispatcher. In this section we will consider just two of them: First-Come-First-Served (FCFS) and Round Robin.

(1) First-Come-First-Served

With FCFS scheduling, the process at the head of the Ready list is always the one chosen to run next. Once selected, a process retains control of the CPU until it 'voluntarily' relinquishes it, either by blocking for an I/O operation or when the process terminates. This is called *non pre-emptive* scheduling. Although this is very simple and easy to implement, it gives unfair advantage to processes that do a lot of calculations with little I/O (CPU bound processes). It also suffers from the fact that if a process fails to relinquish control of the CPU, possibly due to a bug in the program, then the whole system is brought to a standstill. With *pre-emptive scheduling*, such as Round Robin, this can usually be avoided.

(2) Round Robin

Round Robin (RR) is the form of scheduling we tacitly assumed when we discussed the concept of multiprogramming, a process being selected from the Ready queue on a FCFS basis and then allocated the CPU for a fixed time quantum. Unlike FCFS, the process is 'forced' to relinquish control of the CPU when its quantum expires and for this reason is described as pre-emptive scheduling.

The size of the quantum can be altered through program control, a value of 20 ms being quite popular. In choosing the size of the quantum, consideration must be given to typical process interaction times and the types of processes involved. Very short or very long values for the time quantum are always avoided.

TQ 9.4 By referring to Figure 9.2, why should a very short quantum be avoided?

9.7 Inter-Process Communication (IPC)

A process needs to communicate with one or more other processes when competing for shared resources or when co-operating on joint tasks. This section introduces the problems this poses for the operating system and describes some of the methods used to overcome them.

9.7.1 Mutual exclusion

The resources managed by an operating system can be classified as either *physical resources*, such as CPU, keyboard and printer, or *logical resources*, such as shared memory segments and files. A resource is *pre-emptable* if ownership can be taken away from one process and given to another. If this is not the case, the resource is said to be *non-pre-emptable* or *critical*.

TQ 9.5   How would you classify a printer?

The section of program code used by a process to access a critical resource is called its *critical section*. Mutual exclusion is concerned with ensuring that, at any moment in time, there can be no more than one process in its critical section on the same resource. This necessitates some form of signalling between competing processes, as we shall see in a moment.

9.7.2 Synchronisation

Another situation in which processes need to communicate is when they need to co-ordinate their actions. For example, if two processes P_1 and P_2 share a buffer in which P_1 deposits data *(producer)* and P_2 removes data *(consumer)*, then steps must be taken to prevent data being consumed when the buffer is empty and to prevent data being produced when the buffer is full. Once again, some form of signalling is needed between the processes.

9.7.3 Achieving mutual exclusion

As a first approach to implementing mutual exclusion, let us consider using a variable called *flag*, to indicate when a resource is available (*flag* = 0) or in use (*flag* = 1). The following pseudocode illustrates how a flag could be used by a process to gain access to a critical resource.

```
begin
    repeat
        read flag;
    until flag = 0;
    set flag to 1;
    < Critical Section >
    set flag to 0;
end
```

After examining the flag and finding the resource free ($flag = 0$), the process sets the flag ($flag = 1$) and enters its critical section. If a second process now tried to gain access to the resource, then finding the flag set, it would be effectively locked out and remains in the repeat loop until the flag changed. We describe a process in this condition as *busy-waiting*. When the first process finishes using the resource and leaves its critical section, it clears the flag ($flag = 0$) allowing the second process to gain access. Unfortunately, this first approach has a fatal flaw, which we can illustrate with the following scenario.

1. Process P_1 examines the flag and finds it free. Just as it is about to set the flag, it is pre-empted by another process P_2 that also wants to access the resource.

2. P_2 examines the flag and finding it free, sets the flag and enters its critical section. Before it manages to finish with the resource, it too gets pre-empted and P_1 is rescheduled.

3. P_1 now proceeds from the point where it was last pre-empted, by setting the flag and entering its critical section.

   P_1 and P_2 are now both in their critical section and mutual exclusion has been violated!

TQ 9.6   What are the basic causes of this problem?

---

(1)   Hardware support

One hardware solution to the above problem is to 'turn off' all interrupts before testing and setting the flag. The CLI instruction will mask all maskable interrupts. This will not work however if the dispatcher uses the unmaskable interrupt and/or the process is in protected mode as the CLI instruction will not then be available. This mechanism therefore only provides a partial solution to the problem. A second solution is to use instructions that can read, modify and write-back a stored variable in a single *indivisible* operation. Some processors provide such an instruction, called *Test And Set* (TAS). (There is no equivalent to this in the 8086 instruction set.) The TAS instruction operates upon a byte-sized operand, which it tests before setting the most significant bit (bit-7) to 1. If during this test the byte is found to be negative or zero, then the N and Z flags of the Flags register are set. The following assembly code illustrates how the TAS instruction can be used to implement mutual exclusion.

```
Wait    TAS    flag
        JNE    Wait              busy-wait
                                 Critical Section
Exit    MOV    0, flag
```

Although this technique works, it introduces the possibility of two problems called *deadlock* and *indefinite postponement*. To illustrate deadlock, consider the following scenario, where we assume the dispatcher uses a priority scheduling algorithm.

1. A low priority process, P_L, is in its critical section on a resource.
2. The dispatcher schedules a process, P_H, which has a higher priority than P_L.
3. The dispatcher continues to schedule processes, but never chooses P_L because P_H is always able to run.

Neither process can make any more progress because deadlock has occurred!

TQ 9.7 Would this problem have occurred with RR scheduling?

The problem of indefinite postponement may arise even if processes are of the same priority.

1. The first process, P_1, may try to access its critical section and enters.
2. The next process, P_2, tries to enter its critical section but gets blocked and keeps looping on the wait loop until it is pre-empted.
3. While P_2 is on the Ready queue, P_1 may exit its critical section then loop round and enter the critical section again or another process enters the critical section before P_2 gets a chance to enter the critical section.

In the worst case, P_2, despite being the second process to attempt to access the critical section may continually be overtaken by new processes.

(2) *Software support*

To eliminate the need for hardware support, several purely software solutions exist for implementing mutual exclusion. These are based on various algorithms, such as Dekker's algorithm and Peterson's algorithm, which are described in texts listed in the references at the end of this book. As with the hardware solutions, software solutions continue to impose 'busy-waiting' conditions on processes and are prone to deadlock.

9.7.4 *Semaphores*

A *semaphore* is a flag, bit or combination of bits used to signal various events, such as whether a resource is free/in-use or whether a buffer is empty/full. In some systems semaphores are implemented in hardware, while in others they are implemented as software constructs (usually non-negative integer variables). A *binary semaphore* can have just two values, 0 or 1, while a *counting semaphore* can have values between 0 and N, where N is a positive integer. If the semaphore is a non-zero positive value, the resource is available and if the semaphore is zero, then it is unavailable. Semaphores are stored in the operating system's address space and accessed by a running process through the *primitives* signal and wait. Primitives are very basic processing steps, often consisting of moving or altering bits. The operating system implements these system calls as *indivisible* or *atomic* operations, possibly by turning off interrupts or using the TAS instruction we described earlier. The operations on a semaphore, s, are defined below.

wait (s):   if (s > 0) then (s := s − 1)   [:= means 'is assigned the value']
            else add process to queue of processes blocked on s
signal (s):   if queue is empty then (s := s+ 1)
            else move a process from queue into the Ready state.

To illustrate the use of semaphores, let us consider how they can be used to implement mutual exclusion. We shall assume that the resource is initially available (s = 1).

The first process to request access, P_1, performs a wait(s) and enters its critical section. The execution of wait(s) decrements s, so that (s = 0). If a competing process, P_2, is now scheduled, then on performing wait(s) it gets blocked. When P_1 is rescheduled, it completes its critical section and executes signal(s). This causes P_2 to be moved back into the Ready state, so that when it is rescheduled it has immediate access to the resource and enters its critical section. If by the time P_2 is finished there are no further processes blocked on (s), then when it performs signal(s), s is incremented (s = 1) to indicate that the resource is free for use.

TQ 9.8   How does the use of semaphores overcome the 'busy-wait' problem we mentioned earlier?

9.7.5 *Other techniques*

There are other techniques used for inter-process communication, such as monitors and message passing. These techniques are discussed in the texts listed under references at the end of this book.

9.8 Threads

In Section 9.3 we discussed multiprogramming and in Section 9.4 we discussed processes. In these two sections we assumed that a process would have instructions, data and a single *thread* of control. What we mean by this is that there is a single context with an IP value associated with the process. A process may cause another process to be created which would cause the program code to be loaded into memory along with its data and will have its own context including its own IP value. In an operating system which supports *multithreading*, a new *lightweight* process may be created which shares the same code and data as the initiating process but has a separate

Figure 9.6   Multiprogramming v multithreading

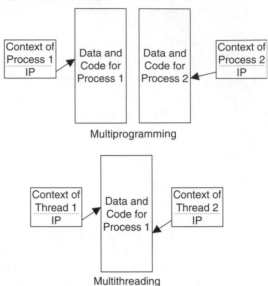

Multiprogramming

Multithreading

context with its own IP value. Each thread will be scheduled separately, have its own context, but share code and data (see Figure 9.6).

9.9   Memory management

In our discussion so far, we have tacitly assumed that all the processes known to the system can be stored together in main memory. In reality, due to its finite size, this is not usually possible and is in fact impossible when the size of an individual process exceeds that of main memory. We have also glossed over other issues, such as how one process is prevented from interfering with another and how processes are able to share common areas of memory such as buffers. Many modern microcomputer systems overcome these problems by using a technique called *virtual memory*.

9.9.1   *Virtual memory*

With this technique, addresses generated by the CPU are not used to access main memory directly, but are converted or *mapped* into real addresses, which can either be main memory locations, secondary memory locations or a mixture of both. This allows main memory to be treated as a form of 'cache' for the secondary storage device (usually magnetic disk), mapping only those portions of a program currently required for execution into main memory and keeping the rest of the program on disk until needed. This is illustrated in Figure 9.7.

As a program runs, the activity of swapping pieces of code or data in and out of main memory is controlled by a part of the operating system called

Figure 9.7   Virtual memory concepts

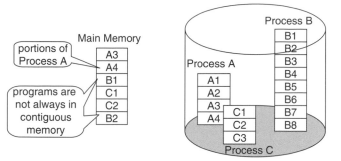

Figure 9.8   Mapping a virtual address to a physical address

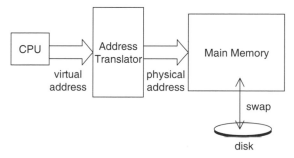

the *memory management system*. The programmer is unaware of this activity and sees his or her program as occupying a set of memory locations in a logical or *virtual address space*, the details of the *physical address space* it occupies being invisible.

TQ 9.9   In Chapter 6, we introduced a general property of program behaviour called the *principle of locality*. How does this apply here?

Because all memory references made in a program refer to a virtual address space, then when a CPU executes an instruction such as:

MOV DH, [2003]

the address 2003, generated by the CPU, is not the physical address in which the byte is stored but its virtual address. To map this into a physical address requires some form of address translation, as illustrated in Figure 9.8. If the byte is in memory, then it can be fetched along the data bus and moved into DH in the usual way. However, if the address translator indicates that the byte is not in memory, then the memory manager must swap a new portion of data from disk into main memory before the byte can be read.

Figure 9.9   Using a page table to perform address translation

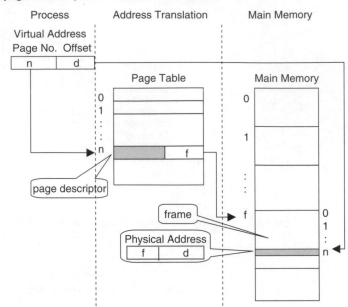

9.9.2 *Paging*

Most virtual memory systems use an address translation technique called *paging*. With paging, each program is divided into equal size portions called pages, typically between 512 and 4096 bytes. Main memory is also divided up in the same way, but this time into *page frames*, each page frame being capable of storing one page. Virtual addresses generated by the CPU are split into a page number (n) and an offset (d) within the page, while each physical address is split into a frame number (f) and an offset (d) within the frame. A page table is used to map the virtual address into a physical address, as shown in Figure 9.9.

The table contains a list of *page descriptors*, each descriptor having a number of bits, which describe and control access to the page (shown shaded), together with a frame number (f). The page number (n) of the virtual address (n, d) is used to index the table and identify the frame number (f) into which the page is mapped. The frame number is then combined with the offset (d) of the virtual address, to form the physical address (f, d).

TQ 9.10   A 24-bit virtual address, 002003, has a 12-bit page number (002) and a 12-bit offset (003). If the first few page table entries are as shown below then to what physical address would this virtual address correspond?

Page Table	
000	05
001	00
002	01
003	FF
004	0A

Included among the control bits of a page descriptor is a *present bit* (P), which is used to indicate whether the page is in main memory and a *modified* or *dirty bit* (M) to indicate whether the page has been altered. If during an address translation, the P-bit indicates that the page is absent, then a trap to the operating system, known as a *page fault*, occurs and a service routine is invoked to load the page from disk. In such cases the virtual address is used to determine the location of the page on disk. Once the page is loaded and the page table updated, then address translation can proceed in the normal way. If there are no spare page frames for the new page, a page must be selected for replacement using some *page replacement algorithm*. We call this form of paging *demand paging*. If the selected page has been modified (M = 1), then before it is overwritten it must be copied back on to the disk.

TQ 9.11   If a page frame used for program code were demanded, then would it need to be copied back to the disk?

Some page frames, such as those used by the operating system kernel, must be kept permanently in memory. To prevent these frames from being paged out, each descriptor also includes a *lock bit*. Because page tables are stored in memory, they can also be subjected to paging, especially when they are large. Unfortunately, the additional overhead of swapping portions of the table to and from disk before an address can be translated can add a significant time penalty to this process.

9.9.3 Hardware support for memory management

When paging is implemented without hardware support, then at least two memory accesses are needed to gain access to an instruction: one to read the page table entry and the other to read the instruction. This effectively doubles the memory access time, making virtual memory systems potentially much slower than systems that address memory directly. To reduce this overhead, most virtual memory systems are supported by hardware.

Figure 9.10 shows how a paged *Memory Management Unit* (MMU) may be used to translate a virtual address generated into a physical address. The MMU reduces the translation time by using a small set-associative address translation cache or *Translation Look-aside Buffer* (TLB). The TLB contains copies of recently used page table entries and can be searched very

Figure 9.10   Memory Management Unit (MMU)

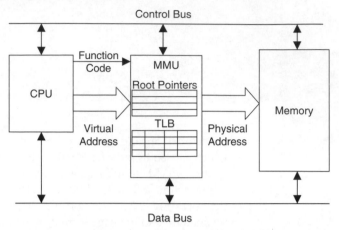

Figure 9.11   Flow chart for the MMU operation

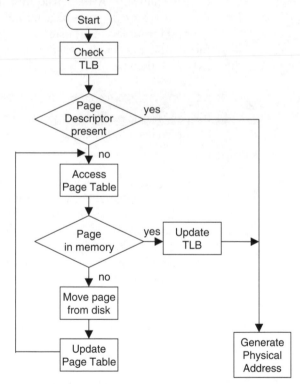

quickly (see Section 6.5 on cache memory operation) to find the appropriate descriptor. If the entry is not present, then the MMU takes control of the system bus and uses one of the *root pointers* to access main memory and retrieve the entry from the stored page table. It then updates the TLB before using the page frame to generate the physical address in the usual way. If a page fault occurs, then the page is fetched from disk and the page table updated before repeating the search. A summary of the main steps involved is shown in Figure 9.11.

Most programs only use a few relatively small segments of their virtual address space. A typical program would probably have a one-program *code segment*, a *data segment* or *heap* and a *stack segment*. Parts of the heap would probably be shared with other programs and also possibly some of the code segment. To support this type of program structure and to provide a more flexible form of paging, some MMUs use *multi-level page tables*, as illustrated in Figure 9.11.

With this two-level scheme, the virtual address is divided into three fields: an A-field, a B-field and an offset field. The A-field is used to index a set of memory pointers contained in the A-table and locate a set of page descriptors held in the B-table. The B-table is then indexed to find the page frame needed to generate the corresponding physical address.

The location of the A-table is provided by one of the root pointers, selected by the function code generated by the CPU (see Figure 9.10). The function code indicates whether the CPU is in user mode or supervisor mode and also the type of cycle (instruction or data) it is currently undertaking. This allows the MMU to select separate A-tables for user code, user data, system code and system data. In this way any invalid operations, such as attempting to write to the user code area, which is designated as read only, can be intercepted and prevented from occurring by trapping to the operating system. The MMU can also provide protection by checking bits in the page descriptor, such as a supervisor only bit, to see if a user is attempting to access an area of memory used by the operating system. It can also support sharing, by allowing multiple entries in the A-tables of different processes to point at the same entry in the B-table (see Figure 9.12).

Some MMUs, such as the Motorola MC68851, can be programmed to allow three or four different levels of paging, giving even greater flexibility to this type of implementation.

Figure 9.12   Two-level page table

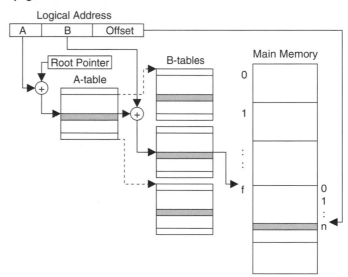

9.10 Operating system traps

The principle function of the operating system is to manage the computer system's resources. It can do this successfully only if it has sole control over these resources. The operating system wants to prevent, as much as it can, user processes accessing I/O devices and interrupt handling in particular. If a user process can access a disk drive directly, it can bypass any restrictions or controls the operating system may wish to impose. If a user process can access the interrupt mechanism, then it can gain complete control of the processor and bypass any scheduling policy implemented by the operating system. Ensuring the user processes run in user mode, with its restricted instruction set, helps in this respect as the instructions for performing I/O operations and controlling the interrupt mechanism are not available in user mode. The operating system, which needs to be able to perform I/O and control interrupts, runs in supervisor mode, where these instructions are available. So how does a program that needs to perform an I/O operation arrange for its data to be input or output?

When an application program is compiled, I/O operations, such as print or read, do not result in code to perform the print or read operation being inserted into the executable program. What is inserted is a call to an operating system function that will perform the operation on behalf of the user program. The operating system functions reside in the operating system's address space that will be protected from user processes by the operating system's memory management. It will also be necessary to switch from user mode to supervisor mode. The operating system will not want a user process to be able to switch modes itself.

In order to resolve these two problems, the user processes will access operating system functions through the use of interrupt calls or traps. When a program wishes to perform an input operation, such as a read from a file, it will invoke a software interrupt. This will cause an action similar to those described in Chapter 8. The processor will switch to supervisor mode, save the context of the interrupting process and start the function, or routine, associated with the interrupt. In the case of an interrupt request that is associated with a file read, a routine, which will retrieve data from a disk file will be run. When the routine has finished, a return from interrupt instruction is executed which will reload the context of the interrupting process and switch the processor back to user mode. This means that a user program has been able to call upon the operating system to perform an I/O operation on its behalf without having to access the operating system address space or to execute any of its own code in supervisor mode.

If an 80x86 program, running under MS-DOS, wishes to read data from the keyboard it will invoke interrupt 21_{16}. The interrupt handler for this interrupt contains a number of routines for performing I/O. One of the routines is for reading from the keyboard. This particular routine is selected by placing $0A_{16}$ in the AH register. The address of the keyboard buffer is placed in the DX register. When the INT 21_{16} instruction is executed, the context for the calling program is saved but is not overwritten, except for the IP. The interrupt handler then has access to the values in the AH and DX registers. On handling the interrupt, the processor switches to real mode. The data is then read from the keyboard and placed in the buffer. At the end of the keyboard input, the routine executes IRTN instruction, which will reload the context of the calling program and switch back to protected mode.

Appendix 2 contains examples of programs that make use of operating system routines.

9.11   File systems

Data is stored on disk in files. Files are collected together into *directories* or *folders*. Each directory may contain not only files but also other directories called *sub-directories*. This results in a hierarchical structure with a directory, usually called root, at the top, as illustrated in Figure 9.13. Any file or directory can be located by specifying all the directories between the desired file and the root directory. This list of directories is called the *path*. The path for file *f8* in Figure 9.13 would be *root/d3/d8/d9/f8*. The use of directories is useful to collect together related files and sub-directories. An operating system must provide file system management to decide where files are stored on the disk and to control access to the files.

9.11.1   File allocation techniques

The file manager must know which areas of disk are free and which have been allocated, and which areas of disk have been allocated to a particular file. We will briefly consider two ways of doing this.

(1)   File map

In the file map approach, the operating system maintains a data structure where each entry represents a disk block or *cluster*. The value of the entry is the number of the next cluster. Each cluster is a fixed number of disk sectors. Figure 9.14 shows a system where a file has been allocated cluster 4. There is a field in the directory entry for the file that indicates the first cluster allocated to the file. When this cluster was full it was then allocated cluster 5. The value

Figure 9.13   Directories, sub-directories and files

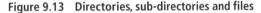
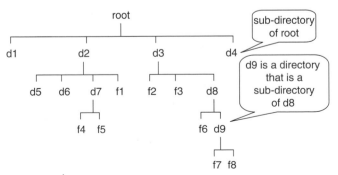

Figure 9.14   File map

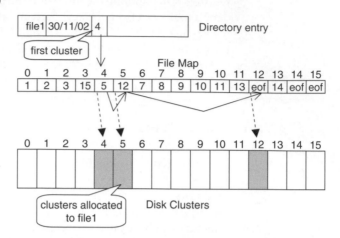

of element 4 in the map is thus 5. Cluster 12 was then allocated to the file so element 5 has the value 12 in it. Cluster 12 is the last cluster allocated to the file so there is a value representing *end-of-file* in element 12.

As disk sizes increase so the size of the file map must increase due to the increase in the number of sectors. To stop the file map become excessively big, the number of sectors per cluster can be increased. The problem here is that the minimum size of a file is determined by the number of sectors in a cluster. If, for example, a sector is 0.5 KBytes and there are 16 sectors per cluster, the smallest file size is 8 KBytes even if the file contains only a single byte of data.

This is the type of system used in the Windows operating system (excluding NT and 2000 versions). The file map in Windows is called a *File Allocation Table* (FAT).

TQ 9.12   The FAT in versions of Windows up to Windows 98 osr2 (a major upgrade to the original release of Windows 98) has 16 bits per entry. If the maximum cluster size is 16 sectors, where each sector is 0.5 KBytes, what is the maximum disk size supported by this file allocation technique?

(2) Indexed file blocks

If we divide a disk into blocks (equivalent to clusters in the previous section) each block can be used to hold data or pointers to blocks containing data. Blocks containing pointers are called *index* blocks. The entry for a given file in a directory will contain a field that will be a pointer to an index block. As data blocks are allocated to a file, a pointer to the block is placed in the index. Eventually the index may become full, so the last entry in the index will be a pointer to another index block as illustrated in Figure 9.15.

Figure 9.15   Indexed file blocks

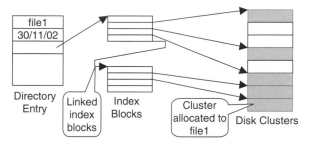

Figure 9.16   Unix i-node structure

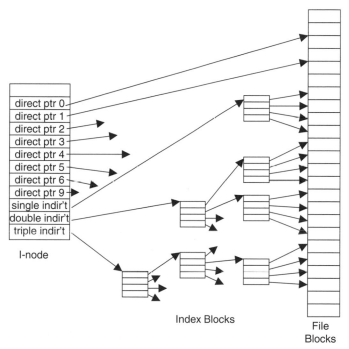

The Unix operating system uses a variation on this approach. Each file is allocated a data structure called an *i-node*. Within each i-node is a set of 13 pointers. Each of the first 10 pointers, points to a file block (or disk cluster) that has been allocated to the file. The next pointer is a single indirection pointer. This points to an index block that contains a set of pointers to file blocks. The next pointer is a double indirection pointer which points to an index block which contains pointers to further index blocks that contain pointers to file blocks. The final pointer in the i-node is a triple indirection pointer which points to an index block with pointers to index blocks with pointers to index blocks with pointers to file blocks. This is illustrated in Figure 9.16. This approach enables Unix to manage small files without large levels of management overhead while still being able to support very large files reasonably efficiently.

9.11.2 *File access control*

In a single-user operating system access control is quite simple. MS-DOS, for example, allows a user to specify a file as system, hidden or read-only. These primarily enable the user to put some controls on a file to reduce the chances of the user corrupting a file accidentally.

When an operating system allows access to a network, the user then has the opportunity to share files and directories with other users. The Windows operating system, for example, does this by enabling the user to share files and place optional read-only access and password on the file. Access control over the file is thus through the security of the password.

Providing access via passwords is awkward to manage and offers limited security. A more sophisticated approach is offered in operating systems such as Unix. In Unix, access rights can be allocated to the user, other members of the group to which the user belongs and then anybody else (i.e. there are three sets of rights allocated to the file or directory). Each class of user may be allocated no rights or any combination of read, write and execute rights. Users may, for example, give themselves read, write and execute rights; other members of the group read rights and no rights to everybody else.

The approach used in Unix gives very coarse control over allocating file access. A user may belong to a number of groups but different groups may need to be given different rights. There may be some groups the user does not belong to, but wishes to give them some access. There may be some individuals that require access to the file. Operating systems or network managers such as Novell Netware, support a list of access rights to be defined for each file or directory. This list is known as an *Access Control List* (ACL). Each user or user group can be given specific rights. In Netware the rights allocated may include supervisor, access control, create, delete, modify, write, copy, read, and file scan.

9.12 Summary

In this chapter we have introduced several key features of an operating system and explained how it provides services and manages the resources of the system. We explained the concept of a process and described how an operating system, with the aid of an interrupt handler and dispatcher, can support multiprogramming. The need for process synchronisation and mutual exclusion were then discussed together with two forms of hardware support. Semaphores were then introduced as a mechanism for synchronising processes and for enforcing mutual exclusion, together with the primitive operations, wait and signal. We then discussed memory management and introduced the concepts of virtual and physical address spaces and explained how a page table could be used to map virtual addresses into physical addresses. We described how hardware support, in the form of a paged MMU could be used to assist the operating system in performing this task. The problem of restricting access to system resources was explored and how software interrupts can be used to allow user programs to invoke operating system routines to perform I/O operations. Finally some techniques of file management were introduced, specifically techniques for allocating areas of disk to files using file maps and indexed file maps, and techniques for file access control ranging from simple single-user systems to access control lists.

Answers to in text questions

TQ 9.1   DMA allows I/O to take place without the intervention of the processor. Therefore one process can be running on the processor while another is performing an I/O operation in parallel with it.

TQ 9.2   The PCB for process 5 would be updated to Ready and added to the Ready list. The PCB for process 1 would be updated to Running and replace process 5.

TQ 9.3   To prevent the scheduler from running out of processes and halting.

TQ 9.4   If the time quantum approaches the switching time, then the CPU spends more time switching than it does performing the useful work of running processes.

TQ 9.5   A printer is a critical resource, because once a process has started to print a file, it cannot be assigned to another process until the complete file has been printed.

TQ 9.6   a) A process can be interrupted at any time.

　　　　　b) Testing and Setting the flag is performed in two operations.

TQ 9.7   No, because RR scheduling makes the implicit assumption that processes have equal priority.

TQ 9.8   By blocking these processes.

TQ 9.9   The principle of locality refers to the fact that during program execution, certain localised groups of instructions tend to be referenced much more frequently than others. By keeping these portions of a program in main memory and the rest of the program on disk, a reasonable performance can be expected with only occasional delays caused by page swapping.

TQ 9.10   The frame number corresponding to page number 002 is 01. Therefore the physical address would be 01003.

TQ 9.11   No, program code is not modifiable and therefore could not have been changed.

TQ 9.12   16-bit FAT entries enable addressing of 2^{16} or 65536 clusters. If each cluster is 16×0.5 KBytes then the maximum disk size is 65536×8 KBytes — 524288 KBytes or 512 MBytes (assuming 1K = 1024).

EXERCISES

1 What is the difference between a process and a program?

2 Draw a diagram to explain the various state changes a process goes through from the time it is first created.

3 If the time quantum used in RR scheduling becomes too large, then what form of scheduling takes place?

4 How does pre-emptive scheduling differ from non pre-emptive scheduling?

5 Explain the terms critical resource, critical section and mutual exclusion. In what ways can hardware be used to guarantee mutual exclusion?

6 What is a semaphore and what advantages does it offer when used to implement mutual exclusion?

7 A computer using virtual memory has a main memory with just 4 page frames. If the following sequence of virtual page numbers is encountered:

0 1 2 3 4 3 2 5 6 3 4 5 6 3 5 0

then if a Least-Recently-Used page replacement policy is used, how many page faults will occur?

8 What purpose does a Translation Look-aside Buffer serve in a Memory Management Unit? Why should caching be disabled on those pages that contain memory-mapped I/O device registers? [Hint: consider programmed I/O that we discussed in Section 8.4.]

9 Explain why a multiprogramming system may be compromised if a user program has access to

   (a) I/O machine code instructions and

   (b) the interrupt mask.

10 A Unix i-node file system uses 2 KByte file blocks and 32 bits per block pointers. Calculate the maximum file size and maximum disk size that can be supported by this file system. Assume index blocks and file blocks are the same size.

10

Reduced instruction set computers

Two of the best known families of microprocessor are those based on the Motorola 68000 and Intel 8086 architectures, the 680x0 family gaining popularity through its association with the Apple Macintosh and the 80x86 family through association with the original IBM PC. By adopting this family approach, first introduced for IBM mainframes in the mid-sixties, processor designers have been able to take advantage of the implementation techniques and speed increases offered by advances in Very Large Scale Integration (VLSI) technology, while continuing to support a common architecture. Supporting a common architecture is important because it allows software written for older machines to run on newer ones and thus protects the customers' software investment.

Being locked into a particular architecture, designers have tended to increase the power of their processors by increasing the size and complexity of the instruction sets and by adding new features, such as 'on-chip' caches, memory management units (MMU), and floating point coprocessor units. In principle, increasing the power of the instruction set eases the burden on the compiler writer and allows shorter and more efficient code to be generated. This is because shorter code reduces the number of memory fetches and hence reduces the processor–memory bottleneck. It also occupies less memory and therefore reduces the number of page faults generated by the MMU.

Based on research, first started in the late 1970s with the IBM 801 project, designers began to question this 'complex instruction set' approach to processor design, particularly after overwhelming evidence suggested that the richness of the instruction set was not being used. A compiler translates high-level code, such as C, into machine code. Compiler programmers, when deciding which machine code instructions a high-level instruction will be translated to, would only use a small subset of the machine code instructions available. This research has culminated in the emergence of a breed of commercial machines called Reduced Instruction Set Computers (RISC). This name arises because these processors use a much smaller streamlined instruction set than their Complex Instruction Set Computer (CISC) rivals. At the time of writing, virtually all CISC manufacturers have developed at least one RISC chip, which is a good indication of the importance of the RISC approach in building high-speed machines. In this chapter, we examine the philosophy that underpins this approach and give some examples of its implementation.

10.1 CISC characteristics

Although there is no precise definition of a CISC processor, most of them share the following characteristics:

1. A large number of instructions – typically between 100 and 250.
2. Instructions that perform specialised tasks together with instructions that support memory-to-memory operations.
3. A large number of addressing modes – typically between 5 and 20.
4. A range of variable length instruction formats with variable execution times.
5. A microprogrammed control unit.

10.2 Instruction usage

Because RISC and CISC processors are designed to support the execution of programs written in high-level languages (HLLs), the interaction of compilers with HLLs significantly affects the way in which the processor's instruction set is used. Several studies on CISC instruction set usage have revealed that only a relatively small portion of the instruction set is ever used by programmers of CISC compilers. For example, one report found that roughly 71% of the MC68020 instruction set was not used when a variety of programs were compiled using Sun and Gnu C compilers. Table 10.1 demonstrates that although the actual instruction usage depends upon factors such as the language and type of program, there is clear evidence that certain types of instructions are used far more frequently than others.

Thus HLL assignment statements, such as $A \leftarrow B$, which are implemented using data movement primitives like *MOV A, B* are used more frequently than logical *AND* or *OR* instructions. Also of importance are program modification instructions, such as Branch and Jump instructions, which are used to support HLL iteration in the form of *WHILE* and *FOR* loops and also for calling procedures. Other studies carried out on the use of program variables indicate that the majority of operands accessed by HLL

Table 10.1 Typical CISC instruction usage

Instruction type	Average usage (%)
Data movement	46.3
Branch and subroutine call/return	27.6
Arithmetic	14.1
Compare	10.4
Logic	1.6

programs are of the single or *scalar* type and that over 80% of these are local procedure variables.

Based on this evidence, processor designers began to develop new architectures designed to be highly efficient in supporting a small (reduced) set of regular instructions and addressing modes, together with efficient ways of storing and retrieving simple operands.

10.3 RISC architectures

The following characteristics are typical of pure RISC architectures:

1. Relatively few instructions, with single-cycle instruction execution
2. Relatively few addressing modes
3. Fixed length easily decodable instruction formats
4. Memory access is limited to *LOAD* and *STORE* instructions
5. Relatively large general purpose register sets
6. Instructions that operate upon operands stored in registers rather than in main memory
7. A hardwired control unit.

Other characteristics, not exclusively attributed to RISC are:

8. Extensive use of pipelining, including instruction pipelining
9. Powerful compilers to optimise program code and make good use of the pipelined architecture
10. Complex functions implemented in software rather than hardware.

TQ 10.1 If a program is compiled to run on a RISC machine, would you expect it to be longer or shorter than if it is compiled to run on a CISC machine?

10.3.1 *MIPS R3000 and R4400*

The R4400 64-bit RISC processor has 32×64-bit general-purpose registers. It also has a 64-bit Program Counter and two 64-bit registers for holding the results of integer multiply and divide operations. The R4400 is binary compatible with the earlier 32-bit R3000 (i.e., the R4400 will run R3000 machine code without alteration). All R3000 instructions are 32 bits long and there are only three instruction formats to simplify decoding. These formats are shown in Figure 10.1.

All formats have a 6-bit opcode to specify the operation and the particular format to be used.

(1) *Load/Store instruction example*

The R3000 supports a *Load/Store architecture*, as only Load and Store instructions are used to access memory. Load and Store instructions use the

Figure 10.1   MIPS R3000 instruction formats

ccccccsssssttttt oooooooooooooooo

(a) I-type (immediate)

ccccccaaaaaaaaaa aaaaaaaaaaaaaaaa

(b) J-type (jump)

ccccccsssssttttt dddddhhhhhffffff

(c) R-type (register)

cccccc = 6-bit operation code
sssss = 5-bit source register; ddddd = 5-bit destination register
ttttt = 5-bit source or destination register
hhhhh = 5-bit shift amount; ffffff = 6-bit ALU/shift function
oooooooooooooooo = 16-bit immediate data, branch or address offset
aaaaaaaaaaaaaaaaaaaaaaaa = 24-bit target address

I-format to move data between main memory and the processor's registers.

lb Rt, address   Load the byte at *address* into register Rt and sign extend it by one byte.

The addressing mode used is base register (Rs) plus 16-bit signed immediate offset.

Instruction format: 011000sssssttttt oooooooooooooooo

(2) Jump instruction example

Jump instructions use the J-format, as shown below:

j label   Jump unconditionally to address label.

The address is found by shifting the target field two bits and then combining it with the upper four bits of the program counter.

Instruction format: 000010aaaaaaaaaa aaaaaaaaaaaaaaaa

(3) Computational instruction examples

Computational instructions can use either the I-format or the R-format, as shown in the following examples.

add Rd, Rs, Rt   Add the contents of registers Rs and Rt and copy result into Rd.

Instruction format: 000000sssssttttt ddddd00000010100

addi Rt, Rs, Imm   Add the immediate 16-bit signed literal to the content of Rs and copy result into Rt.

Instruction format: 001000sssssttttt oooooooooooooooo

TQ 10.2   How do the instruction formats of the 80x86 (see Section 5.4) compare with those of the R3000?

Table 10.2   MIPS R3000 integer instruction types

Instruction type	Number
Load/store	12
Jump and branch	12
Arithmetic and logic	18
Multiply/divide	8
Shift	6
System call/break	2

The R3000 uses 74 instructions: 58 basic integer instructions, as shown in Table 10.2, together with several others to support coprocessor and system control.

10.3.2   *The memory bottleneck*

One of the major problems with von Neumann style machines is the bottleneck caused by the processor–memory interface. This bottleneck arises because main memory is slower than the speed at which the processor can manipulate and process data internally. We can illustrate this by considering the instruction cycle timing for an *ADD* instruction, using figures typical for a modern microprocessor based system. We assume that one of the operands to be added is stored in memory.

[MAR] ← [PC]	5 ns
[PC] ← [PC] + 2	5 ns
[MBR] ← [M([MAR])]	70 ns
[IR] ← [MBR]	5 ns
Decode Instruction	10 ns
[MAR] ← Operand Address	5 ns
[MBR] ← [M([MAR])]	70 ns
Add Operation + set flags	30 ns
Test exceptions	5 ns
Total	205 ns

TQ 10.3   How much time is taken up accessing memory?

Although the actual time taken for each sub-operation depends upon the VLSI technology used, we can still see that a substantial fraction of each instruction cycle is dominated by the memory access time.

The fact that RISC systems have large sets of general-purpose registers and use register–register and not register–memory operations for computational tasks tends to alleviate the problems associated with this bottleneck and reduces instruction execution time. Also, because RISC instructions are equal to the width of the data bus, each instruction can be fetched in one *memory cycle*, unlike many CISC instructions that often need to be fetched using multiple memory cycles. To reduce the effect of the bottleneck even further, processor designers have adopted various strategies including increasing the width of the data bus to increase the rate at which information is read from or written to memory (*memory bandwidth*) and by using caching techniques, as we described in Section 4.3.2. Some designers have also resorted to using separate memories for instructions and data, called a *Harvard Architecture* (see Section 4.3.2), each memory being served by a separate address and data bus.

10.3.3 *Parameter passing*

The fact that programs tend to make extensive use of procedure call/returns has led some RISC designers to include hardware support for parameter passing between procedures. Processors based on the open RISC architecture specification, called SPARC (Scalable Processor ARChitecture), manage this through the use of overlapping *register windows*. A SPARC implementation may have up to 528×64-bit registers, partitioned into as many as 32-register windows.

Each window consists of 32 registers, only one window being 'visible' or active at a time, as shown in Figure 10.2. Procedure B occupies the active window, which is pointed to by a 5-bit *Current Window Pointer* (CWP). Registers R16, ..., R23 are used to store local variables, while registers R0, ..., R7 hold global variables that are visible to any active procedure.

If Procedure B wishes to pass parameters to Procedure C, it first copies them to registers R8, ..., R15 before calling it. Decrementing CWP on entry to Procedure C, causes the window to slide 'upwards', exposing a new set of registers R16, ..., R23 and with registers R8, ..., R15 becoming R24, ..., R31 in the called procedure. When a return is made, the same registers R24, ..., R31 are used to pass parameters back to the parent procedure, the CWP being incremented on exit from the procedure.

TQ 10.4 Why can the SPARC processor only have 32 windows?

In contrast to SPARC architectures, the MIPS R3000 architecture does not provide hardware support for procedure call/returns; instead it employs its *optimising compiler* to undertake this task. Using special optimisation

Figure 10.2 Parameter passing using SPARC's register window

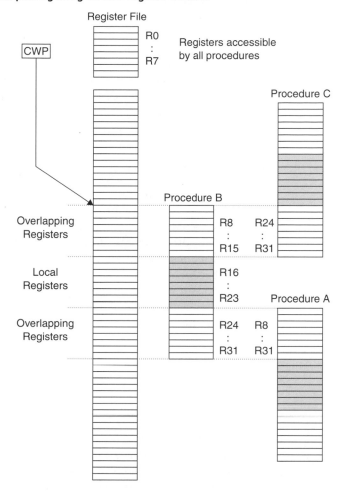

techniques, such as *procedure merging*, which replaces the call by the procedure code itself, the compiler can either eliminate or at least alleviate the problem. This illustrates the special role that compilers play in RISC systems.

10.4 The control unit

In Chapter 4, we described the internal organisation of a typical von Neumann style CPU and illustrated how the control unit sequenced the flow of data between the various registers and the ALU, which we call the *data path*. One important characteristic that tends to distinguish RISC from CISC architectures is the implementation of the control unit. Due to the complexity of their instruction sets, CISC designs use a *microprogrammed* control unit, while RISC designs are able to take advantage of a simpler and faster *hardwired* control unit.

10.5 Pipelining

Pipelining is the key implementation technique used to make faster CPUs and is extensively used in RISC processors. RISC processors allow instructions to be executed in stages, the stages being implemented using separate hardware. The stages are connected together to form an *instruction pipeline*, which allows more than one instruction to be processed at the same time. *Arithmetic pipelining* uses the same technique, allowing the operation to be broken down into smaller stages and implementing each stage with separate hardware. In a typical pipelined RISC design, each instruction takes one clock cycle per stage, allowing the processor to accept a new instruction into the pipe after each clock cycle. Although this does not significantly alter the *latency* or number of cycles needed to complete an instruction, it does improve the overall throughput, one instruction completing per clock cycle. The R4400 processor has an eight-stage integer instruction pipeline while the SPARC processor has a four-stage instruction pipeline. Instruction pipeline techniques were discussed in Section 4.3.1.

Section 4.3.1 discussed the problems of resource hazard. The R3000 processor reduced this problem by having separate instructions and data caches. Some implementations of the SPARC processor however, use a dual instruction buffer for multiple instruction fetching.

10.6 Hybrids

Nothing is ever quite as clear-cut as we would like. There are processors that are purely CISC, with very rich instruction sets and microprogrammed control units. There are processors which adhere closely to the principles of RISC design with a few very simple instructions and hard-wired control units. There is an ever increasing number of processors, which combine some aspects of both. There are CISC designs with the most common instructions decoded by hard-wired logic while the remaining instructions go through a microprogrammed control unit. There are RISC designs that have incorporated some more complex instructions. Most processors are therefor something of a hybrid.

10.7 Performance and benchmarking

It is often necessary to try to compare different processors. This may be comparing two processors in the same processor family to determine the improvement of the latest generation over the previous. It may be desirable to compare competitive products. It may be necessary to compare different processors of different architectures to determine which would be the best in a given environment. Just looking at clock speeds and bus widths is not sufficient.

AMD stopped rating their Athlon XP processors on simple clock speeds as Intel were delivering processors with greater clock speeds but the AMD processors were found to deliver similar performance because they were able to do more work per cycle. AMD decided to use model numbers (such as 2800+), which gives a figure that indicates speed relative to earlier AMD processors.

Comparing CISC and RISC processors is particularly difficult. RISC processors have slower clock speeds but can do more per cycle. To compare CISC and RISC processors it is necessary to come up with some sort of *benchmark*. A benchmark is a value against which other systems can be measured. A common benchmark for processors is the SPEC CPU2000 benchmark. SPEC benchmarks are developed by an independent organisation called Standard Performance Evaluation Corporation. Details of their benchmarks can be found at www.specbench.org. SPEC CPU2000 is in two parts, integer and floating point. These are designed to test the CPU performance specifically by performing a set of numerical problems. The code can be compiled to run on any processor. This enables manufacturers and users to compare processor performance even if they are of significantly different architectures. Two values can be produced from these benchmarks. The first is generated by using a standard set of compiler options. This means that a standard software configuration is used across all processors tested. The second value is produced when the compiler optimises the code for the specific processor being tested. Any special characteristics of the processor under test can be utilised to achieve the best performance possible. The benchmark for this suite of tests is the Sun SPARC Ultra5 300 processor, which is rated at 100. All other tested processors are rated relative to the SPARC processor. The same processor in different systems can produce quite different performance. This is due to other system components, such as I/O, memory, disk and network components affecting the performance of the system as a whole. To give a better indication of performance, computer systems to be compared are given a set of tasks to complete and the timings for these tasks are compared. SPEC provide a set of benchmarks for a range of different application types so that systems can be evaluated under conditions similar to those for which they are to be used.

10.8 Superscalar and superpipelined architectures

With *superpipelining*, instruction execution is broken down into even finer steps by lengthening the pipeline to increase *granularity*. For example, the MIPS R4000 processor uses a superpipelined eight-stage instruction pipeline that is able to deliver 50 MIPS at 50 MHz, compared with only 20 MIPS at 25 MHz offered by its non-superpipelined predecessor, the R3000. The increased performance arises because each stage can execute in under half a clock cycle. By doubling the internal clock speed, two stages and hence two instructions can be completed in one external clock cycle. In the case of the R4300, an on-chip frequency divide circuit is used to clock the pipeline at 100 MHz from an external 50 MHz clock source. One drawback of these long pipelines is that they are more susceptible to data dependency and require more 'intelligent' compilers to reduce the overhead introduced by flushing the pipeline (see Section 4.3.1).

An alternative way of increasing internal parallelism is to allow multiple instructions to be issued in the same clock cycle. This requires the duplication of various pipeline stages and the inclusion of multiple execution units, so that, for example, an instruction requiring a floating point add operation can be executed concurrently with one requiring an integer arithmetic operation. Processors that support this type of architecture are called multiple-issue processors. There are two basic types of such processors. The first is the superscalar processor such as the Intel Pentium, which schedules parallel execution within variable length blocks of five or so instructions using static/dynamic scheduling. The second is the Very Long Instruction Word (VLIW) processor, which uses static scheduling techniques to issue fixed size blocks of instructions or instruction words of between about 128 and 1024 bits, each field being used to encode an operation for a particular execution unit. Using sophisticated *trace scheduling* and other compilation techniques, these VLIW processors take advantage of program-wide parallelism among the instructions and are potentially much faster than superscalar processors. Their main drawback is that the compilers for these processors are slow and expensive and also the code is specifically targeted for a particular architecture and cannot be ported to a similar architecture unless the number of execution units and their respective latencies can be matched.

The Transmeta Crusoe TM5800 VLIW processor has a 128-bit instruction word. It makes use of a ROM-based interpreter, that uses a technique Transmeta call *code morphing*, to provide a very efficient mapping of Intel 80x86 instructions into the 128-bit instructions used by the Crusoe processor.

10.9 Summary

In this chapter we have described the main characteristics that distinguish RISC processors from conventional CISC processors. We explained the differences between their instruction sets and the control units used to decode their instructions. Because of the simplicity and regularity of the RISC instruction set, we explained how RISC designs used instruction pipelining to speed up the instruction execution rate.

Answers to in text questions

TQ 10.1   You would probably expect RISC programs to be longer, because several simple instructions would be needed to do the same job as one complex instruction. This is called code expansion. However, through the use of code size optimisation, RISC compilers can usually generate code that is at least within 15% and sometimes even shorter than the equivalent CISC code.

TQ 10.2   The 80x86 has a number of variable-length formats and several instruction coding schemes.

TQ 10.3   The two operations [MBR] ← [M(MAR)], use 140 ns and therefore over half the instruction cycle is spent accessing memory.

TQ 10.4   Because the CWP only uses 5 bits.

EXERCISES

1   List the important characteristics that could be used to distinguish RISC from CISC architectures. Why do RISC architectures tend to use large register files?

2   Describe how register windows are used with SPARC architectures to pass parameters between procedures. How does the R3000 deal with this problem?

3   What is meant by a superscalar processor?

Networked systems

In Chapter 1, the idea of a networked system was introduced as a mechanism intended to enable computers to be connected together so that resources could be shared. Resources in this context consist of processing power, computer memory, secondary data storage, the data itself and peripheral devices. This chapter covers both *wide area networks* (*WANs*) and *local area networks* (*LANs*), and then introduces the concept of distributed systems. It ends with a brief coverage of the security issues associated with networked systems.

11.1 Introduction to networked systems

11.1.1 *Communications basics*

An important characteristic of all communication links is the data rates that they will support. This is determined by the physical properties of the media used to make the link, of which *bandwidth* is one of the most important. The bandwidth of a link is the difference between the lowest and the highest frequency signal that can be sent on the link. The frequency characteristic of any type of link is shown in Figure 11.1.

The graph shows the output power from a link that is fed with a constant power signal of varying frequency. At very low frequency, there is a large loss on the link and so the output power is quite low. As the signal frequency increases, the losses in the link reduce and much of the input power is transferred to the output until an upper frequency is reached where the link

Figure 11.1   Frequency characteristics of a communication link

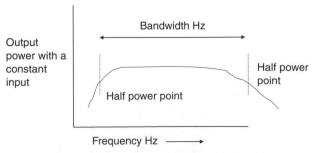

losses again start to increase. The bandwidth is the frequency range between the points where the output power has fallen by 50% of the value for the central frequencies. For any link, the data rate that is attainable is directly proportional to the bandwidth, so a fibre optic cable, which has a higher bandwidth than a twisted pair cable will provide a higher data rate capability. The story does not end here because another important factor to consider is the background noise that is inherent in any communication system. Noise is produced by thermal agitation of the atoms that make up the transmission medium, induced interference from sources such as power transmission systems and crosstalk from adjacent channels. The effect of noise is to reduce the maximum attainable data rate of the link. Noise is normally expressed as a ratio of the signal power to the noise power and so if in a link, the signal power is 10 Watts and the noise power is 0.01 W, the signal to noise ratio will be 1000. The signal to noise ratio is normally expressed in a unit called a decibel (db). Expressing a signal to noise ratio in db is done by using the following formula:

$$\text{ratio in db} = 10 \log_{10} (\text{power of signal/power of noise})$$

Using the above example of a signal to noise ratio of 1000 : 1

$$\log_{10} (1000) = 3$$
$$10 \log_{10} (1000) = 30 \text{ db}$$

TQ 11.1   What is the value in db of a signal to noise ratio of 100000 to 1?

Two important people in the field of communications, Nyquist and Shannon, produced equations linking bandwidth to data rate with Nyquist's equation just considering links without noise and Shannon including noise in his equation.
    Shannon's equation is:

$$C = W \log_2 (1 + P/N) \text{ bits per second}$$

where C is the link capacity or data rate in bps, W the bandwidth in Hz and P/N the signal to noise ratio mentioned above with P being the signal power and N being the noise power.
    Consider an example. The maximum data rate for a link, which has a bandwidth of 5 KHz and a signal to noise ratio of 40 db, which is 10000, is calculated as follows:

$$5000 \log_2(1 + 10000) \text{ bps}$$

which is approximately $5000 \log_2 (10000)$

$$= 5000 (\log_{10} (10000)/\log_{10} (2))$$
$$= 5000 (4/0.3)$$
$$= 66.5 \text{ Kbps}$$

11.1.2 Network connection modes

Computers can be connected to a network in one of two modes, either peer-to-peer or server based. We will now look at these two modes in a little more detail.

In a peer-to-peer network, every connected computer is of equal standing and inter-computer communication can be carried out on a direct computer-to-computer basis. The original computer networks, introduced in the early 1960s, used this mode of connection. In a big organisation with many large computers, some of which may be mainframe systems, the computers are often connected into what is known as a *cluster* by means of a peer-to-peer network. The machines can work independently but they can also work together, sharing data and their processing power. With a server-based network, a powerful controlling computer, called a server, forms the heart of the network and the other connected computers make all their communications through this server. The server provides *services* for the network users such as printing, controlling who may use the network, known as access control and a central file store for data and software. In a server-based network, the task of sending a file from computer A to computer B has to be done as follows: computer A sends the file to a common storage area in the server's file store and then computer B retrieves the file from the server's common area.

11.1.3 Network media

Network media is the term used to describe the connection material used to form the links of the network. Because the signals used in most networks are electrical, cables of various types are used but light signals over fibre optics and radio signals over the air are also used.

(1) Copper cables

There are two common types of copper cables used in networking, coaxial cables, known as coax and twisted pair cables. Twisted pair cables may have an outer screening layer to protect the twisted pairs from external electrical interference that may corrupt the data being transferred. The unshielded variety is known as Unshielded Twisted Pair (UTP). Figure 11.2 shows the two types of copper cables. Early types of LAN made use of both thick and

Figure 11.2   Network cable types (a) twisted pair (b) coaxial (c) fibre optic

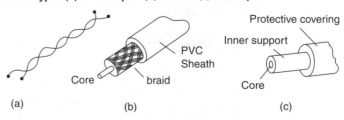

thin coax cable but the trend now is to use UTP cables as these are cheaper and easier to work with. WANs have used coax cables for years but fibre optic cables are the favourite for new installations.

Thin coax cable is about five millimetres overall diameter and thick coax cable is about 12 millimetres overall diameter. Their construction is almost identical. The inner copper conductor is stranded or solid and is supported and insulated from the outer copper braid by a polythene sleeve. The braid is made of thin strands in the thin version but the thick version uses much heavier strands, which makes the thick coax cable very rigid and difficult to handle. Both types of cable have an outer protective PVC sheath. The cables use different types of connectors, the thin cable using bayonet type BNC plugs and the thick cable using screw on plugs. Thick coax is much more expensive but has a lower signal loss per metre of length compared with thin coax. A typical data rate for coax used in LANs is 10 Mbps.

Twisted pair cables used in LANs are known as CAT 5 cables and consist of four sets of twisted pair insulated wires in a single PVC sheath. The copper wires are solid conductors and each wire is insulated with a different colour to aid identification when making connections. The connectors used with twisted pair cables are known as RJ45 connectors and these look very much like a telephone cable plug but are a little bigger. CAT 5 cables are cheaper than thin coax, are quite flexible, are easy to handle and require little skill to fix to the RJ45 plugs. CAT 5 cables can operate up to 1000 Mbps when used in conjunction with special equipment.

(2) Fibre optical cables

The physical properties of fibre optic cables are complex. A more detailed description can be found in material listed in the references at the end of this book. The following few words give some idea without too much technical detail. A fibre optic cable consists of an inner core of finely drawn glass or plastic, thinner than a human hair, which acts as a light pipe. Surrounding the core is a glass or plastic cladding, which supports the core, and over the cladding is a PVC sheath (see Figure 11.2(c)). Fibre optic cables are unidirectional and a pair of cables is needed for two-way transmission. To send a digital signal along a fibre optic cable requires the electrical pulses at the sending end to be turned into light pulses, using a light source, and a light detector to turn the light pulses back into electrical pulses at the receiving end. Light sources commonly used are *Light Emitting Diodes* (LED) for short distances, up to 1 km under favourable conditions, and *semiconductor lasers* for longer distances, up to 30 km.

Fibre optic cables using LEDs as light sources are sometimes used in LANs but the main area of application for fibre optics is in WANs. When used in WANs, the cables are multi-core, which are expensive and require a high level of skill and special equipment to join them. The advantage of fibre optic cables is that they have a high bandwidth and so support a very high data transfer rate, up to 1 Gbps and a single core can carry many hundreds of simultaneous signals using a technique known as *multiplexing*.

(3) Radio

The importance of radio for all types of communication systems is well known, even more so with its use for mobile telephones. LAN systems based on radio communication are becoming popular, especially where users wish to be mobile, and a little more will be said about this later. Radio, either direct path or via communication satellites, is an essential part of all worldwide data networks. A little more will be said on the way in which radio is used when discussing LAN systems.

11.1.4 *Network topologies*

In a network, the connected devices are known as *nodes* rather than computers because devices other than computers are connected to networks. The topology of a network is to do with the way in which it operates and the way in which the network is structured and how the nodes are connected. There are two aspects to the structure. The first aspect is to do with the way in which the wiring for the connections among the nodes is physically laid out and this is known as the *physical topology*. The second aspect is the way in which the communication among the nodes is carried out and this is known as the *logical topology*. The installers of the wiring for the network need to know about the physical topology whereas those who specify and administer the network need to know about the logical topology. There is a tendency to mix these two aspects thus causing confusion in the early stages of learning about networks.

The main topologies are *bus, mesh, ring and star*, see Figure 11.3.

(1) Physical topologies

We will first use Figure 11.3 to illustrate physical topologies. A physical bus is effectively a single cable that is used to connect nodes in much the same way as peripheral devices are connected using Firewire, see Section 8.5.5. With a star, all nodes are connected to a common central device using individual links for each connected node. A ring has all nodes connected such that a circular route is produced. A mesh can be *fully interconnected*, where every

Figure 11.3 Network topologies (a) bus (b) mesh (c) ring (d) star

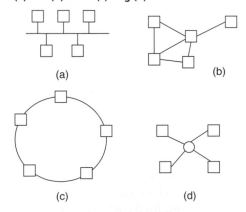

node is directly connected to every other node, or *partially interconnected*, where not all nodes have a direct connection to every other node. Figure 11.3(b) shows a partially interconnected mesh. Connecting a new node to a bus is simply a matter of connecting the new node to the single cable. Connecting a new node to a star requires a new link to be provided between the node and the central point. Connecting a new node to a ring means re-routing two links to accommodate the new node. Connecting a new node to a fully interconnected mesh requires the provision of as many new links as there are nodes in the original network. Because of the large number of links, fully interconnected mesh networks are expensive and this is the reason for the existence of partially interconnected mesh networks. In spite of the expense, mesh networks are widely used and more details will be given later.

(2) *Logical topologies*

Before we give details of logical topologies, it is necessary to explain *broadcast transmission* and *point-to-point transmission*, which are the two methods of data transmission used in networks. In a broadcast transmission system, when a node wishes to send a message to another node, it transmits the message in such a way that all nodes receive the message but only the node for which it is intended takes it in. This is how broadcast radio and TV operate. Obviously, for a broadcast system to work, the transmission medium must be suitable.

With point-to-point transmission, a message is sent from one node to the next in line, and so on, until the message destination node is reached. At each node, the message is stored and its destination address inspected before it is sent on to the next node.

(a) A logical bus

A logical bus type system has a single link to which all nodes are connected. It operates as a broadcast system. Bus systems can use cable with a layout, which can be a physical bus, or a physical star or the connection can be by radio signals over the air.

(b) A logical mesh

The mesh topology uses point-to-point transmission. The actual action needed to send a message from one node to another node depends on the actual physical topology. In a fully connected mesh, there is a direct connection between every node and so the message is sent directly. This is called a *single hop*. In a partially connected mesh, the path could be a single hop or the message may have to be sent via several intermediate nodes resulting in several hops. When a message is sent to an intermediate node and then on to another node and so on, process is known as *store and forward* and this is a characteristic of point-to-point data transmission.

(c) A logical ring

The ring topology needs some careful consideration. The ring normally consists of links connecting *ring interface units* (RIU), one for each node. A node wishing to send a message to another node, adds the address of the destination node to the message and sends this, via its RIU, to the next RIU

Figure 11.4   Possible internal connections for a cable connection box

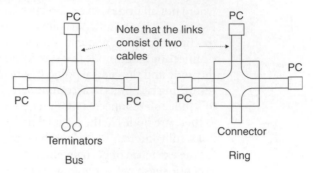

in the ring. This RIU reads the address and if the message is for this node, the message is sent to the node. If the message is not for this node, the RIU passes the message to the next RIU in the ring and so on until the message reaches its destination node. So far so good but there is a problem. There are a number of different ways of implementing ring networks and the RIUs for each implementation operate in different ways. We will look at details of the most popular type later but for now we can just say that some RIUs use store and forward while others just read the address and pass on the message, if it is not for that address, without storing it. So depending on the type of RIU, we could have a point-to-point system or a broadcast system, which are two different logical topologies that operate in totally different ways, but both look like a physical ring. Here is an illustration of why it is important to know the difference between a physical and a logical topology.

(d)   A logical star

We have a problem with the star topology. The type of device, which forms the common point, needs to be known before any comments on the logical topology can be made. If the central point device is a server or a *switch* connected to a server, then we have a point-to-point system, forming a logical star. Switches will be covered later. If the central point device is simply a cable connecting box, then the internal connections could be such that a logical bus or even a logical ring is formed, see Figure 11.4, but physically we see a star. Note that the links for this type of connection consist of two cables.

11.2   Local area networks

There are a number of definitions for a LAN mainly based on size. We believe that our definition is more helpful. A LAN is a network used by an organisation that normally covers a small area, typically a single building or a single site, such as a hospital, factory or university campus. The entire network is owned and controlled by the organisation and does not make use of external communication services provided by a service provider. To look at our definition in another way, if a network uses the communications services of a service provider then it is not a LAN.

11.2.1 *Ethernet*

One of the earliest forms of LAN is based on the *Ethernet* system. This uses a common communication path to link a group of computers together. Figure 11.5 gives a logical representation of the network. Ethernet is based on a logical bus topology and uses broadcast transmission. Each computer is fitted with a *Network Interface* device. This can take the form of a printed circuit card that plugs into an ISA or PCI slot or it can be an integrated part of the motherboard. In either case, an externally accessible socket is provided at the back of the processor box to which the network cable can be attached. Every network interface device manufactured has a unique 48-bit hardware address built into it. When a card is used, it is called a Network Interface Card (NIC). The type of cable used in early networks was thin coax cable. A special cable connector called a 'T' piece was connected to the BNC coax connector on the NIC thus providing two coaxial connectors per NIC. Connecting cables were made up into the required lengths to connect the computers together and these were connected to the 'T' pieces. The outer arms of the 'T' pieces on the computers at each end of the cable were fitted with a cable terminator to prevent electrical reflections in the cable, see Figure 11.6. The cabling forms a physical bus topology and Figure 11.5 shows this.

In an Ethernet network, all computers share the same single cable for communication. The way the NICs function is as follows. Assume computer A in Figure 11.5 wishes to send data to computer D. NIC A listens to the cable to see if it is being used. If there is no signal on the cable, NIC A sends data. All NICs connected to the network 'see' the data but only the NIC in computer D actually receives the data. This is because the data sent by A has attached to it, the unique address of the NIC in computer D. The data also

Figure 11.5 Ethernet bus topology

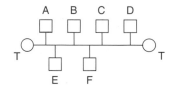

T is a Terminator

Figure 11.6 Ethernet using thin coax cable

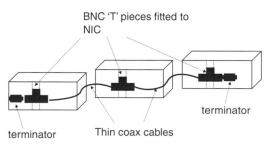

has the address of the sending NIC so that a reply can be sent back if it is needed. If the NIC in computer A had found the cable busy, that is a signal on it, when it wanted to send data, then it would have waited until the cable was free before sending any data. So far so good. Now assume that computer A wished to send data to D and C wished to send to B. NICs A and C listen to the cable and as soon as it is free they both start to send data. Electrical signals travel very fast on the cable but it takes a few microseconds for the signals to meet and collide and by that time a few bits have been sent. This collision of signals means that the transmission is corrupted. To overcome this problem, the NICs are designed to send data and at the same time 'listen' to what is on the cable. If what a NIC 'hears' is what it is putting on the cable, all is well, if not a collision is detected and the NICs stop transmitting. After a NIC detects a collision, it waits for a short random period of time before it starts to 'listen' to the cable once more. The period of time that a NIC transmits data and listens at the same time is known as the *contention* period and this period is fixed by the Ethernet standard. The reason that a random wait period is used is to reduce the possibility of both NICs trying to re-transmit at the same time and so cause another collision. The Ethernet system is often called a Carrier Sense Multiple Access with Collision Detection (CSMA/CD) system. CSMA/CD systems are simple to implement and work very well for networks that are not heavily loaded with communications traffic. This is because as the traffic load increases, there is more likelihood of a collision occurring thus wasting transmission potential. Another problem is that under very heavy traffic load conditions, a NIC wishing to use the cable could wait a very long time before it can gain access to the cable. Ethernet systems are sometimes described as *non-deterministic* because there is no maximum time limit before access can be guaranteed. For this reason, Ethernet systems should not be used for *real time* applications.

In the descriptions above, no mention has been made of the amount of data that is being sent between nodes or the sizes of the messages. In fact, all data transmission systems send the data in small chunks, using a technique known as *packet switching*. Packet switching was devised for wide area networks and will be covered in more detail in Section 11.3.

For the benefit of our discussions on LANs, it is important to understand that unless the amount of data or the message to be sent is quite small, it will be split up into what are called *frames*. For Ethernet, the maximum amount of data that can be sent in a frame is 1500 bytes and when we have said above that a message is sent, what is actually sent is a frame. Figure 11.7 shows an Ethernet frame that conforms to the IEEE 802.3 frame format. IEEE 802.3 is a widely used standard for Ethernet systems. Messages or data too long for a

Figure 11.7   The format of an IEEE 802.3 Ethernet frame

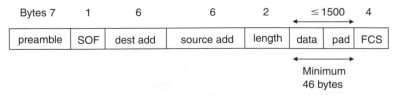

frame will be split into frame-sized pieces at the transmitting end and reassembled at the receiving end. The frame starts with a 7-byte pattern of alternate zeros and ones, called the preamble, which enables the NICs on the network to synchronise with the signal. A single byte, with the bit-pattern 10101011, then announces the start of the frame. The source and destination addresses are the 48-bit addresses of the sending and intended receiving NICs. The length is a 2-byte binary value indicating the number of bytes of data that are to follow. The data field, sometimes called the *payload*, has a minimum of 46 to a maximum of 1500 bytes. The Frame Check Sequence (FCS) is a 4-byte value, obtained by a calculation involving the destination address, the data and a special bit pattern specified by the standard being used. The FCS provides error checking at the receiving end by carrying out the same calculation as was done at the sending end and if the FCS that is received is the same as that calculated at the receiving end, it is assumed that no error has occurred during transmission. Returning to that minimum of 46 bytes in the payload the IEEE 802.3 standard states that an Ethernet frame must be at least 72 bytes long. This is to ensure that NICs that are sending and listening for a collision are transmitting for sufficient time to be able to detect a collision. The fixed length contention period is one of the reasons for there being limits to the length of cables used for Ethernet systems. If the amount of data to be sent is less than 46 bytes, then pad bytes must be added to the data to make the number of bytes in the data field up to at least 46.

TQ 11.2   Why is it that an Ethernet system can have only one frame passing over the cable at any one time?

TQ 11.3   An Ethernet frame is to hold 26 bytes of data. What is the length of the frame in bytes?

The Standards for Ethernet systems specify a number of different data rates. These include 10 Mbps, 100 Mbps and a new 1000 Mbps. Typically coax cable is used at 10 Mbps, UTP at 10 Mbps, 100 Mbps and 1000 Mbps and fibre optic at 1000 Mbps.

11.2.2   *Token ring*

The token ring LAN is the most popular of a family of LAN-ring topologies. Figure 11.3(c) shows a sample token ring system. There are a number of variations and our description gives the general idea rather than giving details of a specific system.

Nodes are connected to the links by means of a RIU as explained in Section 11.1.4(2). Some ring systems use a dedicated master control node, while others use an *election algorithm* to make one of the normal nodes on the network perform the master control function. The token is the key to the way in which this ring LAN operates. At start-up, the master control node generates a special

Figure 11.8 Example token ring frames

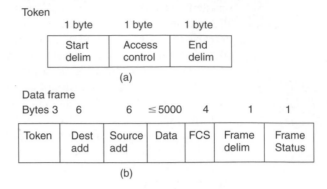

Token

1 byte	1 byte	1 byte
Start delim	Access control	End delim

(a)

Data frame

Bytes 3   6   6   ≤ 5000   4   1   1

Token	Dest add	Source add	Data	FCS	Frame delim	Frame Status

(b)

3-byte frame, which is the token and our version of its format is shown in Figure 11.8(a). The start and end delimiter bytes consist of special bit patterns that are not used for data. The token is passed round the RIUs and finally arrives back at the master control node where it is checked to make sure it is still a valid token. If node A wishes to send data to node D, it starts to send the data to its RIU which makes up a data frame and stores it in an internal buffer. The RIU uses a handshake mechanism to stop the node sending data when the frame is full. Typically, ring data frames can hold up to 5000 bytes of data. Now the RIU waits for a token to arrive. On receiving a token, the RIU converts the token to a loaded data frame, see Figure 11.8(b) and sends the data frame on its way. The data frame has a frame delimiter byte to mark the end of the data rather than a length field as used in the Ethernet system. As the data frame passes each RIU, the destination address is tested to see if the frame is intended for that RIU. If it is, then the data is copied from the frame and a received bit is set in the Status byte of the frame and the slightly modified data frame continues round the ring. If the data frame is not for the RIU, the data frame passes through the RIU. Eventually, the data frame will arrive back at the sending RIU where first the received bit is checked and then the data is compared with what was sent. If the data matches, it is assumed that the data arrived without error. The received bit being set, tells that the receiving RIU was active and that the frame was received. The sending RIU must now generate a token, which it passes on to the next RIU. By doing this, every RIU is given a chance to send a data frame in turn, if it has one to send. This process ensures that any RIU has a maximum waiting time equal to the time taken for all RIUs to send a frame. A set of operating rules, such as those described above, is known as a *protocol* and networks make use of many different protocols. Ring LANs work very well under heavy traffic load, as there are no collisions to degrade their performance. Ring LANs are classed as *deterministic* and are ideal for real time applications. The node performing the Master Control function monitors the token or data frame as it passes and if neither type of frame passes in a certain time, then it assumes that a corruption has occurred and it generates a new token frame. Should the node that is performing the Master Controlling function fail, the functioning nodes run an election process to elect a new node to take over the Master role. Only one token or one data frame can be on the ring at any one time with this type of ring system.

Ring networks can use any of the four media types introduced in Section 11.1.3 and in fact, the links between RIUs can be of different types on the same ring. The most common are UTP for standard 16 Mbps data rate systems and fibre optic cables for high speed systems, which can operate at data rates in excess of 600 Mbps. A special, high-speed ring system, that uses fibre optic cables, is known as Fibre Distributed Data Interface (FDDI) and this type of ring is sometimes used in interconnecting multiple LANs.

11.2.3 Wireless LANs

Until quite recently, all LANs used cables for their links. However, there is increasing interest in the use of radio links to produce what is often referred to as a wireless LAN. The greatest benefit is that nodes on the network can be placed almost anywhere, and can in fact be mobile, within the confines of the LAN area. Even desk bound PCs can be moved without the need for any re-cabling. Almost all wireless LANs are based on server-based Ethernet systems using the radio *channel* as the shared communication medium. The wireless system requires a radio transmitter/receiver (*transceiver*) to be fitted to each node, acting as a NIC. At a convenient central place is installed a radio base station, to which is connected the server, with the base station acting as the server NIC. There is a set of IEEE standards for wireless LANs, which allows operation at data rates similar to standard Ethernet. The most common application for wireless LANs is in large open plan offices with users having wireless NICs in their desk top standard PCs or portable/notebook computers. The high frequency used for wireless LANs means that the range between nodes and the base station is a little restricted, particularly inside multi-roomed buildings.

Another area of use that is growing rapidly is where hand held devices need to communicate with a central server. A typical scenario would be a small factory site or works yard or inside a warehouse where the nodes are palmtops or Personal Data Assistants (PDAs were briefly mentioned in Chapter 1). These devices are often fitted with bar code readers and small touch sensitive displays.

There are ring type systems that can make use of a broadcast radio channel for connecting all the nodes to the master control unit. These systems are more expensive than Ethernet-based wireless LANs but they are deterministic and ideal for real time control applications.

11.2.4 LAN wiring systems

This section is about physical topologies used by LAN systems.

(1) Basic wiring

You will recall that a physical topology describes the way in which the cabling used to interconnect the nodes is laid and this will depend on the geography of the site where the network is to be installed. The Ethernet bus topology, illustrated in Figure 11.5, is appropriate for a logical topology but how would the cables be run in a real situation. If the network is required for a computer lab in a college, with PCs being placed on tables round the wall, then thin coax links could be used to link the 'T' pieces on the NICs thus forming an obvious physical bus. Now consider a single floor of an office building that house a number of individual offices where each office is to have a PC. The thin coax cabling system used for the computer lab could be used here but a more convenient system would be to provide each office with a network connection point which is connected, via its own individual cable, to a central wiring cabinet. Now if a fault occurs with the wiring, each individual link can be tested from the cabinet without having to visit every office, which would be the situation if the computer lab wiring system were to be used. The office wiring system forms a physical star with the wiring cabinet as the central point of the star. Inside the wiring cabinet, the links can be connected so that they form a logical bus, see Figure 11.3.

Some NICs are manufactured with connectors for thin coax and UTP cable and occasionally with a 15-pin Access Unit Interface (AUI) socket, for use with thick coax cable. However, the current trend is just to provide a RJ45 UTP connector.

The physical star topology, using UTP cable rather than thin coax, is currently the most popular method for wiring LANs. So much so that new buildings such as office blocks and even hotels have the UTP cable installed alongside telephone and TV cables in such a way as to provide outlets at convenient points throughout the building. These cables are brought into a central wiring cabinet, which acts as the distribution and control centre for the network, telephone and TV services for the building. This method of wiring is known as *structured wiring*.

Let us take a closer look at the wiring cabinet. There are a number of different devices that can be installed to provide the connections for the links. Figure 11.4 shows the actual wires being connected using a device called a patch panel. The problem with this type of connection is that every link is directly connected and if an electrical fault occurs, the whole network fails. Current systems use devices, variously called *hubs* or *switches*, which provide a degree of electrical isolation between the links but still provide signal connectivity. In essence, these devices have four, eight, 16 or 24 sockets, typically UTP RJ45 type, to which are connected the individual links. If there are more than 24 links in a network, extra hubs can be daisy chained together.

The basic wiring cabinet device is the hub and this simply connects the cables into a physical bus and is used for Ethernet systems as described above. An advanced device, becoming popular for server-based LANs, is a switch or *intelligent hub* to which the server, as well as every other node in the network, are directly connected. There are various types and they all use the Ethernet principle. The basic concept is that the switch samples each of its connected links to look for a NIC that is starting to send a frame. When the start of a frame is detected, the switch directly connects the node to the server for the duration of the frame and all other NICs get a 'busy' signal from the switch. The server, when requiring to send a frame to a node, has priority over other nodes. As soon as the 'busy' signal is removed all NICs can contend for access just like a bus Ethernet system. However, we now have a central device, the switch, which is controlling some of the network access rather than the NICs controlling all access. This is a logical star and is similar to a type of early LAN topology where a central computer acted as a server and user nodes were directly connected to it and were accessed using a polling technique.

There are now switches and hubs that work at standard Ethernet (10 Mbps) and high-speed Ethernet (100 Mbps) and some can work with a mix of standard and high-speed NICs on the same network.

The token-ring system described above could also be wired as a physical star by using appropriate hubs but the use of switches is not appropriate for ring systems.

(2) Interconnecting LAN segments

It is sometimes appropriate to split a network into smaller physical sub-networks, often called *segments*, and then connect these into one large logical network. An example is where a building has a number of floors and each floor has its own segment, possibly with its own servers, but overall connectivity among the floors is required. Another example is where departments in a company could have their own segments or even their own networks, again with their own servers, but some cross department traffic provision is needed. Convenience in wiring, network traffic distribution and security are the issues that need consideration. There are a number of devices that are available to provide interconnection for LANs and even more for interconnecting WANs. We will look at LAN devices here and WAN devices in Section 11.3.

(a) Repeaters

These are the simplest devices for interconnecting segments and are used for Ethernet-type systems. They provide electrical isolation between the connected segments and they also provide signal regeneration.

Figure 11.9(a) shows two simple two-port repeaters connecting three segments and Figure 11.9(b) a multi-port repeater connecting four

Figure 11.9 LAN interconnection using repeaters

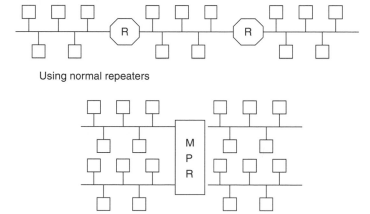

Using normal repeaters

Using a multi-port repeater

201

segments. The simple repeater takes the electrical signal it sees on port A and sends it out on port B. Likewise electrical signals seen by port B are sent out on port A. The Ethernet standards set an upper limit of five segments that can be connected together using simple repeaters, with the maximum length of the cables being limited to that specified in the standards. The effect of the repeater is to connect the segments into one network. A multi-port repeater works in exactly the same way to produce a single network and also provides electrical isolation. This type of repeater does the same job as a hub but for network segments rather than single nodes. Typically, multi-port repeaters are available with four or eight ports.

Repeaters are occasionally used in ring systems where the ring geography requires a particularly long link between two RIUs. The repeater boosts the signal and this is why this type of repeater is sometimes called a *line driver*. It should be remembered that frames travel only in one direction in a ring and so the repeater used in a ring is unidirectional.

(b) Bridges

Bridges are intelligent devices that actually look at and interpret the frames that they see, unlike the repeater, which just handles bits. There are various types of bridges and we will look at a few of the most common. When a bridge is used to connect two network segments, the segments remain two separate networks as far as access control is concerned and each can have a frame on it without the frames being corrupted. Figure 11.10 shows a bridge being used to connect two Ethernet networks together. Each of the bridge ports has a buffer, which is used to store a frame and a routing table to store routing information. Each port sees every frame on the network just like a NIC does.

The simplest type of bridge is called a self-learning bridge and it operates in the following way. Refer to Figure 11.10. Assume that node A wishes to send a frame to node F. The frame will contain the destination node NIC address. The frame will be broadcast and all NICs on network X will receive it as will the left hand port of the bridge. The bridge buffers the frame and inspects the destination address. The bridge then inspects its routing table to see if the destination node is connected to its right or left hand port. Now when the bridge is first powered on, its routing table is empty, remember this type of bridge is called a learning bridge. So the bridge, not knowing which side the destination node is on, passes the frame to its right hand port and sends it on network Y. However, it now knows which side node A is on and it puts this information into its routing table. Also node F NIC receives the frame that was destined for it. Almost certainly, node F will wish to respond

Figure 11.10 LAN interconnection using a bridge

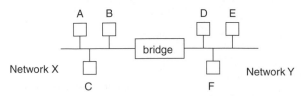

to the frame sent from A and so it transmits a frame with A as the destination address. This is received at the right hand port of the bridge and because of the learned entry in its routing table, it knows that it must pass the frame to its left hand port for transmission on network X. The bridge now knows where node F is.

Now assume that node C wishes to send a frame to node A. Node C NIC transmits the frame and node A NIC receives it. Also the bridge receives the frame, on its left hand port, and upon looking at the destination address it knows not to pass the frame over to its right hand port. As nodes on the network exchange frames, the bridge either passes the frames over, if it does not know where the destination is, or it actually knows that it must pass the frame over by referring to its routing table, or it does not pass the frame if the destination is on the same side as the transmitting node. The bridge is also adding entries to its routing table until it knows where each node is located. What happens if someone physically moves a NIC from one side of the bridge to the other? The bridge notices and changes its routing table entry accordingly. What the bridge is doing is confining traffic that is between nodes on one side to that side only and only passing frames that need to cross from one network to the other. Careful use of bridges in a large network can help to distribute the traffic and prevent overloading. This process is known as filtering.

Figure 11.11 shows how four bridges can be used to interconnect four networks on each of four floors of a building using what is called a *backbone*. This is a convenient way to install the cabling. The four networks, each with their own servers, operate as independent networks, but have the ability to interchange cross network traffic should the need arise. Some bridges can be programmed such that they only allow certain nodes to send frames outside their own network or will only allow frames in from other designated nodes. By using this type of network, some level of security can be implemented. The backbone cable can be the same as the network cable, typically UTP, but if there is likely to be a large quantity of inter-network

Figure 11.11 Using bridges and a backbone to connect networks

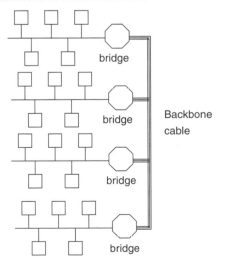

203

traffic, the backbone could be high-speed Ethernet or even an FDDI ring, thus preventing the backbone from being a bottleneck. Obviously, appropriate bridges would have to be used.

Bridges are normally used to connect similar types of network together, so there are bridges suitable for connecting two token ring networks as well as Ethernet connecting bridges. However, there are special bridges, called translating bridges, which enable a token ring and an Ethernet network to be connected. This has extra work to do as the frame formats are different for the two systems and so frame format translation is required.

Figure 11.12 shows how another type of bridge, known as a remote bridge or half bridge, can be used to connect a LAN on one site to a LAN on another site via a telephone or other service provider facility. The diagram shows a leased line being used for the interconnection. Leased lines will be covered in the next section. Note that a remote or half bridge is needed at each site. Each half bridge consists of a port and its associated buffer and a routing table with addresses of those nodes connected to it. The operation is exactly the same as for a normal bridge except that transferred frames pass over the interconnecting line. The half bridge must have an in-built device to allow the digital network signals to be converted to the type of signals that the line will transport. A *modem* is the device needed for telephone lines and these will be discussed in the next section.

Bridges may be used to connect more than two networks and Figure 11.13 shows how three networks can be connected using two bridges.

Figure 11.12   Connecting remote LANs

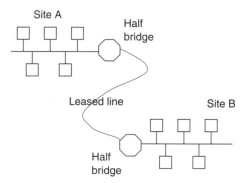

Figure 11.13   Connecting more than two networks

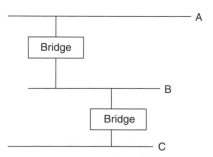

The problem here is that if network B fails, there will be no connectivity between networks A and C. It is a temptation to connect a third bridge between networks A and C thus providing some redundancy and hence a way of overcoming single network failures. However, normal bridges cannot be connected such that a circular route is formed because the node locating process would get confused as frames could approach from either direction. Special types of bridges are available, that make use of a different type of frame routing mechanism and these can be used in a situation where a circular route is formed in the interconnected networks.

11.3 Wide area networks

WANs are almost entirely based on point-to-point mesh topologies and make use of a store and forward mechanism. WANs have been in existence for many years and predate LANs by about 20 years. The original WANs were used to interconnect some government research establishments and universities in the USA and UK, providing the facility to exchange research papers and similar documents. WANs grew steadily in size and number of connected nodes until the early 1990s when the idea of the Internet was born. Since then, the number of WANs and their size has dramatically increased. WANs tend to operate at slower data rates than LANs and the error rate, caused by interference, is also higher. Special action must be taken to reduce the error rate and this will be discussed later.

Most WANs use fibre optic cable for the node-to-node links but twisted pair copper cables, coax, point-to-point radio and communications satellites are also widely used.

The world telephone system is a very large WAN, originally intended for voice traffic, but increasingly used for data transfer. Telephone *subscribers* form the end nodes and telephone exchanges provide the switching capability that enables calls to be routed and connected. In data transfer, computers form the end nodes and the exchanges switch data traffic.

WANs cover all the countries of the world, use many different and often incompatible systems and use equipment made by many different manufacturers yet they need to inter-communicate. To get sufficient co-operation to achieve world wide telephony took many years and to achieve world wide data transfer took longer. The real problem was that many *communication networks* had their own way of operating with their own protocols. Ideally, a single standard defining a universally agreed protocol would solve all interconnectivity problems. The success of the Internet has been made possible only by a universal adoption of a suite of protocols used in some of the early WANs that used UNIX as the operating system for the end node computers. The suite is known as TCP/IP and more will be said of this later.

11.3.1 *Packet switching*

Packet switching was briefly mentioned in Section 11.2. It is now time to look into this a little more deeply. The concept of packet switching is that a message to be sent from A to B is split up into small chunks, called packets,

Figure 11.14   A mesh connected WAN

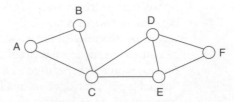

and it is these packets that are sent through the network from source to destination. Obviously, if a long message is to be sent and it is split into packets at the transmitting end, then the packets need to be rejoined in the correct order at the receiving end.

(1)   *Virtual Circuit and Datagram services*

Consider the mesh network shown in Figure 11.14. Nodes A and F are end nodes and nodes B through E are intermediate switching nodes. Assume a message, which is to be split into three packets, is to be sent from A to F. There are two ways in which this can be done. Firstly, a connection could be set up, as is done in the telephone system, by setting switches in say C and E to connect A to F. Now the three packets could be sent over this circuit in sequence and they will arrive at F in the order in which they were sent. Remember that a store and forward mechanism is being used, which means that each packet would be received in full at C, before it is transmitted to E and so on. This sort of system is known as a *Virtual Circuit* because it looks like a direct circuit has been established between the two-end nodes. The second way of sending the three packets, known as a datagram service, is to put the destination address (F) and a sequence number for the packet at the front of each packet of data and then send the packets on their way either via B or C. At each intermediate node, the packet would be received and the destination address inspected and a decision made as to which path to use to forward the packet. Eventually the packets arrive at F but, depending on the *Routing* decision made at each node, individual packets could have travelled different routes and the order of arrival at F could be different to the sending order. This is where the sequence number is required to enable the packets to be placed into the correct sequence.

What are the relative advantages and disadvantages of these two types of service?

The Virtual Circuit system needs the circuit to be set up before any data is sent and then it ties up the links between the switching nodes for the whole time that it takes for the message to be transmitted. After the last data packet has been sent, the circuit needs to be *torn down*, to release the links for others to use. However, the individual packets are not involved with routing decisions at each intermediate node and the packets arrive in the correct order at the destination without need for any reordering. With the datagram system, there is no circuit set up and tear down activity as packets are just sent with the destination address embedded in them. No reservation of links is needed as any link that can forward the packet towards its destination can be used by the intermediate nodes thus increasing the utilisation of link resources. However, the order of packet receipt is not guaranteed and packet reordering at the destination node may be required.

For the service provider, Virtual Circuit takes more resources and so a higher price is charged for this service whereas a datagram uses fewer resources and the user is charged less.

For the user, if the message can be put into one packet, datagram is best because it is cheapest, whereas if the message is long, then Virtual Circuit may be best as packet order delivery is guaranteed, which means that packet reordering is never needed.

(2) *High data rate services*

Packet switched services have been offered for many years, conforming to a standard known as X25. The underlying network that provides these services is the normal telephone system and the data rate available is 64 Kbps.

TQ 11.4   Assuming a signal to noise ratio of 40 db, calculate the bandwidth required to provide 64 Kbps transmission speed.

With the demand for much higher data rates growing, a number of new services have become available relying on the fact that telephone network companies have been replacing their old analogue networks with high bandwidth digital networks using fibre optic cables. Amongst these new services are Integrated Services Digital Networks (ISDN), Asynchronous Transfer Mode (ATM) and the xDSL family of services.

(1) ISDN is a digital service that is intended to provide multiple 64 Kbps telephone circuits into a subscriber's premises. Circuits can be combined to provide higher data rates up to a level where the bandwidth is sufficient for good quality video conferencing. The service is a virtual circuit system, like the telephone, but can be used to send packetised data. The service is rather expensive involving an initial installation fee, a monthly service charge and in some cases a charge for traffic carried. Data rates of 155 Mbps and 622 Mbps are available.

(2) ATM is the underlying system upon which ISDN is based. It was first used on WAN systems but has subsequently been introduced into some LAN systems. The system is quite complicated and we will just give an overview. ATM relies on good quality communication channels that have very low-error rates and high data transfer rates. It is most often used with fibre optic cables. The idea is to use very small packets, typically 48 bytes of data and a 5-byte header. In ATM the packet is called a *cell*. The user 'sees' a Virtual Circuit service but in fact, a type of datagram service is used. The big advantage is that with such a small cell, many users can share the links and, even more important, some users can have more cells per second than other users if the type of traffic being carried needs more capacity. Voice and video packets need a high bandwidth and cannot tolerate packet delay, whereas data transfer is not

Table 11.1 Some xDSL services

Service	Up load rate	Down load rate
ADSL	1.544 Mbps	1.5–8 Mbps
ADSL Lite	512 Kbps	1 Mbps
HDSL	1.544 or 2 Mbps	1.544 or 2 Mbps
VDSL	1.5–2.3 Mbps	13–52 Mbps

affected by packet delay. ATM systems, with their ability to dynamically vary cell allocation, are very good at handling *mixed traffic*.

(3) The xDSL family of services is an attempt to bring digital services into the domestic market as well as providing a business offering. Table 11.1 shows some of the services available.

xDSL services are permanent digital connections suitable for voice and data. The various services in the family provide different data rates that may be different in each direction. The service is of particular benefit for access to the Internet where short requests for pages from a website result in large quantities of data being downloaded, hence the relatively slow up rate and faster down rate.

Asymmetric Digital Subscriber Line (ADSL) is ideal for the small business where the traffic is not too heavy. ADSL Lite is intended for domestic use. H, High bit rate, and V, Very high bit rate, are intended for businesses with a larger demand for digital services. The cost of provision depends on the bit rate provided and as this service is permanently connected, there is no connection time charge.

11.3.2 Public and private networks

Figure 11.15 shows a representation of a public WAN. The communications subnet is provided by a network services provider and access to it is provided in much the same way as to the public switched telephone network (PSTN). Note that the term *host* has been used rather than user or subscriber as the user will normally be a computer, or even a LAN with a number of computers connected to it, to which many users may be connected. A virtual circuit as well as a datagram service is provided and a charge is made for usage, see Section 11.3.1. The actual content in terms of the switching nodes and the links is totally the responsibility of the network provider and the way in which hosts both connect and send traffic over the network must conform to the protocols specified by the network supplier. Packets entered into the network for delivery, must have appropriate destination addresses and the

Figure 11.15 A diagrammatic representation of a public network

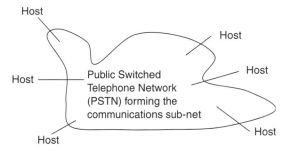

Figure 11.16 A diagrammatic representation of a private network

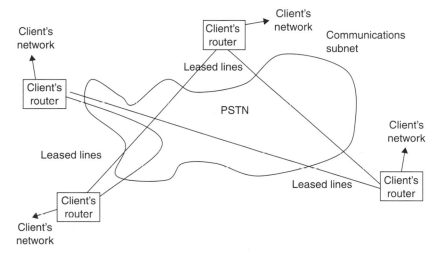

protocol will specify the packet format that must be used in order that the address can be extracted.

Virtual circuit services guarantee ordered delivery of correct packets but a datagram service makes no guarantee of delivery. If confirmation of delivery is required, then the receiving host must send a *confirmation of receipt*. This type of operation requires the sending host to start a timer when a packet is sent and if a reply has not been received within a certain time, then the sender assumes that the packet was lost and resends the packet.

Large organisations such as banks and multinational companies have many sites that contain computers and networks and they wish to join them together to enable easy transfer of data. They do not wish to use the public network because of security concerns and so they set up a private network. Figure 11.16 shows how this might be done. The first thing to remember is that it is not possible to just dig up roads to lay your own cables as there are strict regulations governing who can do this sort of work. This means that to connect sites together, organisations must lease dedicated lines from network service providers. The *leased lines* are the same as those used for the public network except that at the intermediate switching nodes, the switches are permanently set and the links cannot be accessed by public network users. In spite of the system being called a private network, because a network service provider's lines are being used, strict adherence to the permitted protocols must be observed. Private networks can use virtual circuit and datagram systems as appropriate for the applications being supported. At each site, there may be several leased lines provided and unlike the public network, where the routing of traffic is determined by the intermediate nodes of the subnet, the host must select the appropriate leased line on which to send the traffic. This is done by devices called *routers* and one is required at each site where there is more than one leased line.

11.3.3 Protocols

As mentioned in Section 11.2.2, protocols are sets of agreed rules and operations that are used to ensure that devices can interoperate. They are normally defined as *standards* and a *standards body* or other organisation takes responsibility for maintaining the definitive version of their standards. A great deal of effort has been put into generating what are known as *open standards* which are standards that are not specific to a particular manufacturer or small group of organisations. The problem with an open standard is that everyone must agree with it and agree to use it. Getting a good level of agreement usually takes years and in the mean time, because interconnectivity is required, a particular manufacturer or a small group of interested parties suggests an *interim standard*. This allows some interconnectivity to be achieved but can cause problems if another group comes up with a different standard. For the Internet to succeed, a suitable set of protocols needed to be found. The Internet started life as a network used by academics and researchers at universities and research institutions. These people worked on computers that had the UNIX operating system. One of the facilities provided as a part this operating system allowed a machine to transfer files to another machine over a network using a *protocol suite* known as TCP/IP.

TCP/IP is named after two of the protocols in the suite. The set of protocols forms a series of layers where each layer uses the facilities of the layer below it. By dividing the overall process of communication into separate layers, the complexity of the communication system can be handled in a much simplified manner in much the same way as a complex computer program can be split into manageable parts. Layered protocols are best illustrated by a diagram, Figure 11.17, and an example of how it is used.

(1) The International Standards Organisation, Open Standards Interconnect (ISO OSI) model

In any network, the actual communication takes place along a wire or optical cable. For the sake of simplicity, we will just describe the operation using a wire. The message consists of a series of bits and on the wire these bits are electrical signals. This is the physical level of the communication link and gives its name to the *physical layer* of the *protocol stack*. The physical layer is also concerned with the types of wire and the types of connectors used. The physical layer can be implemented in a particular way that is then defined as

Figure 11.17   The ISO Open Standards Interconnect layered model

Application layer
Presentation layer
Session layer
Transport layer
Network layer
Data Link layer
Physical layer

a standard. If you refer back to Ethernet, we spoke of thin coax cable and UTP and the types of connectors used. This is all part of the physical layer for Ethernet. The physical layer is applicable for all networks.

Again referring to Ethernet, we explained how messages were actually split into frames and the format of an Ethernet frame was shown in Figure 11.6. We also explained how these frames were put onto the bus by the NIC. This set of activities constitutes what is called the *data link layer* and again there is a standard that defines these functions for an Ethernet system. In fact the data link layer consists of two sub-layers, a lower sub-layer called the *Media Access Control* (MAC) layer and an upper sub-layer called the *Logical Link Control* layer (LLC). The MAC layer is concerned with the way in which NICs gain access to the bus and LLC layer is concerned with the frame format, addressing and how the FCS is to be used. All networks have some form of data link layer. For the data link layer to operate there must be a physical network for it to use and this is specified by the physical layer standard for the type of media being used. Put another way, the physical layer defines the *functionality* upon which the data link layer functionality relies.

It must be emphasised that the standards do not define how to implement the functionality but what the functionality is.

For the next layer in the model, we need to look at Figure 11.15. When we described public networks, we spoke of packets and not frames being transmitted through the network from node to node and that at each node a routing decision needed to be made. We have moved outside the LAN here and the NIC addresses do not mean anything, so a new method of host addressing is required. We will give more details of this when we look at TCP/IP later. In essence, a packet is a frame with a header and a trailer added to it. The header contains a destination host address, and some other information, so that the packets can be routed through the network from node to node. The layer that deals with this activity is called the *network layer*. The network layer also deals with congestion control in the network and attempts to uniformly distribute the traffic so that no part is overloaded.

Long messages need to be split up into packets, and for a virtual circuit system a connection between the source host and the destination host needs to be set up before and torn down after use. These activities are the concern of the next layer, which is the *transport layer*. The transport layer has many other areas of concern and more details of these can be found in the material listed in the references at the end of this book.

Now what happens if a very large file is to be sent over a network and half way through, the network connection fails? To start all over again would be a waste of resources. If after say 10% of the file has been sent, a special mark packet is sent and similarly after 20% and so on, the receiving host will be able to keep track of the file transfer process. Now if connection failure occurs between the 50% and 60% marks, the transport layer can be asked to remake the connection. A simple enquiry packet can then be sent to the receiver asking what was the last mark received, to which it replies the 50% mark. The sender can then restart sending the file from the 50% mark. What is being described here is setting up a connection *session* with efficient restart in the event of a connection failure. This is the main activity covered by the *session layer*.

Assume that the file transfer had to be carried out in a secure way by encrypting the file and obviously decrypting the file at the receiving end. This is one of the areas covered by the *presentation layer*. The *application layer* is the final layer and effectively provides an interface for applications that have need to use a network connection.

The lower three layers are concerned with node-to-node data transfer whereas the top four layers are concerned with end-to-end connection.

Figure 11.18 shows how the layers of protocol are used in a host-to-host connection that passes through two intermediate nodes in a communications sub-net. Referring to Figure 11.18, host A wishes to send a file to host B using encryption for security. Host A starts to send the file to an encryption program, which starts to produce a stream of encrypted data. This is a presentation layer function. As the encrypted data stream emerges from the encryption program, numbered marks are placed in it at 10000 byte intervals. This is a session layer function. The transport layer sets up a virtual circuit through to the destination address by sending a special circuit set-up packet into the communications sub-network. The set-up packet works its way through the nodes of the network, using the destination address to determine the actual route, and reserving buffer storage at each node on its way. When the receiver responds to acknowledge that the connection has been made, a transport layer program starts to form packets from the encrypted data stream. The packets are turned into frames with a FCS being

Figure 11.18   Protocol layers used in a host-to-host connection

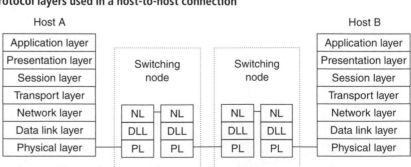

calculated for each frame by a data link layer program. The bits of each frame are then sent to the first node in the sub-net.

At the first node in the sub-net, the received bit stream is formed into a frame and the FCS is checked to determine if there are any errors. If errors are detected the frame is discarded and a time out and retransmission mechanism is invoked. If there are no detected errors, the frame is formed into a packet and the destination address is checked and correct outward link buffer is loaded with the packet. The packet is formed into a frame and then the bit stream is sent on the link to the next node. The process is repeated at the next switching node. If a frame error is detected at this node, the retransmission is from the first switching node, not the host, as the frame was correct when it arrived at the first switching node. When the bit stream arrives at the destination host, it is formed into a frame then a packet. The receiving end transport layer joins the packets into an encrypted file. Any breaks in the connection will be dealt with by the session layer and retransmission restarted at the appropriate point. A presentation layer program decrypts the encrypted data and the file is loaded into the receiving host's file system by an application layer program.

The above description illustrates a theoretical protocol stack, now we will look at TCP/IP.

(2) TCP/IP

Figure 11.19 shows the TCP/IP family of protocols and their relative positions in the layered architecture. TCP/IP predates the ISO OSI model. Because it took so long for the OSI committee to come to an agreed framework, and TCP/IP worked and was acceptable to many involved with networking, it was used as an interim *Reference Model* and subsequently adopted as the protocol suite for the Internet. The protocol layers make use of any underlying network that provides packet switching. The lowest layer, the *internet layer*, has a protocol that specifies a packet format, which contains the source, and destination host addresses in a form known as an *IP address*. The task of the internet layer protocol, IP, is to provide a routing strategy that is able to get packets through the network. The protocol simply allows packets to be entered into the network and hopefully, they appear at the destination but with no guarantee that the delivered order is the same as the entered order.

On top of the IP layer are two protocols, a reliable, virtual circuit protocol, *Transmission Control Protocol* (TCP) and a *User Datagram Protocol* (UDP). TCP specifies the set up, packet transfer and tear down phases of the virtual

Figure 11.19   TCP/IP family of protocols

	Equivalent OSI layer
TELNET FTP HTTP SMTP DNS	Application layer
TCP UDP	Transport layer
IP	Network layer
Any network	

circuit between the end hosts and ensures that packets are delivered in order and is quite a complicated protocol. On the other hand, UDP just provides for individual packet transfer between end hosts. UDP is a simple protocol and is ideally suited for single packet messages. The upper layer, the application layer, consists of a number of commonly required applications that make use of the TCP or UDP facilities as appropriate. *TELNET* provides the facility to make a local terminal or PC the I/O device for a remote computer. This is how many time sharing systems are accessed. FTP is a *file transfer protocol* that specifies a mechanism for sending a copy of a file from one computer to another or for obtaining a copy of a file from another computer. *HyperText Transfer Protocol* (HTTP), is a protocol that specifies a mechanism that can be used to fetch pages from Web servers. *Simple Mail Transfer Protocol* (SMTP), is the basis for e-mail systems and specifies how e-mail messages are formatted and sent and retrieved to and from *mailboxes* on *mail servers*. *Domain Name Service* (DNS), is the facility that converts the names that we give to our host machines to the IP addresses mentioned earlier. More about this later.

The TCP/IP suite does not have Session and Presentation Layer protocols as the designers of the suite felt that the facilities associated with these layers were very rarely needed. However, if any of the facilities were needed then they could be provided by the application using the network.

11.3.4 *IP addresses*

When we discussed LANs, it was stated that all NICs and RIUs had a unique hardwired address embedded in them. Using these addresses was OK for small networks but they are useless for worldwide networks. It would be just like trying to locate someone in the world by just using their name. The concept of an IP address is that every network in the world is uniquely numbered and every host on each network has a unique number on their network. IP network addresses are governed by a world body and network administrators allocate the host numbers on their networks. The IP address is independent of the hardwired address.

There are two current IP address formats, Version 4 (IPv4), consisting of 32 bits and the emerging version 6 (IPv6) consisting of 128 bits.

IPv4 has five classes of address as shown in Figure 11.20. Class A addresses are for large networks with very many hosts connected to the network. Class B networks are for medium sized networks with a good many hosts connected to the network. Class C networks are for small networks with only a few hosts connected. Multicast addresses are used for sending messages to groups of hosts and will not be discussed here.

The *dot notation* that gives the decimal equivalent of each 8-bit byte, used in the host address range makes it easy to write the address rather than using a binary bit pattern. Note that there are a few gaps in the address ranges for class A, B and C networks as some addresses are reserved for special purposes.

Figure 11.21 shows the number of hosts and networks that are possible when using the IPv4 addressing format.

Figure 11.20   IPv4 address classes

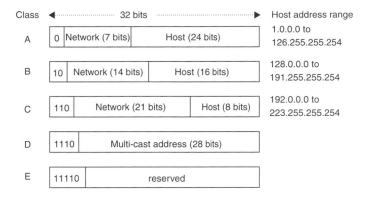

Class	32 bits	Host address range
A	0 | Network (7 bits) | Host (24 bits)	1.0.0.0 to 126.255.255.254
B	10 | Network (14 bits) | Host (16 bits)	128.0.0.0 to 191.255.255.254
C	110 | Network (21 bits) | Host (8 bits)	192.0.0.0 to 223.255.255.254
D	1110 | Multi-cast address (28 bits)	
E	11110 | reserved	

Figure 11.21   Numbers of hosts and networks possible with IPv4 addresses

Class	Max number of networks	Max number of hosts
A	128	16777216
B	16384	65536
C	2097152	256

TQ 11.5   To what class of network does the IP address 169.15.25.6 belong?

With the increasing number of computers in the world, each needing a unique address, IPv4 addresses have all but run out. IPv6, with its 128-bit addresses will solve this problem. Much of the address space has yet to be assigned and work is ongoing in determining how this is to be handled.

11.3.5   Domain name service

When we send an e-mail or request a page from a website we do not specify an IP address, we use a symbolic name or *Universal Resource Locator* (URL) for the computer. This makes using the system much easier for humans. However, the computers are actually identified by their IP address, which means that some facility must be provided to convert the symbolic names to IP addresses. This is the job of the DNS.

The following is a simplified explanation of how the Service works. Let us assume that it is required to send an e-mail to a person in a distant university. The person's e-mail address will contain the name of the host where their mailbox is located. Distributed throughout the Internet are computers that have a list of some, mainly local, computer names and their IP addresses.

These are called *domain name servers* and collectively they provide the worldwide directory that is required to enable e-mail and the Internet to work. The e-mail system, on the sender's machine, sends a query to its local DNS server asking for the IP address of the destination host and if this information is in its database, the server returns the IP address. If the local DNS server does not have the required IP address, it sends a request to its nearest DNS server and asks for the IP address and so on until a server is reached that knows the IP address requested. When the sender's e-mail system has the destination host IP address, it can then send the e-mail. This process is called *name resolution.*

11.3.6 *Routers and gateways*

A router is the name given to the interconnecting device that inter-links all the nodes in a network. It receives packets, inspects their destination address and then forwards them on the appropriate link to get them nearer to their destination. Routers use a routing algorithm to determine the appropriate link. Routing algorithms can be static or dynamic and adaptive. Static routing algorithms make use of a table that the network designers load into the router when it is installed. If the network is changed, then the table content must be updated. Dynamic and adaptive algorithms watch packets moving through the network and exchange routing information with adjacent routers and then make routing decisions based on the accumulated information. Routers of this type are able to adapt to changes in the network that could include link failure and congestion. Dynamic adaptive routing requires more powerful routers and the exchange of routing information uses some of the link bandwidth to the detriment of the data traffic. Figure 11.16 shows how routers are used in a private WAN.

Routers can be used in a LAN to do the same job as bridges with the advantage that routers are able to handle the situation where there are circular routes in the network. Figure 11.22 gives an example of the way in which routers can be used to interconnect five LANs at three different sites. Only two links are actually needed, but to provide single link failure protection, the extra link is installed and hence the circular route. Packets intended for inter-network transfer must be sent to their router as the first hop of their journey. In this simple example, each network would have an IP address, as would each node on each network. The router could use static routing and the content of the tables for R1 and R2 are shown in Figure 11.23. Notice that the table shows a first choice and a second choice to handle the link failure protection mechanism.

A gateway is a network interconnecting device that enables two networks with completely different and incompatible protocol stacks to be connected together. The device consists of a processor, which runs software that provides the translation between the two network systems. Translation may be required at all layers including the Physical Layer where incompatible electrical signalling systems could be involved. For the gateway to be effective and not be a bottleneck to the inter-network traffic, a fast powerful processor is required. Gateways are expensive and are the most complex of all the interconnecting devices.

Figure 11.22   Interconnecting LANs using routers

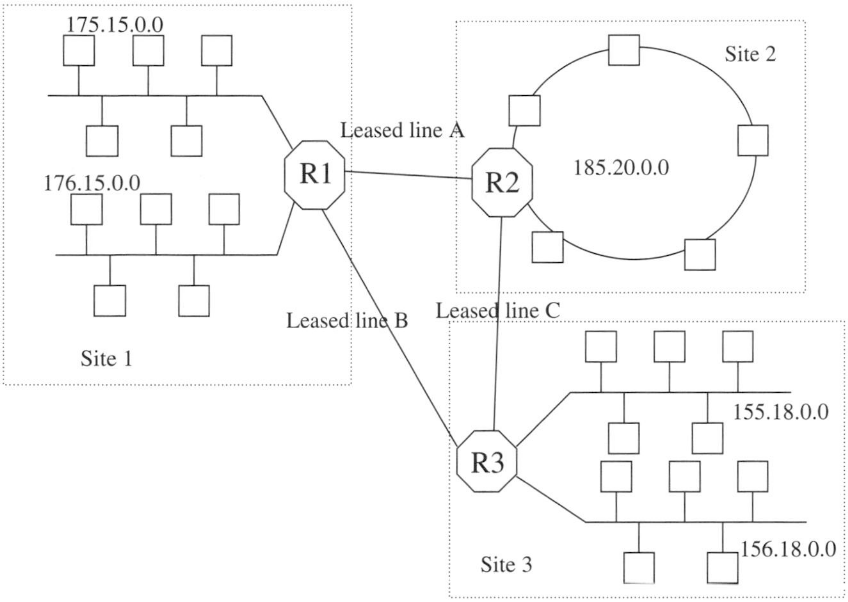

Figure 11.23   Router tables for Figure 11.22 R1 and R2

Router 1				Router 2		
Packets to	1st choice line	2nd choice line		Packets to	1st choice line	2nd choice line
175.15.0.0	–	–		175.15.0.0	A	C
176.15.0.0	–	–		176.15.0.0	A	C
185.20.0.0	A	B		185.20.0.0	–	–
155.18.0.0	B	A		155.18.0.0	C	A
156.18.0.0	B	A		156.18.0.0	C	A

Figure 11.24   Using modems to connect computers using a telephone service

| PC |—| modem |— Normal phone line —| modem |—| Remote computer |

11.3.7   Modems and dial-up systems

Figure 11.24 shows how a modem is used to connect a PC to a remote computer via a telephone connection. The problem with using a telephone line is that it is intended for analogue speech signals and the computer uses digital signals. The modem (MODulator DEModulator), is a two-way device that turns the zeros and ones of the digital signal into a *modulated* analogue signal and vice versa, so that digital signals can be transferred over the telephone line. *Modulation* involves changing the characteristics of a signal. For example, the zeros and ones of the digital signal could be turned into two different frequency tones, this is known as *Frequency Shift Keying* (FSK). A modem is required at each end of the communication channel. There are a number of different standards used for modems amongst which are the CCITT V series of standards. The standard designation is a V followed by a number and an example would be V90. This is the standard for modems operating up to 56 Kbps. The different standards are for the different types of telephone lines being used, the different types of modulation and the speed of operation. The important point is that the modems on each end of the communication channel have to be compatible or one end has to be able to adjust its characteristics to those of the modem at the other end. Modems come in three varieties, a plug-in PCI card, an external box that is connected to the serial or USB port or as a built-in component of the motherboard of a PC. The modem is connected to the telephone socket via a lead with a standard telephone plug. Almost all new PCs have the motherboard version.

Modems require a software program to control them. The program will be able to instruct the modem to connect to a telephone line, detect the dialling tone and then dial the telephone number of the remote computer. Next will follow a short handshake process that enables the modems at each end to adjust to each other's characteristics. With the virtual circuit set up, the application, which may be e-mail, Web access or file transfer, takes over and uses the connection to transfer packets as required. When the application is finished, the modems close the connection at each end.

11.3.8   *The Internet*

The Internet is a public, worldwide network of connected computers, that uses a packet switched communication system operating with TCP/IP protocols. The connected computers are often referred to as *Internet Servers* because they provide a service to the Internet users. The Internet provides the underlying network that allows applications such as The World Wide Web, e-mail, file transfer and electronic commerce to be implemented. Individual organisations, including business, industry, learning institutions and research centres connect their computers to the network and give access to data that they wish to share with everyone. Companies known as *Internet Service Providers* (ISPs) have servers permanently connected to the network and provide storage space, e-mail boxes and Internet access for individuals and companies that do not have their own Internet servers. ISP subscribers can build their own websites using their allocated storage space or the ISP staff can build websites for them. The ISPs exist by charging for the facilities they provide, often recovered from the network system provider's call charge, or from advertising revenue.

As far as a connected computer is concerned, the Internet is just another WAN that provides the opportunity to connect to another computer. As mentioned earlier, all connected computers must have an IP address and

Figure 11.25 Connecting to an ISP from home

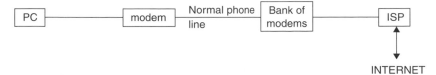

packet transfer is made possible by the use of DNS. Figure 11.25 shows how a home PC can be connected to an ISP using a modem and a dial up telephone connection. With a dial up system, the local PC is connected only when there are packets to be sent or received and so is not a permanent member of the connected computer population. Allocating a dedicated IP address to each and every PC would be a waste of precious IP addresses (until IPv6 becomes widely used) and so each ISP has a pool of IP addresses from which it allocates an IP address to a PC when it connects. When the PC disconnects, the allocated IP address is returned to the pool for reuse. The ISP server will have a number of incoming telephone lines, connected to a bank of modems to enable it to handle multiple simultaneous connections.

TQ 11.6   How can an ISP have multiple telephone lines, each with its own modem, yet have only a single telephone number? Hint, you will need to read about telephony to find an answer to this. Try line hunters!

Alternatives to a dial up service are the new offerings of so-called broadband services consisting of ISDN and the xDSL family of services as discussed in Section 11.3.1. ISDN and most of the xDSL services are normally used for business facilities, but ADSL Lite is gaining popularity with the domestic market. It is normal practice for ISDN and xDSL terminations to be allocated permanent IP addresses as quite often, LANs are connected to these. However, for domestic use, the allocation of a permanent IP address for the termination is dependent on the service provider and the ISP being used. These broadband services are digital throughout and special termination units rather than modems are required. These units are often supplied and installed by the service provider.

11.3.9 Intranets

This is the term used for in-house or private internets and is normally based on a private network. The intranet consists of one or more servers that provide Web type sites and users access the material using WEB browsers in the same way as they would access Internet websites. The intranet provides in-house e-mail facilities and bulletin boards and is often used for providing computer-based training packages for use by staff within the organisation. The intranet is not directly connected to the Internet and so is not accessible to the public at large. Access to the intranet may be obtained by using a

Figure 11.26   An intranet with Remote Access Service

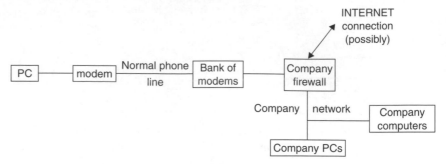

Remote Access Service system (RAS) and this is useful if the organisation owning the intranet has employees working away from the organisation's premises. Figure 11.26 shows how an intranet with RAS may be set up. The company firewall is a powerful security device that prevents unauthorised access to the company network. Firewalls are discussed in Section 11.5.

11.4   Distributed systems

The Internet is often described as an enormous distributed system. We will look briefly at distributed systems and see why the Internet is so described.

The term *distributed system* needs to be qualified to state what is distributed. A number of computers can be inter-linked in such a way as to provide collective processing power, known as *distributed processing*. The inter-linked computers may well have individual file stores but these can be combined to produce a single virtual file system that is distributed and consequently called a *distributed file system*. Again, a number of interconnected processors can each have their own RAM but the interconnection allows the memory to be shared among the processors. Such systems are classed as *distributed shared memory systems*. We will look briefly at distributed processing and distributed file systems.

(1)   *Distributed processing*

At the heart of current distributed processing is the *client/server architecture*. What this means is that a computer, a client, requests some processing to be done by another computer, a server. The workload distribution between the computers can vary greatly and has led to several models being defined. The first is where the client just acts as a user interface, typically driving a GUI. The client computer accepts requests from the user and sends these in an appropriate form to the server where the real processing is carried out. The server then sends the results of the processing back to the client for it to display to the user. This model uses *thin clients* and *fat servers*. Typical applications have clients forming queries that are then sent to powerful *database engine servers*, with the results being sent back to the client for display. The opposite end of the spectrum is a *fat client* that does most of the

Figure 11.27   Client/Server architecture

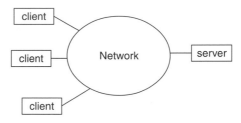

Figure 11.28   Three layer distributed processing system model

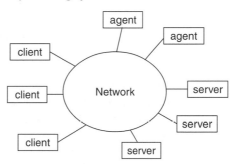

work and a *thin server* that does a small amount of processing. An example here would be a PC doing some heavy calculation processing on a spreadsheet and then sending the finished spreadsheet to a *print server* for printing. In both cases it can be seen that servers provide processing power for a number of clients and if server power is in heavy demand, the servers must queue the requests and keep track of which client to send the processed results back to. Figure 11.27 shows the general idea.

Network performance is a critical aspect of distributed systems and most distributed systems use LANs that have a relatively high data rate. Reflecting back to the Internet, we can see now that our PC is a client that runs the browser software, which presents the GUI. The browser sends requests to Internet sites, which are servers that retrieve pages from their databases and send them back for display by the client. The network here is a WAN and we all know the problems of slow downloads due to the restricted bandwidths of WANs. It is hoped that *Broadband* connections will help with this problem. So the Internet qualifies as a type of distributed system.

The two layer distributed system model described above can be extended to a three-layer model by introducing a middle layer sometimes called a *broker* or *agent layer*. Figure 11.28 shows such a system. In this model the network contains a number of processors that act as agents or brokers as well as clients and servers. In this model, the clients send requests for services to the agents. The agents either refer to information they have collected and stored about server resources or search the network for available server resources or a mixture of both and then arrange for the client to be connected to the most suitable server. This architecture is one way of achieving what is known as *load distribution*, in that an agent can select a server that is lightly loaded in preference to one that is heavily loaded for connection to a requesting client.

(2) Distributed file systems

Databases are implemented as physical files and so the following discussion relates to both distributed database systems as well as distributed file systems. Distributed file systems exist for one of two reasons. First, separate systems are in existence and because of circumstances such as company mergers and so on, there is a desire to join the systems together to make them look and act as one system but the component parts are distributed geographically. The second reason is concerned with a mixture of efficiency of access, security and storage capacity.

In the first example, if the file systems are of the same type, producing what is known as a *homogeneous system*, and a fast reliable network is interconnecting the distributed components, then the distributed system will work well. However, if the file systems are not of the same type, producing what is known as a *heterogeneous system*, and the interconnecting network is unreliable and slow, many problems will be encountered. General advice in the latter case is do not try to do it.

With the second system we have already looked at RAID systems which have been developed to provide enhanced access speed, security through redundancy and convenient increase in storage space at a relatively low price. However, RAID systems are either in a single box or distributed among a group of processors, sometimes called a *cluster*, that are in very close proximity with each other. Figure 11.29 shows an example of a distributed file system in diagrammatic form. The concept is that the distributed nature of the components is not visible to the user or applications using the system. There will be a single file naming system that has no element of location involved. Physically, files can be relocated in the system without having any effect on file access. This is known as *location transparency* and is a very desirable, although hard to achieve, quality of distributed file systems.

Figure 11.29   A distributed file system

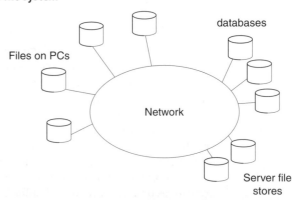

TQ 11.7 In a server-based network, the server filer system can be mapped as the Z drive for PCs connected to the network. Does this system have location transparency?

11.5 Security of networked systems

The whole idea of the Internet is to provide everyone with easy access to a vast array of resources. The purpose of security is to restrict access to only those entitled to have access. So to have a secure Internet is an impossibility. The subject of network security is vast and there are many books that are dedicated to security. We have limited space available and so our coverage will be limited to general issues.

11.5.1 Threats

First it must be stated that most of the threats to any computer system, networked or otherwise, are from those who have the authority to use it. Damage can be caused accidentally or deliberately and a security system will provide very little protection, if the damage is deliberately or intentionally done by those who have authority to access the system. A security policy, carefully designed, accepted and practised by all those who have authorisation to use the system is the best protection from inside security risks.

A network that either goes outside the premises of an organisation or is connected to the outside world has a number of points of exposure. These security risk points include switching nodes and interconnecting devices; the communication links themselves and outside terminal nodes. Figure 11.30 shows the points of vulnerability.

Figure 11.30 Points of attack in a network

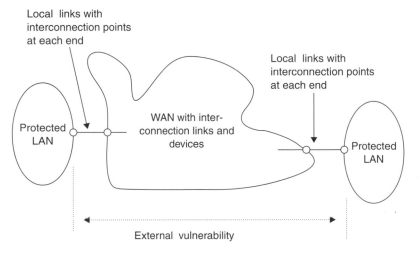

Damage can take several forms and includes unauthorised access to data, corrupting data, changing data, deleting data and denial of service. Probably the most well known form of damage is caused by computer viruses that are propagated via the Internet through e-mails, downloads and through infected exchangeable disks. The openness of the Internet makes planting viruses easy. Using virus scanning software, not opening e-mails and only downloading from reliable sources are sensible precautions to take. There are many websites dedicated to providing guidance on how to avoid virus attacks.

Attacks on interconnecting devices and links have two forms. The first is a passive attack in which no damage is done to the data itself and the intention is to obtain secret information. The second is an active attack, where damage to the data is done. The first is very difficult to detect whereas the second tends to be a little easier to.

The most common method of dealing with passive attacks is to encrypt the data so that anyone listening in on the link or interconnecting device can make no sense of what is seen. There are several types of active attack and we will look at a few of these. The first type consists of destroying data that is being transferred. This is easily detected as expected data does not arrive. The cure is to retransmit the data. The second type of attack is altering the data. This attack is difficult to hide as most transmitted data has some form of error detection mechanism that involves a checksum calculation. The mechanism involves calculating a binary value based on the bit pattern of the data in the frame being transmitted and attaching the binary value to the end of the frame. This is the frame check sum FCS mentioned in Section 11.3.3. When the frame arrives at its destination, the FCS is recalculated and compared with the value that was sent. Any discrepancy signals an error or possibly the result of an active attack. A third type of attack is known as *masquerading* where an attacker pretends to be an authorised user and injects data into the network hoping that this illicit data will not be noticed.

11.5.2 *Protection mechanisms*

Two main methods, *private* and *public* key encryption, are employed in network communication for encryption to change the original *plain-text* into *cipher-text*.

(1) *Private or* secret key *encryption*

This makes use of a single key, known by the sender and the receiver, and a reversible process that is used one way to convert plain-text to cipher-text and in reverse to convert cipher-text back to plain-text. The security is based on the process being complex and that the communicating parties keep the key a secret. The problem with this type of encryption is keeping the key secret when it has to be sent from sender to receiver, possibly over a network, where it could be intercepted and used either to decrypt sent messages or by a masquerader. Two of the most common versions of private key encryption are the Data Encryption Standard (DES) and the International Data Encryption Algorithm (IDEA).

(2) *Public key encryption*

This uses two keys, a receiver's key (secret key) and a sender's key (public key) and a non-reversible process. The person wishing to be sent a message, the receiver, generates a receiver's key and applies the process to it to generate a sender's key. The sender's key and the process are then placed into the public domain. The receiver's key is kept secret. Anyone wishing to send a message to the receiver uses the process and the public key to encrypt the message that is then sent to the receiver. The receiver then uses the secret receiver's key to decipher the cipher-text. Because of the non-reversibility of the process, it is not possible to decipher the cipher-text knowing the public key and the process. The secret key is never sent anywhere, so it is not at risk of interception. Public key encryption is no protection against masquerading. A common version of public key encryption is RSA, so named after the initial letters of the three people responsible for its development, Rivest, Shamir and Adleman.

(3) *Authentication*

To protect against masquerading, some form of authentication is required, which means that a receiver can be assured that a message has come from the person they think is the source.

We will look briefly at three methods of authentication that are in common use. The first is used to allow remote users to access central networks and computers and is called *call back authentication*. The second is used for general communication and is based on research work that went under the name of *Kerberos* and uses *third party authentication*. The third makes use of a *digital signature* and is used for transferring valuable documents.

(a) Call back authentication

Users are supplied with a tiny authentication device that has a miniature numeric LCD display. The device is programmed prior to issue and runs through a numeric sequence governed by an embedded algorithm and driven by an internal clock. The device is sealed and has a life of about two years. The system the user is authorised to use has a copy of the initial load details and the algorithm. The user can either use a desktop PC or a portable computer, connected to a normal telephone network, to gain access to their remote system. Users dial in to the system they are authorised to access from telephone numbers that they are authorised to use, and they log on using an ID and a password. The system now breaks the connection but after a few moments it rings back the user on the authorised phone number. The system displays a randomly generated number that the user types into an authentication device and then the user types the number displayed on the authentication device. The system beats masquerading and use from a telephone that is not authorised for use. This is a rather complex system, but worthwhile if high security is required. Obviously, all transmissions are encrypted to secure the link.

(b) Third party authentication

This makes use of a trusted third party to provide authentication. Consider the diagram in Figure 11.31. The third party consists of two servers, an authentication server and a ticket-granting server. Consider A wishing

Figure 11.31 Third party authentication mechanism

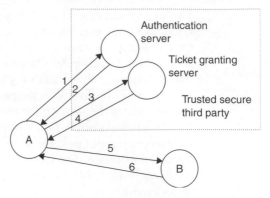

to send a message to B. A sends a message (1) to the third party authentication server saying that it wishes to send a message. The authentication server sends back an encrypted message (2), containing an *authority* for A to communicate with the ticket-granting server and a *session key*, using A's public key for the encryption. A is the only one able to decrypt the message using its secret key. When the message arrives back at A, A enters a password which is used to calculate A's secret key. The returned message (2), can now be decrypted and the *authority* and the *session key* can be retrieved. The password is not stored at A but simply used for calculating the secret key. Now A indicates that it wishes to communicate with B and sends a time stamped message (3), encrypted with the ticket-granting servers authority and containing the session key, to the ticket-granting server, asking for a ticket to communicate with B. The time stamp prevents copy and replay of the message. The ticket-granting server knows that the message (3) has actually come from A because of the encryption used and session key included in the message. The ticket-granting server then sends an encrypted message (4) back to A containing a key for A to use in the communication with B. A can now send the message (5) to B encrypted with B's key and time stamped. B responds (6) to A to confirm that it is really B that has received the message.

(c) Digital signatures

These are used for documents and are the electronic equivalent to a signature. The electronic system must convince the receiver of three things.

(i)   That the document is from the person it is supposed to be from (authentication);

(ii) Be sure that the sender cannot claim that the document did not come from them (non-repudiation);

(iii) Convince the sender that the receiver could not have produced the document (sender protection).

A private key can be used in place of the signature if a secure and trusted central server can be provided to both issue and confirm the authenticity of the secret keys accompanying documents. If this is not considered to be sufficiently safe, because of the need to distribute secret keys, then a system based on public/secret key pairs can be used similar to the system used for the third party authentication described above.

11.5.3 Firewalls

These are special routers used to protect an internal network, by preventing unwanted packets from entering the network from outside. This is achieved by the firewall filtering the traffic. The firewall can also prevent certain packets leaving the internal network on route to an external destination. Their capabilities vary considerably in terms of the level of sophistication of the filtering they do. The simplest types contain a table indicating which IP addresses are able to send out packets and which IP addresses are allowed to send packets into the network. This type of filtering is foiled by masquerading. A more secure form of filtering is obtained if packets arriving at the firewall are dissected and their content analysed. The filtering process looks for particular words or combination of characters. This sometimes intercepts viruses embedded in e-mails. This type of filtering is unreliable if the traffic includes encrypted messages. Another strategy that can be used by the firewall is to allow only certain selected protocol traffic to be transferred. SMTP used for e-mail and HTTP used for Web access could be allowed whereas FTP, for file transfer and TELNET for remote access could be barred. Figure 11.26 shows the location of a firewall in a network.

TQ 11.8 How can a firewall prevent e-mails being sent outside an organisation's network?

It must be understood that a single modem inside a network will destroy any protection that a firewall can provide by bypassing the controlling nature of the firewall.

A good firewall will make a log of all packets rejected. Analysis of this log will show the level of attack that the network has been subjected to and even the source of the attack may be revealed. Frequent and regular inspection of this log is essential if network security is to be taken seriously.

11.6 Summary

This chapter started with a look at some of the basic principles of communication systems including the concept of bandwidth and its relationship with the data rate that it is possible to achieve. We discussed various types of media and what was commonly used in LANs and WANs. Physical and logical topologies were introduced with emphasis being placed on the differences between them. Ethernet and token ring LANs were covered including NICs and RIUs and typical wiring systems for them. Interconnecting devices for LANs were introduced and covered repeaters and bridges and remote bridges. WANs were discussed next, with a description of packet switching and virtual circuit and datagram systems setting the scene. High data rate services such as ISDN and xDSL were explained. A brief comment was made regarding private and public WANs and the use of leased lines. A section on protocols then followed with the ISO OSI and TCP/IP layered models starting the discussion. The format of IP addresses was presented and mention made of IPv6. Routers and gateways were explained and the way in which routers are used for both WANs and LANs was described. The use of modems was explained as was the different types that were available and a brief comment on modem standards. The Internet was discussed in terms of its networking aspects.

Various types of distributed systems were then explained and the areas of application they were best suited for was mentioned. The last section covered a number of aspects associated with network security including areas of vulnerability, use of encryption and the need for authentication. The section concluded with a brief outline of the role of firewalls in interconnected networks.

Answers to in text questions

TQ 11.1 50 db

TQ 11.2 If there were more than 1 frame in an Ethernet system at the same time they would collide and both frames would be corrupted.

TQ 11.3 72 bytes. The data field must be at least 46 bytes long so the data will need to have 20 padding bytes appended to bring the field up to its minimum length. The preamble, addresses, length and FCS will take 26 bytes. The total is 26 + 46 = 72 bytes.

TQ 11.4 8 KHz approx.

TQ 11.5 Class B

TQ 11.6 The incoming multi-line service is connected to a device called a line hunter, which has a sequence of telephone numbers allocated to it, starting at the single number given. When the given single number is dialled, the hunter connects the call to the next available free modem. The hunter acts as a switch.

TQ 11.7 No it does not have location transparency because you have to access the file by telling the system, which drive the file, is on and if you moved it to another server, then you would have to remap it.

TQ 11.8 The firewall can be programmed to block any SMTP traffic from leaving the network.

EXERCISES

1   Calculate the maximum data rate that can be provided by a communication link that has a bandwidth of 200 KHz and a signal to noise ratio of 50 db.

2   If an interconnected network suffers a link failure and this divides the network into two separate networks, the network is said to be partitioned. Explain, with the aid of diagrams, how this can never happen in a fully interconnected mesh but it may happen in a partially interconnected mesh.

3   Carry out some research and from this draw up a table that shows for each of the CCITT standards for modems, V21, V22, V22bis, V26, V32, V34, V42bis and V90, the line types, the data rates and the method of modulation the standard specifies.

4   Investigate amplitude, frequency and phase modulation and with the aid of diagrams, explain the differences among them.

5   What are the relative advantages and disadvantages of having a modem built into the motherboard of a computer compared with having an external modem?

6   Explain, with the aid of a diagram, how a modem connected to a PC in a network can compromise the security service provided by a firewall.

7   Explain why a router needs to look at packets rather than frames to apply its routing mechanism.

8   Explain why private key encryption does not give 100 per cent protection against masquerading.

9   A router interconnecting two networks will have two IP addresses. Explain why this is so.

10 As hosts connected to a network are given IP addresses and these are independent of the hardwired NIC address, is there any reason for attempting to ensure that every NIC manufactured has a unique hardwired address?

A look ahead

Computing remains a rapidly developing area of technology with new products being brought to market every day. This chapter consists of a number of items that cover some of the emerging products and ideas that are being written about in research journals, trade releases and computing magazines. Some of the items will be available in the very near future, others may be in their final stages of development and to complete the selection, we include some ideas that are in their early stages of research. The problem with writing a chapter like this is that it soon becomes dated, as development races forward, so one way of treating this chapter is as a snapshot in time, early 2003.

The chapter is presented in six sections covering the main areas of computing, with the content of each section being in no particular order.

12.1 Processors

Although increasing clock speed is the goal of many CPU chip manufacturers, two other areas of concern are emerging as important issues, namely power consumption and parallelism. The power consumption of CPUs needs to be reduced to enable portables and Personal Data Assistants (PDAs) and other small systems to operate longer under battery power and to reduce the amount of heat that has to be dissipated from the CPU chip. Most current CPU chips are fitted with a cooling fan and fans are noisy. In a desktop system, the fan noise level is considered to be a slight annoyance but if the fan cooled processor is inside a home entertainment system or a laptop being used in a public place, then even a slight noise is not acceptable. A number of options are being tried as the alternative to fan cooling. These include heat pump semiconductors and heat sinks that look like hedgehogs. Work on developing quieter fans is ongoing but the real answer is to lower the dissipation to a point where a fan is not needed. Current research is concentrating on reducing power consumption. This also helps with the battery drain problem. Reducing the size of the transistors on the CPU chip reduces the dissipation but this tends to motivate those who wish to increase the complexity of the CPU and the heat dissipation is back to its original level. Interconnecting the components inside the CPU by means of light paths eliminates the heat that is generated by resistive losses in the current metallic interconnections, but a commercially viable totally optical CPU is some way off, although the technology to manufacture optical gates has been around for a long time. Higher clock speeds generate more heat and although the current top end clock speeds of around 4 GHz seem fine for near future applications, processor power hungry applications involving interactive graphics are likely to absorb this apparent over capacity. An alternative to increasing the clock speed is to increase the work that can be done in one clock cycle and this was discussed in Chapter 10 and is the basis of RISC technology.

Here are a few items worthy of note: 64-bit CPUs that are backwards compatible with their 32-bit architectures for use in high-end PCs are going into production. Providing backwards compatibility, can present a time penalty but it allows current 32-bit applications to be used in the transition to a pure 64-bit architecture.

Very soon, processors that are capable of processing eight instructions in parallel will be on the market, doubling the current four instructions at a time. This is made possible by using special pipelined systems and fast parallel access memory. The clock speed is likely to be around 2 GHz but this reinforces again the statements in Chapter 10 that it is not just clock speed that counts when comparing processing capability.

A system that uses 4000 Intel-based chips connected as a cluster is being built to process geological data for oil exploration. This is an example of a distributed system based on a Very Local Area Network (VLAN). Even with this level of parallelism, typical calculations are likely to take several weeks of continuous processing time.

Research is under way to investigate the use of alternatives to silicon for chips. Among the alternatives are new semiconductor materials and biological organisms that can be used to grow computer components. The drive here is for faster switching times, easier fabrication and lower power demand. It has long been recognised that a particular architecture may well suit certain applications but not be very efficient with other applications. Investigations are under way to look at the possibility of dynamically adjustable architectures that can adapt to demand. The first goal in developing such a CPU could be to produce a universal programmable chip that could be set in the last stage of manufacture to fulfil a particular need such as controlling a car engine or the next generation mobile telephone. The final goal could be that the chip detects its current application and adapts itself to operate in the most efficient manner for the task. Efficiency could be measured in terms of power consumption or speed.

Intel is working on what they call 90 nm chips, a nanometre is 1×10^{-9} m, containing in excess of 100 million transistors and expects to be able to operate these at up to 1000 GHz. Intel expects the 1000 million-transistor CPU to be in production in a few years time.

CPU chips with built-in radio transceivers are on the near horizon. Computers containing these radio-enabled chips would be able to communicate via Bluetooth, cellular telephone networks and wireless LAN systems with no extra devices being needed.

Mini motherboards (170 mm $\times$ 170 mm), designed for incorporation into home entertainment systems are now available with CPUs running at 500 MHz. The boards include network and Firewire connection capability as well as all that is required for multimedia entertainment systems. A currently available board has a near silent fan for cooling the CPU. A 1 GHz CPU is planned that will not need a cooling fan.

Experiments are being carried out with carbon monoxide molecules which when arranged into an appropriate pattern can perform a sorting function. Is this the way forward for CPU chips?

12.2 Primary memory

The drive here is to produce memory that can keep up with the demand placed upon it by the CPU. As explained in Chapter 6, various techniques are currently being used to split memory into parts that can be accessed in parallel. Currently, memory for bus speeds of 370 and 434 MHz in capacities up to 512 MBytes is available, based on traditional silicon, and at a very cheap price. Nanotechnology with silicon has provided us with a single atom memory cell, but this needs to have additional material to support it physically.

Experiments with biological organisms are being carried out to see if these could be the breakthrough we are looking for. Researchers say that biological memory modules are a long way off. Interest in optical and magnetic storage goes in cycles and it would seem that we are currently experiencing a lull in activity on this front.

12.3 Secondary memory

Development of fixed disk magnetic storage devices is progressing steadily with the price per GByte falling rapidly. Current standard PC disk drive capacity is around 80 GBytes with access time of 4 to 8 ms. Microdrives for PDAs and similar devices are due soon in 20 and 40 GByte capacities and a version for a Compact Flash II slot with 4 GByte capacity is almost ready for the market.

Development of exchangeable disk systems is progressing mainly with optical CD and DVD disks but a revisit of the magneto-optical disk technology is also in hand with a 30 GByte double sided CD-RW system, that uses *Blu-Ray* technology (a blue laser), almost on the market. Optical DVD-RW disks, at up to 30 GBytes capacity, are being developed that also use the Blu-Ray laser technology. Current thinking is that these disks will need to be provided with a protective case.

A new technology is being investigated with storage being based on holography. These systems use two laser sources to create a series of interference patterns within the thickness of a special optical medium. Each pattern represents a 1 Mbit block of data. Initial research indicates that a storage density of about 8 GBytes per cubic centimetre can be achieved. The medium is like a CD disk and at present only a worm device is being discussed. Holographic drives, as they are being called, will operate at read/write speeds of 1 Gbps and could have up to 1 TBytes capacity and the stored data life is expected to exceed 50 years. Investigations indicate that

500 GByte disks, using a material called holonide are about two years away. The systems should be as cheap as current DVD-RW systems.

12.4 Peripheral devices

The ways in which data is input to and output from computers have not changed much over the last 10 years. Probably the most noticeable fact is that peripheral device prices have been steadily falling. Scanners, still and video cameras are now commonplace input devices. Touch sensitive screens, especially on PDAs and portables, come almost as the standard configuration. This section will concentrate on screens and two new types of input devices.

12.4.1 Screens

Digital Light Processor (DLP) micro-mirror chips used in low cost projectors are now being used in 50- and 60-inch wide screens. The displays are truly flat but they are nearly 18 inches deep. Plasma screens that are 42 inches wide are just entering the market but the price is very high. The next generation of screen will be plastic, very thin and able to be rolled up. There are currently two types of material being researched, carbon and Light Emitting Polymers (LEPs). These are used to produce what are known as organic displays.

The carbon technology uses a carbon-based material to make Organic Light Emitting Diodes (OLEDs). The technique is to use vacuum deposition to plant the material that makes up the OLEDs onto a flexible plastic sheet. The screens so formed use very little power and small versions are being used in mobile phones. The low power consumption could enable solar powered screens to be produced. LEPs are used to make plastic LEDs. The polymer material can be dissolved in ink and printed onto a plastic sheet using an inkjet printer. These screens have a very fast response time but they use more power than OLED screens. However, they give a very bright display with a 5-V supply.

Monitors and TV screens in sizes up to 20 inches that use these technologies are likely to be available in a few years time.

The big advantages of both these technologies over LCD displays is their cheapness and the fact that they emit light rather than selectively blocking light from a back light as is the case with LCD displays.

12.4.2 Drawing pads

An input device type of growing popularity is the drawing pad or digital paper. These are not touch sensitive screens. The simplest device consists of a detection unit that clips on the top of a clipboard and the user writes on the paper on the clipboard with a special pen. The detector acts as a short-range radar, using infra red and ultrasound, to pick up the movement of the pen over the paper. The detected movements are then turned into a digitised

Figure 12.1 Digital paper system

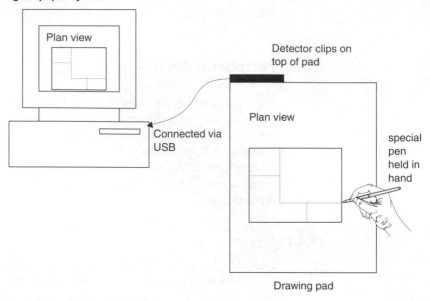

image. A similar device clips on the top of a white board and picks up images drawn and words written. The detector can either be connected to a PC or PDA and the images displayed on their screens or the images can be stored in the detector's memory and downloaded later. Once the images are in the PC or PDA, they can be processed in much the same way as images obtained from a scanner, with handwriting being converted to a word processed document and sketches being input to a Computer Aided Design package. Figure 12.1 gives a diagrammatic representation of this type of device.

12.4.3 *Virtual keyboards*

With practice, considerable speed can be achieved entering a text message via a mobile telephone keypad but a qwerty style keyboard would make input so much easier. Carrying a keyboard around in one's pocket is not an option, unless it is a virtual keyboard. A virtual keyboard has been developed as part of a mobile telephone. The mobile telephone is stood vertically on a flat surface. Built into the mobile telephone is a projector that projects an image of a qwerty keyboard onto the flat surface in front of the phone. The users can now use their fingers to type on the projected keys. The phone has a detector, similar in concept to that used in the drawing pad described in Section 12.4.2, that picks up the finger movements and translates these into the key characters. The concept can be used with Tablet PCs, described in Section 12.6, and PDAs, with the addition of a projected mouse block and mouse buttons to give full input functionality. Figure 12.2 shows the concept of a projected keyboard.

Figure 12.2 **A projected keyboard system**

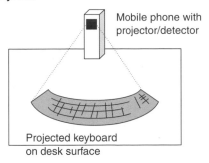

12.5 Networks

Two areas dominate the network development arena, ultra fast Ethernet and wireless networks. We will say little on Ethernet because 1000 Mbit Ethernet is already with us. The only real development is that there is now a category 6 UTP cable, which looks very similar to Cat 5 cable except that the copper wires are a little thicker, the twists are a little tighter and the cable is manufactured to a tighter physical tolerance. The way in which old-fashioned copper cables can deliver such a high data rate is because of the special NICs and interconnecting devices used in the network. These devices provide what is known, in the telephony field, as line conditioning. Line conditioning is a technique for overcoming problems such as electrical echoes and reflections that occur when using copper cables at high data rates. This is achieved by using clever electronic circuits in the NICs and hubs. Turning now to wireless, mention has been made above of CPU chips having radio transceivers built in and the need to '*unwire*' connected computers is said to be the way forward. Wireless connection is the obvious choice for portables and PDAs, whether used in a LAN or WAN environment. Until recently, the problem has been with the available bandwidth and radio links have tended to be slow. All is changing now with new radio frequency bands being made available, making use of digital encoding to optimise the bandwidth. 802.11 is the IEEE series of standards that cover wireless networks and it is the additions to this family of protocols that has paved the way for a predicted dramatic growth in wireless connections and networking. The new 802.11a and g standards provide 55 Mbps in the 5 GHz band and 54 Mbps in the 2.4 GHz band respectively. A fivefold increase in data rate over the previous standards. Some manufacturers are proposing special equipment that will take the data rate to 150 Mbps. How long before 1 Gbps is achieved?

For those on the move with their portables and PDAs, wireless communication hotspots, known as WiFi hotspots, are being provided in many public places such as mainline railway stations and airports. WiFi stands for Wireless Fidelity meaning high performance wireless, the usage being similar to Hi-Fi for high quality audio systems. The hotspot is a radio connection point, which gives access to the Internet. The advantage here is

Figure 12.3   A meshbox system

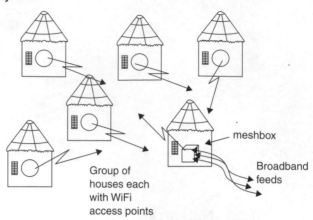

Group of
houses each
with WiFi
access points

meshbox

Broadband
feeds

the high data rate that is available, which is much higher than can be achieved with operation over the current mobile telephone networks. Will advances in the next generation of mobile telephones, with their claimed higher data rates, make hotspots redundant?

A concept, under the name of a meshbox, is being tested in a number of locations. Figure 12.3 shows the idea. The topology is that a number of households in a small area have wireless connections to the meshbox, which can be located anywhere in the local area. The meshbox has a few, say four broadband services connected to it. The idea is that rather than each household paying for its own broadband connection, the broadband service can be shared amongst the householders. The target application is mainly video on demand, where a high data rate download is infrequently required. The system also provides Internet access for all connected households. Satellite TV service providers are getting in on the broadband service market in competition with cable service providers. Similar services to Asymmetric Digital Subscriber Line (ADSL) are on offer at cheaper rates than cable services for 1 Mbps download data rates.

To return to Ethernet, this last network item could show the way forward if radio does not satisfy demand. A small neighbourhood has been wired with fibre optic cables to a central switching node, which is in turn connected to TV, telephone and broadband Internet services. In each home, the fibre optic cable is connected to a distribution box that feeds the telephone TV, PC and digital entertainment centre. The fibre network provides broadband local interconnection, using Ethernet technology, and shared access to the outside world. This is like a fibre optic version of the meshbox.

12.6   Complete systems

Having looked at a number of computer components, it is time to look at a few items that can be described as whole system developments.

As mentioned above, the flat screen display is gradually replacing the CRT display even with desktop systems. Closely following this trend is the adoption of what is called the Tablet PC. Tablet PCs are flat screens with the computer built into the display housing. The screens are touch sensitive and can be used as an input device by allowing the user to write on the screen with a special pen as explained above. Near future developments will also allow speech input. Tablet PCs are intended to be battery powered and portable and have built-in wireless networking capability, but they may be mains powered if used in a desktop application. They can have keyboards and mice connected if required. A thin client version of a tablet PC is in development, whereby the tablet is just a display and input device and the processing is carried out by a shared server that is at the other end of a wireless connection. The big advantage of this is the much reduced battery drain.

Our last item is the Ultra PC, which is the latest in miniaturisation. A full function, palm held, PC running a full Windows operating system, 10 GByte hard disk and wireless connectivity. The screen is touch sensitive and has pen write-on capability with speech input coming shortly.

12.7 Summary

This chapter has described briefly a number of products, concepts and ideas that are likely to come into common use either very soon or in the very near future. It is difficult to predict what new technologies will emerge from the research establishment but a few things are certain and they are that new devices will be smaller and faster and processors will get more complex and applications will rapidly exploit any gain in processing power that is achieved.

EXERCISES

1   Devices exist that can pick up the minute electrical signals in the human brain and these have been used to enable physically handicapped people to control such things as lights and heating systems by just thinking about the required action. Research these systems and comment on the possibility of using a similar mechanism for everyone to communicate with a computer.

2   What would be the benefits and drawbacks of using a meshbox in a small community such as a block of flats?

3   What would be the benefits and drawbacks of using a virtual keyboard for a desktop PC?

4   Discuss any drawbacks that might result from every CPU having wireless connection capability.

5   Investigate Blu-Ray technology and compare it with the technology used for standard CD and DVD systems.

Appendix 1
Introduction to logic circuit minimisation using Karnaugh map methods

A1.1 Introduction

When analysing a logic problem the result may be a long and complex logic expression. Before trying to implement the expression it would be desirable to try to simplify the expression. The process of simplification is called *minimisation*. It is possible to use algorithmic rules to carry out the minimisation process but it can be difficult to identify the best approach to achieve the optimal solution. Karnaugh maps are a way of achieving an optimal result using a graphical approach.

A1.2 Two variable expressions

Minimising two variable problems appears a relatively straightforward process. Generating the truth table for the expression will result in the characteristic output pattern for a basic gate. Consider the two expressions

$F_1 = (Y \text{ AND } \overline{Z}) \text{ OR } (\overline{Y} \text{ AND } Z)$

$F_2 = (Y \text{ AND } Z) \text{ OR } (\overline{Y} \text{ AND } Z)$

The truth tables for these two expressions are given in Table A1.1. The truth table for F_1 has generated the output of an XOR function (see Figure 3.2). F_2 however does not produce output that can be matched with any of the basic gates in Figure 3.2 and thus would not appear to be reducible.

We will now try mapping the output of the truth table on a Karnaugh map. The map is a 2×2 grid. The first column represents $\overline{Y}$; the second column represents Y. The first row represents $\overline{Z}$; the second row represents Z. Figure A1.1 demonstrates this layout. Data from the truth table for a function can be transcribed onto the Karnaugh map. The result for Y = Z = 0 is placed in the top left box. The result for Y = 1,

Table A1.1 Truth tables for (a) F$_1$ = (Y AND $\overline{Z}$) OR ($\overline{Y}$ AND Z) and (b) F$_2$ = (Y AND Z) OR ($\overline{Y}$ AND Z)

Y	Z	F$_1$
0	0	0
0	1	1
1	0	1
1	1	0

(a)

Y	Z	F$_2$
0	0	0
0	1	1
1	0	0
1	1	1

(b)

Figure A1.1 Two variable Karnaugh map

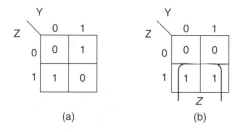

Figure A1.2 Karnaugh maps for (a) (Y AND $\overline{Z}$) OR ($\overline{Y}$ AND Z) and (b) (Y AND Z) OR ($\overline{Y}$ AND Z)

Z = 0 is placed in the top right box and so on. The resulting Karnaugh map for the two functions F$_1$ and F$_2$ above are shown in Figure A1.2.

The diagonal pattern in Figure A1.2(a) is typical of an XOR function. The pattern in Figure A1.2(b) shows two adjacent 1 values. It is this sort of pattern, which we are interested in. What this pattern demonstrated is that if Z = 1, then it does not matter what the value of Y is, the output will be 1. We can now rewrite F$_1$ and F$_2$ as

$$F_1 = Y \text{ XOR } Z$$
$$F_2 = Z$$

Let us now consider a third function

$$F_3 = (\overline{Y} \text{ AND } \overline{Z}) \text{ OR } (\overline{Y} \text{ AND } Z)$$

The truth table and Karnaugh map for this function are shown in Figure A1.3.

From the Karnaugh map it can be seen that the output of this function will be 1 if Y = 0, irrespective of the value of Z. The output is therefore the inverse of Y, or $\overline{Y}$. F$_3$ can thus be rewritten as

$$F_3 = \overline{Y}.$$

Figure A1.3 Truth table and Karnaugh map for F₃ = ($\overline{Y}$ AND $\overline{Z}$) OR ($\overline{Y}$ AND Z)

Y	Z	F₃
0	0	1
0	1	1
1	0	0
1	1	0

	Y=0	Y=1
Z=0 ($\overline{Y}$)	1	0
Z=1	1	0

A1.3 Three variable expressions

This technique can be extended to cover three variable expressions. The layout of the Karnaugh map for these expressions is shown in Figure A1.4. It can be seen from the Karnaugh map in Figure A1.4 that the top row represents Z and the bottom row is $\overline{Z}$. The left half of the map represents $\overline{X}$ and the right half is X. The middle two columns represent Y and the outside two columns represent $\overline{Y}$. The Karnaugh maps in Figure A1.5 illustrate the pattern we would expect for F₄ = X and F₅ = $\overline{Y}$ AND Z. In Figure A1.5(a) the four cells containing 1 all fall within the area where X = 1. Two of the cells are in the region where Z = 1 and two in the region where Z = 0. Similarly two are in the region where Y = 1 and two where Y = 0. All four cells therefore only have X = 1 in common. This means that the expression produces a TRUE result whenever X is TRUE. Note that in Figure A1.5(b) the cells of the right-most column are thought to wrap round and be adjacent to the left-most column. It is thus possible to group the bottom-left cell with the bottom-right cell. The two cells in which there is a 1 have Y = 0 and Z = 1 in common and thus the expression will return TRUE if Y is FALSE and Z is TRUE. As an AND gate will return TRUE (1) only when all its inputs are TRUE then the expression will return TRUE if $\overline{Y}$ is TRUE and Z is TRUE. Figure A1.5(c) illustrated the pattern for F₆ = X OR ($\overline{Y}$ AND Z). The expression X OR ($\overline{Y}$ AND Z) is formed by taking the expression for each of the groupings (which will be made up of a number of terms connected by ANDs) and connecting them via ORs. This type of expression is known as *sum-of-products* form. The reason for this name is obvious if you remember that AND can be replaced by '.' and OR by '+'.

The objective when grouping the 1's together is to create the biggest group of adjacent 1's as possible. In Figure A1.5(c) it can be seen that the bottom-left cell is counted twice. This does not matter; the important things are that every cell containing a 1 is grouped at least once and that it is included in the biggest group possible. It would be possible to group the right half of the map together giving X. The 1 in the bottom-right cell would then be $\overline{X}$ AND $\overline{Y}$ AND Z. The final expression would then be X OR ($\overline{X}$ AND $\overline{Y}$ AND Z) and thus we would have an extra superfluous term.

Figure A1.4 Three variable Karnaugh map

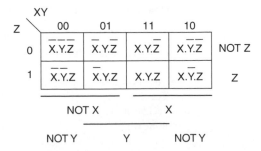

Figure A1.5   **Karnaugh maps for (a) F$_4$ = X, (b) F$_5$ = $\overline{Y}$ AND Z and (c) F$_6$ = X OR ($\overline{Y}$ AND Z)**

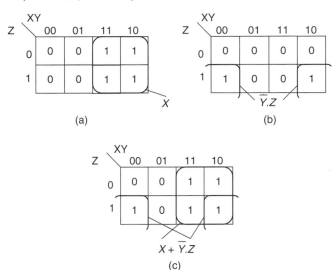

(a)

(b)

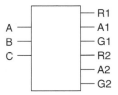

$X + \overline{Y}.Z$

(c)

Figure A1.6   **Traffic light controller**

A1.3.1 *Three variable example*

A traffic signal normally consists of a group of three lamps, a top red lamp, a middle amber lamp and a bottom green lamp and we call this group a *traffic light*. A basic set of traffic lights consist of two pairs of traffic lights at right angles. Let us consider the pair controlling travel in a north–south direction as set 1 and the pair controlling traffic in an east–west direction as set 2. Initially the two red lamps (R1 and R2) will be on. R2 will then remain on while set 1 lamps go through the following cycle. The amber lamp (A1) is turned on. This will be followed by R1 and A1 being turned off and then the green lamp (G1) will be turned on. After a period of time, A1 will be turned on and G1 turned off, then R1 will be turned on and A1 turned off. Set 2 lamps will now go through the same sequence with R1 remaining on. The lamps actually pass through eight states before repeating the pattern. A circuit for controlling the lamps will have three inputs to indicate the current state and an output for each of the six lamps (see Figure A1.6).

The eight states through which the traffic lights pass can be shown on a truth table. A one output for any light indicates that the light is on and a zero output indicates that the light is off. The truth table is shown in Table A1.2.

From this truth table an expression can be determined for each of the lights by mapping the output of each. The Karnaugh maps in Figure A1.7 show the Karnaugh maps for each of the lights in set 1 along with the minimal form resulting from an analysis of the maps. Once we have the minimised form of the expression, the logic circuit, as in Figure A1.8, can be drawn.

Table A1.2   Truth table for traffic light controller

A	B	C	R1	A1	G1	R2	A2	G2
0	0	0	1	0	0	1	0	0
0	0	1	1	1	0	1	0	0
0	1	0	0	0	1	1	0	0
0	1	1	0	1	0	1	0	0
1	0	0	1	0	0	1	0	0
1	0	1	1	0	0	1	1	0
1	1	0	1	0	0	0	0	1
1	1	1	1	0	0	0	1	0

Figure A1.7   Karnaugh maps for traffic light set 1

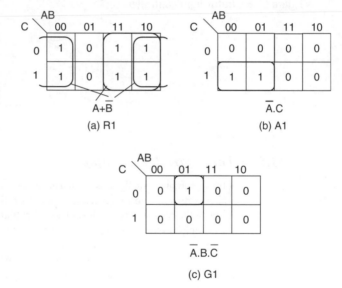

(a) R1   (b) A1

(c) G1

Figure A1.8   Logic circuit for traffic light set 1

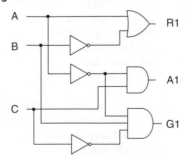

Figure A1.9 Four variable Karnaugh map

<table>
<tr><td rowspan="2">YZ</td><td colspan="4">WX</td><td></td><td></td></tr>
<tr><td>00</td><td>01</td><td>11</td><td>10</td><td></td><td rowspan="2">NOT Y</td></tr>
<tr><td>00</td><td>$\bar{W}.\bar{X}.\bar{Y}.\bar{Z}$</td><td>$\bar{W}.X.\bar{Y}.\bar{Z}$</td><td>$W.X.\bar{Y}.\bar{Z}$</td><td>$W.\bar{X}.\bar{Y}.\bar{Z}$</td><td>NOT Z</td></tr>
<tr><td>01</td><td>$\bar{W}.\bar{X}.\bar{Y}.Z$</td><td>$\bar{W}.X.\bar{Y}.Z$</td><td>$W.X.\bar{Y}.Z$</td><td>$W.\bar{X}.\bar{Y}.Z$</td><td rowspan="2">Z</td><td></td></tr>
<tr><td>11</td><td>$\bar{W}.\bar{X}.Y.Z$</td><td>$\bar{W}.X.Y.Z$</td><td>$W.X.Y.Z$</td><td>$W.\bar{X}.Y.Z$</td><td rowspan="2">Y</td></tr>
<tr><td>10</td><td>$\bar{W}.\bar{X}.Y.\bar{Z}$</td><td>$\bar{W}.X.Y.\bar{Z}$</td><td>$W.X.Y.\bar{Z}$</td><td>$W.\bar{X}.Y.\bar{Z}$</td><td>NOT Z</td></tr>
<tr><td></td><td colspan="2">NOT W</td><td colspan="2">W</td></tr>
<tr><td></td><td>NOT X</td><td>X</td><td></td><td>NOT X</td></tr>
</table>

Figure A1.10 Karnaugh map for $\bar{X}$ AND $\bar{Z}$

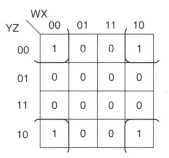

YZ \ WX	00	01	11	10
00	1	0	0	1
01	0	0	0	0
11	0	0	0	0
10	1	0	0	1

A1.4 Four variable expressions

The layout illustrated in Figure A1.9 demonstrates the Karnaugh map for logic expressions consisting of four variables. The principle of transferring the result from a truth table to the Karnaugh map still applies. The objective is to group all the cells containing 1 together in the biggest clusters available still applies. When we were considering three variable Karnaugh maps, it was observed that the left-most column was considered to wrap around and to be adjacent to the right-most column. In the case of a four variable Karnaugh map the top row is also considered to wrap around and to be adjacent to the bottom row. This means that the four corners are adjacent. From Figure A1.10 we can see that the four corners represent $\bar{X}$ AND $\bar{Z}$.

A1.4.1 Four variable example including don't care conditions

Figure A1.11 illustrates a 7-segment display. These displays are used to display the ten digits. Each of the segments is referred to by a letter as shown in Figure A1.11.
A 7-segment display controller will need seven outputs (1 for each segment) and four inputs. Four inputs are sufficient to select between 16 states but there are only ten in the 7-segment display. If there were only three inputs however, only eight states could be used. The truth table for the segment *a* output from the controller is shown in Table A1.3. A one in the result column indicates that the segment is on and a zero indicates that the segment

Figure A1.11   7-segment display

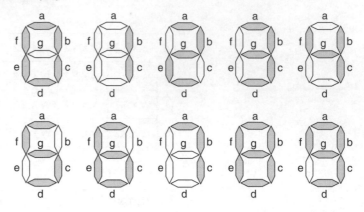

Table A1.3   Truth table for output *a* of a 7-segment display controller

A	B	C	D	a
0	0	0	0	1
0	0	0	1	0
0	0	1	0	1
0	0	1	1	1
0	1	0	0	0
0	1	0	1	1
0	1	1	0	1
0	1	1	1	1
1	0	0	0	1
1	0	0	1	1
1	0	1	0	X
1	0	1	1	X
1	1	0	0	X
1	1	0	1	X
1	1	1	0	X
1	1	1	1	X

Figure A1.12 Karnaugh map for segment *a* of a 7-segment display controller

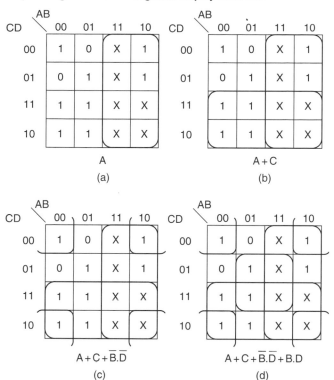

is off. As the final six states are not used, an X is used to indicate that we don't care what the output is. This comes in useful when we come to determine the minimised form for the logic expression for each output.

Figure A1.12 shows how the cells containing a 1 are grouped together to construct the minimised form. A1.12(a) shows how all the don't care cells can be grouped with the two cells in the top-right corner to give the term A. The four cells in the bottom-left corner could possibly be grouped together to give $\overline{A}$ AND C but it is more efficient to group them with four of the don't care conditions, as shown in Figure A1.12(b), to give the term C. That leaves two single cells. The one in the top-left corner can be combined with the four corners, as illustrated in Figure A1.10, to give $\overline{B}$ AND $\overline{D}$ (Figure A1.12(c)). This means that the cell in the bottom-right corner is used three times. This is not a problem as any cell can be used as many times as necessary. The final cell with a 1 in it can be grouped with the other four cells in the middle of the map, as shown in Figure A1.12(d), to give B AND D. It may appear desirable to make a group of six by including the middle two cells of the bottom row. This will not enable us to form a term that includes all six of the desirable cells but exclude the second cell in the top row. The final expression for segment *a* is therefore A OR C OR ($\overline{B}$ AND $\overline{D}$) OR (B AND D). The brackets in the previous expression are superfluous but make it easier to read.

In generating a minimal expression for segment *a*, all the don't care cells were used. It is not necessary to use all the don't care cells provided a minimal expression incorporating all the cells containing 1 is formed. Figure A1.13 shows a truth table and Karnaugh map for the *e* segment. In this case two of the six don't care cells are used. The expression for segment *e* is thus (C AND $\overline{D}$) OR ($\overline{B}$ AND $\overline{D}$).

Figure A1.13   Truth table and Karnaugh map for segment *e* of a 7-segment display controller

A B C D	e
0 0 0 0	1
0 0 0 1	0
0 0 1 0	1
0 0 1 1	0
0 1 0 0	0
0 1 0 1	0
0 1 1 0	1
0 1 1 1	0
1 0 0 0	1
1 0 0 1	0
1 0 1 0	X
1 0 1 1	X
1 1 0 0	X
1 1 0 1	X
1 1 1 0	X
1 1 1 1	X

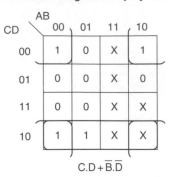

$$C.D + \overline{B}.\overline{D}$$

EXERCISES

1   Produce the Karnaugh maps and minimised expressions for traffic light set 2 in Section A1.3.1 and thus complete the logic circuit for the traffic light controller.

2   Draw up a complete truth table for the 7-segment display controller in Section A1.4.1. From the truth table, produce a complete set of Karnaugh maps and thus the minimised logic expressions for the seven outputs and finally a complete logic circuit for the controller.

Appendix 2
Introduction to debug

A2.1 Introduction

Debug is a utility that has been available to users of MS-DOS systems since the very early versions. Its original function was to offer a tool that would enable developers to identify and fix errors in programs. It has very limited facilities but can be found in the Windows operating systems of today. We will discuss enough of the facilities of debug so that we can write a few simple programs that will give us an understanding of the 80x8s programmer's model and the nature of low-level programming. Assembly language programming and checking are covered in material listed in the references at the end of this book. Rather than listing all the commands and discussing them in detail, this appendix will go through the steps involved in entering and debugging a simple program. Each command will be explained as it is encountered.

When reading through this appendix it must be remembered that all values used are in hexadecimal notation. It should also be noted that MS-DOS is not case sensitive, that is, upper and lower case letters are the same to MS-DOS. In order to make the text easier to read, the commands in the text of this appendix are written as upper case letters. The example provided in the figures however, use lower case letters. In Section A2.3, for example, the command R is exactly the same as r in Figure A2.3.

A2.2 Running debug

As debug is an MS-DOS utility, it is necessary to run it from an MS-DOS window within windows. This can be done by going to the *Run* option in the *Start* menu and entering *debug* in the file text box. This will start debug immediately. Alternatively you can enter *command* (Windows 9x) or *cmd* (Windows 2000) in the text window within the Run utility or select an MS-DOS prompt option in the start menu, if there is one, or click on the MS-DOS icon, if there is one, to start an MS-DOS session. When the MS-DOS window is open you can then enter *debug* (see Figure A2.1). When debug has started the only visible sign that the utility is running as that a simple '-' prompt appears. Debug is now awaiting a command.

Figure A2.1   Starting debug

```
Microsoft(R) Windows 98
   (C)Copyright Microsoft Corp 1981-1999.

C:\WINDOWS>debug
-
```

Figure A2.2   Debug commands

```
-?
assemble        A [address]
compare         C range address
dump            D [range]
enter           E address [list]
fill            F range list
go              G [=address] [addresses]
hex             H value1 value2
input           I port
load            L [address] [drive] [firstsector] [number]
move            M range address
name            N [pathname] [arglist]
output          O port byte
proceed         P [=address] [number]
quit            Q
register        R [register]
search          S range list
trace           T [=address] [value]
unassemble      U [range]
write           W [address] [drive] [firstsector] [number]
allocate expanded memory        XA [#pages]
deallocate expanded memory      XD [handle]
map expanded memory pages       XM [Lpage] [Ppage] [handle]
display expanded memory status  XS
-
```

A2.3   The *?* command

To see a list of all the commands available, the *?* command is useful. It will give all the commands and a brief indication of their syntax. It will not however give an explanation of the function of each command! (This is an old, free command line utility – what do you expect?) (See Figure A2.2.)

A2.4   The R command

The register command (*R*) displays the content of all the CPU registers (see Figure A2.3). The first row of the output shows the value of each of the general-purpose registers. The second row shows the value of each of the segment registers, the instruction pointer and the flags register. The flags register is shown as a series of eight mnemonics representing the value of each of the bits in the flag register. A translation of the mnemonics is shown in Table A2.1. The third row of the *R* command display shows (on the left side) the address of the next instruction to be

Figure A2.3 The _R_ command

```
-r
AX=0000 BX=0000 CX=0000 DX=0000 SP=FFEE BP=0000  SI=0000  DI=0000
DS=18A1 ES=18A1 SS=18A1 CS=18A1 IP=0100 NV UP EI PL NZ NA PO NC
18A1 :0100 00A0A000      ADD     [BX+SI+00A0],AH         DS:00A0=00
-r ip
IP 0100
:0200
-r f
NV UP EI PL NZ NA PO NC  -zr
-r
AX=0000 BX=0000 CX=0000 DX=0000 SP=FFEE BP=0000  SI=0000  DI=0000
DS=18A1 ES=18A1 SS=18A1 CS=18A1 IP=0200 NV UP EI PL ZR NA PO NC
18A1 :0200 A0A700        MOV     AL,[00A7]              DS:00A7=00
-
```

Table A2.1 Flag register values

	OF	DF	IF	SF	ZF	AC	PF	CF
1	OV	DN	EI	NG	ZR	AC	PE	CY
0	NV	UP	DI	PL	NZ	NA	PO	NC

executed, its machine code and the assembly language equivalent. The address is in the form _CS:IP_ where _CS_ is the code segment (CS) register value and _IP_ is the instruction pointer (IP) register value. Figure A2.3 provides an example of the use of this command. It should be noted that at this stage we have not entered any code into the computer. The information relating to the next instruction is going to be random as any data or code may have been placed in the area of memory we are currently displaying. It will also be impossible to determine the CS value in advance. The figure is thus purely illustrative and if you were to try this yourself the information is unlikely to be identical. In Figure A2.3 the address of the next instruction is _18A1:0100_. Debug interprets the memory content at this location as a 4-byte _add_ instruction and displays a disassembled form of the instruction. On the right-hand side of the screen is the text _DS:00A0 = 00_. This shows that the data at the address specified by the operand in the instruction is _00_.

(1) _Changing register values using the R command_

Figure A2.3 demonstrates how it is possible to change register values via the _R_ command. In the figure the IP value is changed from _0100_ to _0200_. The command entered by the programmer was _r ip_. Debug responded by displaying the value of the IP register then a ':' prompt so that a new value could be entered.

(2) _Changing flag values using the R command_

Figure A2.3 then goes on to show that the _r f_ command will cause debug to display the value of all the flags and then allow the user to enter a new flag value. In the Figure A2.3 the zero flag goes from _0_ (NZ) to _1_ (ZR).

Figure A2.4   The *A* command

```
-a 0100
18A1:0100 db 8
18A1 :0101 db 36
18A1 :0102 db 0
18A1 :0103 mov al,[0100]
18A1 :0106 add al,[0101]
18A1 :010A mov [0102],al
18A1 :010D
-
```

Figure A2.5   Tracing through a program

```
-t=0103

AX=0008 BX=0000 CX=0000 DX=0000 SP=FFEE BP=0000  SI=0000  DI=0000
DS=18A1 ES=18A1 SS=18A1 CS=18A1 IP=0106 NV UP EI PL ZR NA PO NC
18A1:0106 02060101      ADD     AL,[0101]                DS:0101=36
-t

AX=003E BX=0000 CX=0000 DX=0000 SP=FFEE BP=0000  SI=0000  DI=0000
DS=1BEB ES=1BEB SS=1BEB CS=1BEB IP=010A NV UP EI PL NZ NA PO NC
18A1:010A A20201        MOV     [0102],AL                DS:0102=3E
-t

AX=003E BX=0000 CX=0000 DX=0000 SP=FFEE BP=0000  SI=0000  DI=0000
DS=1BEB ES=1BEB SS=1BEB CS=1BEB IP=010D NV UP EI PL NZ NA PO NC
18A1:010D 0000          ADD     [BX+SI],AL               DS:0000=CD
-
```

A2.5 The *A* command

The assemble command (*A*) allows a programmer to enter a program using assembly language mnemonics. Figure A2.4 shows a short program to add two 8-bit memory resident numbers and place the result back in memory. The command used was *a 0100*, which tells debug where to start storing the program within the code segment. MS-DOS programs require a 100-byte *program segment prefix* (PSP) at the start of each program so the default start for any code loaded would be *CS:0100*. If the start address is omitted then the code will be stored starting from the IP value.

If no instruction is entered for a particular address, such as location *010D* in Figure A2.4 then the programmer will be returned to the debug prompt.

A2.6 The *T* command

The trace command (*T*) allows a single instruction to be executed. This is often referred to as *single-stepping* through a program. This enables the programmer to study the effects of each instruction. Figure A2.5 shows the effect of stepping through the example program. The first of the trace commands has the format *t = 0103*. This tells debug to trace the instruction at offset *0103* within the code segment. The first three lines of the program entered were data and should not be traced. Debug will

Figure A2.6   Displaying memory locations

```
-d 0100 110
1BEB:0100 08 36 3E A0 00 01 02 06-01 01 A2 02 01 00 00 EB  .6>............
-
```

not know that they are data and will try to interpret them as instructions. After the
T command the registers are displayed so you can see what happened. In this case the
AX value changed from *0000* to *0008*. (Remember that AL is the least significant eight
bits of AX.) The next two instructions do not need an address as they will trace the
instruction determined by IP and IP is incremented after each instruction. Note that
the final instruction should be storing the value produced in AL (3E), which is done
by writing it to memory. The effect of this instruction cannot be seen by just studying
the registers.

A2.7   The *D* command

The display or dump command (*D*) enables the programmer to view the contents of
memory. The *D* command is generally used with at least one argument. A single
argument would tell debug from where to start displaying the contents of memory. A
second argument indicates to debug the number of bytes to display (see Figure A2.6).
This second argument needs to be preceded by an *l* for length. If no argument is
provided then a block of 128 bytes will be displayed.

In Figure A2.6 16 (10_{16}) locations are displayed starting at location *0100*. Each line
displayed by the *D* command will end with the ASCII equivalent of each memory
location. If there is not a printable ASCII character corresponding to that value then
a '.' is displayed. In the example only the locations containing the values *36* and *3E*
have ASCII equivalent characters. These characters are *6>*.

A2.8   The *U* command

It is possible to display the program at a particular location in memory using the
unassemble command (*U*). Some thought needs to be used when applying this
command. The first example in the use of this command in Figure A2.7 shows the
U command unassemblying the program from location *0100*. Unfortunately the first
three bytes are data, which are now being interpreted as instructions so the results are
not valid. The second example *u 0103 010A* will unassemble the code only, as the data
for this program is outside this range.

A2.9   The *G* command

Single-stepping through a long program will be very tedious. An alternative way of
executing a piece of code, which you are fairly certain is correct, is by using the go
command (*G*). This will execute the program from the current IP location or from
an address preceded by an '=' until a *breakpoint*. A breakpoint is an address at which
the execution of the program will finish or pause. Up to 10 breakpoints can be
specified. The example in Figure A2.8 specifies *0100* as the start address and *010D* as
the end address or breakpoint.

Figure A2.7   Unassemble example

```
-u 0100
1BEB:0100 08363EA0     OR        [A03E],DH
1BEB:0104 0001         ADD       [BX+DI],AL
1BEB:0106 02060101     ADD       AL,[0101]
1BEB:010A A20201       MOV       [0102],AL
1BEB:010D 0000         ADD       [BX+SI],AL
1BEB:010F EB13         JMP       0124
1BEB:0111 57           PUSH      DI
1BEB:0112 26           ES:
1BEB:0113 8B3E92DE     MOV       DI,[DE92]
1BEB:0117 26           ES:
1BEB:0118 894DFE       MOV       [DI-02],CX
1BEB:011B 5F           POP       DI
1BEB:011C 3400         XOR       AL,00
1BEB:011E DA1B         FICOMP    DWORD PTR [BP+DI]
-u 0103 010a
1BEB:0103 A00001       MOV       AL,[0100]
1BEB:0106 02060101     ADD       AL,[0101]
1BEB:010A A20201       MOV       [0102],AL
-
```

Figure A2.8   Execute to a breakpoint

```
-g=0103 010d

AX=003E BX=0000 CX=0000 DX=0000 SP=FFEE BP=0000  SI=0000  DI=0000
DS=18A1 ES=18A1 SS=18A1 CS=18A1 IP=010D NV UP EI PL NZ NA PO NC
18A1:010D 0000              ADD       [BX+SI],AL            DS:0000=CD
-
```

Figure A2.9   The *E* command

```
-e 0100 'anything'
-d 0100
18A1:0100 61 6E 79 74 68 69 6E 67-01 01 A2 02 01 00 00 EB anything........
18A1:0110 13 57 26 8B 3E 92 DE 26-89 4D FE 5F 34 00 DA 1B .W&.>..&.M._4...
18A1:0120 04 E8 5A FA 0E 1F E9 F5-B9 E8 40 FE 81 3E 1A 04 ..Z.......@..>..
18A1:0130 00 F0 75 06 C7 06 1A 04-FF FF E9 A7 B6 BF A1 89 ..u.............
18A1:0140 C7 06 8E D3 01 00 E8 E4-03 73 22 0B C0 75 3C E8 .........s"..u<.
18A1:0150 AC 0B 86 F2 89 0E 07 83-89 16 09 83 BA F5 82 E8 ................
18A1:0160 BD 2F E8 FA 00 73 06 0B-C0 74 1F EB 1E 8B 0E BF ./...s...t......
18A1:0170 E1 8A 36 C1 E1 8A 16 C2-E1 51 52 E8 61 04 5A 59 ..6......QR.a.ZY
-e 0110 61 6e 79 74 68 69 6e 67
-d 0100 120
18A1:0100 61 6E 79 74 68 69 6E 67-01 01 A2 02 01 00 00 EB anything........
18A1:0110 61 6E 79 74 68 69 6E 67-89 4D FE 5F 34 00 DA 1B anything.M._4...
-
```

A2.10   The *E* command

The enter command (*E*) is used to enter data. The *A* command is used to enter code so the start address is an offset within the code segment. The *E* command is for data and thus the address argument is an offset within the data segment.

Figure A2.9 shows two ways of entering the text data *anything* into memory. The first shows that debug can accept a literal and store it into consecutive areas of memory. The second shows the programmer entering the data as separate character codes. Data can be entered into the code segment if a full address is given that is *CS:0100*. Debug will then replace CS with the current code segment register value.

A2.11 The *P* command and invoking operating system functions

In order to correctly demonstrate the use of the proceed command (*P*), we need a more extensive example program. The *P* command is used to execute instructions such as the *int* instruction. The *int* instruction causes a software interrupt or *trap*. This type of instruction is used to invoke operating system functions. The example in Figure A2.10 is a program, which will use an operating system function to read a line of text from the keyboard and another function to write the text back to the screen. A third operating system function will terminate the program.

Note that the characters appearing after a ';' are comments and do not need to be entered as part of the program. They are supplied to give a brief indication of what each part of the program is for. The data between *0100* and *0112* are required for the function that will receive the data from the keyboard. The first byte (0100) indicates the maximum number of characters that the program is willing to accept. The next byte (0101) will hold the number of characters actually input. The following 16 bytes will hold the characters input. To accept 16 characters from the user a seventeenth byte is required by the program to hold an end of string character. This character will be a *Carriage Return* (CR) (ASCII code 0D) character.

MS-DOS makes many of its I/O routines available via interrupt number 21_{16}. To differentiate between the different functions, an argument is passed to the interrupt handler via the AH register. To cause the *buffered input from console with echo* function to be invoked AH must contain the value *0A* when *int 21* is executed. In addition, DX must contain the address of the start of the parameter list that is the

Figure A2.10 Extended example

```
0100 db 10          ;max. no character to input
0101 db 0           ;actual no. characters input
0102 db 0 0 0 0 0 0 0 0 0 0 0 0 0 0 0 0
                    ;input buffer
0112 db 0           ;allow for end-of-string

;read buffered input from console with echo
0113 mov ah,0a      ;int 21 function no. oa
0115 mov dx,0100    ;start of param. list
0118 int 21         ;invoke os routine

;place a $ at end of string
011a mov cl,24      ;character 24 = $
011c mov al,[0101]
                    ;al holds number of characters
011f cbw            ;convert al byte to ax word
0120 mov bx,0102    ;initialise bx to start of string
0123 add bx,ax      ;bx now points to end of string
0125 mov [bx],cl    ;place $ at end of string

;output string to console
0127 mov dx,0102    ;dx holds start of string
012a mov ah,09      ;int 21 function no. 09
012c int 21         ;invoke os routine

;terminate program
012e int 20
```

Figure A2.11   Inputting an input string

```
-t=0113

AX=0A08  BX=0000  CX=0000  DX=0000  SP=FFEE  BP=0000  SI=0000  DI=0000
DS=18A1  ES=18A1  SS=18A1  CS=18A1  IP=0115   NV UP EI NG NZ NA PE CY
18A1:0115 BA0001        MOV     DX,0100
-t

AX=0A08  BX=0000  CX=0000  DX=0100  SP=FFEE  BP=0000  SI=0000  DI=0000
DS=18A1  ES=18A1  SS=18A1  CS=18A1  IP=0118   NV UP EI NG NZ NA PE CY
18A1:0118 CD21          INT     21
-p
text input
AX=0A0D  BX=0000  CX=0000  DX=0100  SP=FFEE  BP=0000  SI=0000  DI=0000
DS=18A1  ES=18A1  SS=18A1  CS=18A1  IP=011A   NV UP EI NG NZ NA PE CY
18A1:011A B124          MOV     CL,24
-d 0100 120
1BEB:0100 10 0A 74 65 78 74 20 69-6E 70 75 74 0D 00 00 00 ..text input....
1BEB:0110 00 00 00 B4 0A BA 00 01-CD 21 B1 24 A0 01 01 98 .........!.$....
-
```

maximum number of characters, actual number of characters and input buffer. The code between *0113* and *0119* will cause an input string to be received by the program.

Figure A2.11 shows the first two instructions of the program being traced and then the *P* command being used to execute the *int* command without having to step through it. A *D* command is then used to confirm the contents of the input buffer. The string entered by the user was *text input*. From the dump, it is possible to determine from the value in *0101* that this string is ten characters long. You can also see that a eleventh character is added. This is the *0D* character or *CR* character which is not included in the character count.

The next part of the program needs to replace the *0D* character by a *$* character (ASCII code 24). This is because the routine which outputs strings to the console requires the string to be terminated by a *$*. The instruction at location *011A* places a *$* character in the CL register. AL is then loaded with the length of the string. Because we wish to add this to a 16-bit register we extend AL to the whole of AX by using a *convert binary to word* (CBW) instruction (*011F*). BX is loaded with the start address of the string and then the value in AX is added to it to give the address of the end of the string. The *$* character is then stored at that location (*0125*). Figure A2.12 shows the final part of the program being traced with dumps immediately before and after the *$* character is stored in memory, to show that the *$* has been placed at the correct location.

Now that the string to be output is properly prepared, the routine to output it can be invoked. This is another *int 21* routine but this time the argument in AH must be *09* (*012A*). It is also necessary for *DX* to hold the address of the start of the string (*0127*). Figure A2.13 shows this section of the program being traced and the *int 21* function being executed using a proceed command. There is then another proceed command to execute the *int 20* instruction. *int 20* invokes an operating system routine which terminates the execution of the program.

A2.12   The Q command

The final essential command is the quit command (*Q*). This terminates the debug session.

Figure A2.12 Inserting a string termination character

```
AX=0A0D  BX=0000  CX=0024  DX=0100  SP=FFEE  BP=0000  SI=0000  DI=0000
DS=18A1  ES=18A1  SS=18A1  CS=18A1  IP=011C    NV UP EI NG NZ NA PE CY
18A1:011C A00101        MOV     AL,[0101]                    DS:0101=0A
-t

AX=0A0A  BX=0000  CX=0024  DX=0100  SP=FFEE  BP=0000  SI=0000  DI=0000
DS=18A1  ES=18A1  SS=18A1  CS=18A1  IP=011F    NV UP EI NG NZ NA PE CY
18A1:011F 98            CBW
-t

AX=000A  BX=0000  CX=0024  DX=0100  SP=FFEE  BP=0000  SI=0000  DI=0000
DS=18A1  ES=18A1  SS=18A1  CS=18A1  IP=0120    NV UP EI NG NZ NA PE CY
18A1:0120 BB0201        MOV     BX,0102
-t

AX=000A  BX=0102  CX=0024  DX=0100  SP=FFEE  BP=0000  SI=0000  DI=0000
DS=18A1  ES=18A1  SS=18A1  CS=18A1  IP=0123    NV UP EI NG NZ NA PE CY
18A1:0123 89C3         ADD      BX,AX
-t

AX=000A  BX=010C  CX=0024  DX=0100  SP=FFEE  BP=0000  SI=0000  DI=0000
DS=18A1  ES=18A1  SS=18A1  CS=18A1  IP=0125    NV UP EI NG NZ NA PE CY
18A1:0125 880F         MOV      [BX],CL                     DS:000A=4F
-d 0100 110
18A1:0100 10 0A 74 65 78 74 20 69-6E 70 75 74 0D 00 00 00  ..text input....
-t

AX=000A  BX=010C  CX=0024  DX=0100  SP=FFEE  BP=0000  SI=0000  DI=0000
DS=18A1  ES=18A1  SS=18A1  CS=18A1  IP=0127    NV UP EI NG NZ NA PE CY
18A1:0127 BA0201        MOV      DX,0102
-d 0100 110
18A1:0100 10 0A 74 65 78 74 20 69-6E 70 75 74 24 00 00 00  ..text input$...
-
```

Figure A2.13 Outputting a string and terminating the program

```
-t

AX=000A BX=010C CX=0024 DX=0102 SP=FFEE BP=0000  SI=0000  DI=0000
DS=18A1 ES=18A1 SS=18A1 CS=18A1 IP=012A NV UP EI PL NZ NA PE NC
18A1:012A B409          MOV      AH,09
-t

AX=090A BX=010C CX=0024 DX=0102 SP=FFEE BP=0000  SI=0000  DI=0000
DS=18A1 ES=18A1 SS=18A1 CS=18A1 IP=012C NV UP EI PL NZ NA PE NC
18A1:012C CD21          INT      21
-p
text input
AX=0924 BX=010C CX=0024 DX=0102 SP=FFEE BP=0000  SI=0000  DI=0000
DS=18A1 ES=18A1 SS=18A1 CS=18A1 IP=012E NV UP EI PL NZ NA PE NC
18A1:012E CD20          INT      20
-p

Program terminated normally
-
```

EXERCISES

1   Amend the program in Figure A2.10 so that it will prompt the user with the message 'Input a name': before the user is required to enter a string.

2   Take the program from Exercise 1 and amend it so that when the name is output it is reversed. See Figure 5.16 to see how this might be achieved.

Appendix 3
ASCII and extended ASCII tables

As computer systems developed, different manufacturers used different codes to represent the different types of data to be represented within the computer system. This was found to be a problem when it then became necessary to share data among systems. One of the first standards to be developed to represent data was the American Standard Code for Information Interchange developed by the American National Standards Institute (ANSI). This is a 7-bit code to represent character data. This enables up to 128 characters to be represented. The first 32 codes are used for transmission and device control codes. This leaves 96 codes to represent printable characters.

A 7-bit code was used as the standard as this meant that the code plus a parity bit could be stored within a single byte. Ninety six character codes were thought sufficient when the standard was introduced as applications at the time were rather limited and also computers were being developed in countries where English was the first language. It soon became clear that the 7-bit code was insufficient and an extended version was developed based on 8-bit codes; dispensing with the parity bit. The first 128 codes were unchanged. Initially there was no widely accepted standard for the new 128 codes. Work on standardising the extended character sets was carried out in the late 1980s through Xerox's work on codes for Chinese character sets and Apples work on developing a file exchange standard. The Unicode Consortium evolved from this work. Version 1 of the standard was published in 1991. The current version is version 3 and the consortium has over 50 corporate members.

There are a number of code charts developed by Unicode. The Basic Latin chart is compatible with the 7-bit ASCII chart. This is then extended via the Latin-1 supplement also known as ISO 8859-1. The two charts combine to form a standard form of extended ASCII chart using 8-bit codes. This chart is shown in Figure A3.1. The small square boxes in Figure A3.1(a) indicate where non-printing control codes appear. The first 32 control codes are separately listed in Figure A3.1(b). To determine the code for a particular character, use the row number as the least significant 4 bits, or nibble, and the column number as the most significant nibble. The character 'A', for example, would be code 41.

These charts would obviously be of little use when trying to convey information in non-latin alphabets. The most important work that the Unicode Consortium has undertaken is to develop a fully international character set. To achieve the

Figure A3.1   ASCII chart

	0	1	2	3	4	5	6	7	8	9	A	B	C	D	E	F
0	□	□		0	@	P	`	p	□	□		°	À	Ð	à	ð
1	□	□	!	1	A	Q	a	q	□	□	¡	±	Á	Ñ	á	ñ
2	□	□	"	2	B	R	b	r	□	□	¢	2	Â	Ò	â	ò
3	□	□	#	3	C	S	c	s	□	□	£	3	Ã	Ó	ã	ó
4	□	□	$	4	D	T	d	t	□	□	¤	´	Ä	Ô	ä	ô
5	□	□	%	5	E	U	e	u	□	□	¥	µ	Å	Õ	å	õ
6	□	□	&	6	F	V	f	v	□	□	¦	¶	Æ	Ö	æ	ö
7	□	□	'	7	G	W	g	w	□	□	§	·	Ç	×	ç	÷
8	□	□	(	8	H	X	h	x	□	□	¨	¸	È	Ø	è	ø
9	□	□	)	9	I	Y	i	y	□	□	©	¹	É	Ù	é	ù
A	□	□	*	:	J	Z	j	z	□	□	ª	º	Ê	Ú	ê	ú
B	□	□	+	;	K	[	k	{	□	□	«	»	Ë	Û	ë	û
C	□	□	,	<	L	\	l	|	□	□	¬	¼	Ì	Ü	ì	ü
D	□	□	-	=	M	]	m	}	□	□	-	½	Í	Ý	í	ý
E	□	□	.	>	N	^	n	~	□	□	®	¾	Î	Þ	î	þ
F	□	□	/	?	O	_	o	□	□	□	¯	¿	Ï	ß	ï	ÿ

(a) Extended ASCII chart

	1	2
0	NUL (Null)	DLE (Data Link Escape)
1	SOH (Start or Heading)	DC1 (Device Control 1)
2	STX (Start of Text)	DC2 (Device Control 2)
3	ETX (End of Text)	DC3 (Device Control 3)
4	EOT (End of Transmission)	DC4 (Device Control 4)
5	ENQ (Enquire)	NAK (Negative Acknowledge)
6	ACK (Acknowledge)	SYN (Synchronous Idle)
7	BEL (Bell)	ETB (End of Transmission Block)
8	BS (Backspace)	CAN (Cancel)
9	HT (Horizontal Tab)	EM (End of Medium)
A	LF (Line Feed)	SUB (Substitute)
B	VT (Vertical Tab)	ESC (Escape)
C	FF (Form Feed)	FS (File Seperator)
D	CR (Carriage Return)	GS (Group Seperator)
E	SO (Shift Out)	RS (Record Seperator)
F	SI (Shift In)	US (Unit Seperator)

(b) Control characters

international version it was necessary to move to a 16-bit code. Although this was a great help in supporting most of the languages of the world, the 64000 codes available are insufficient for a truly international standard and so 24- and 32-bit codes are also used. There are now almost 100000 characters represented in Unicode version 3.2. Not all these characters are textual characters; other symbols are also represented. Codes 2700–27BF are used for some useful symbols and fall within the Dingbats code chart. A similar set of symbols can be found on most PCs. If a Dingbats font is not available there will almost certainly be a Wingdings font (see Figure A3.2). Wingdings has a similar set of characters to Dingbats but is not a direct replacement. Unlike Dingbats, Wingdings uses a set of codes which are reserved by Unicode for private use. This means that there is no guarantee that an application on a different system will display a similar character or symbol.

Figure A3.2   Wingdings

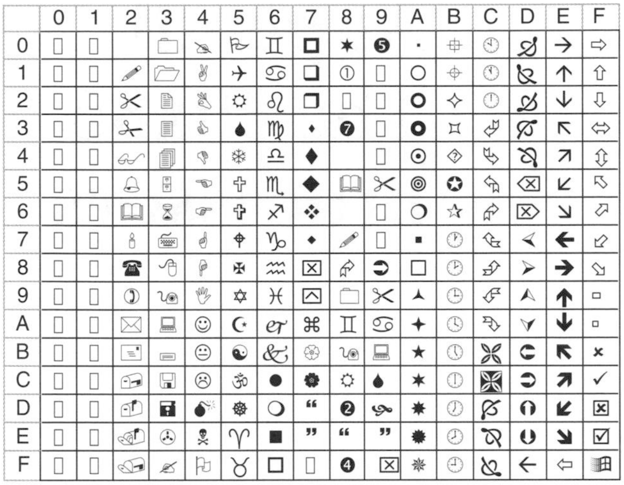

	0	1	2	3	4	5	6	7	8	9	A	B	C	D	E	F
0				📁	✂	✌	♊	□	✷	➎	·	⊕	🕐	⚡	→	⇨
1			✏	📂	✍	✈	♋	❑	①		○	✛	🕑	✂	↑	⇧
2			✂	📄	✍	✿	♌	❏			●	◆	🕒	✍	↓	⇩
3			✂	📄	✍	❀	♍	♦	❼		◉	⌘	✌	✍	↖	⇔
4			✂	📑	✍	❄	♎	◆			◉	◈	✌	✍	↗	⇕
5			🔔	📇	✍	✝	♏	◆	📖	✂	◎	✿	✌	⊠	↙	⇗
6			📖	⌛	☞	✝	♐	❖			○	★	✌	⊠	↘	⇘
7			☊	⌨	✍	✝	♑	♦	✏		▪	🕐	✌	◀	←	⇙
8			☎	🖱	✍	✳	≈	⊠	☞	➲	□	🕘	✌	▶	→	⇗
9			☏	🖲	✋	✶	♓	⬀	💻	✂	▲	🕘	✌	▲	↑	□
A			✉	🖥	☺	☾	ℯ	⌘	Ⅱ	☋	✦	🕙	✌	▼	↓	□
B			✉	💻	☺	☽	&	✪	📺	💻	★	🕙	✂	C	↖	✗
C			📬	💾	☹	✿	●	✸	✿	♦	✹	🕚	✻	➲	↗	✓
D			📭	💾	✍	✾	○	"	❷	∽	✺	🕛	✂	∩	↙	⊠
E			📬	✈	☠	♈	■	"	"	"	✴	🕛	✌	∪	↘	☑
F			📬	✂	♌	♉	□		❹	⊠	✶	🕛	✌	←	⇦	⊞

Appendix 4
The 80x86 family of processors

A4.1 Introduction

The Pentium processor, familiar in today's Personal Computers (PCs), can trace its roots back to the Intel 4004 microprocessor of 1971. This was a *4-bit processor*; that is, it had 4-bit registers and external data bus. In 1972 the 8008, was introduced which had an 8-bit bus. This was followed in 1974 by the 8080, which was faster than its predecessor.

By the end of the 1970s it became necessary to move to 16-bit architectures. Some of Intel's competitors, such as Motorola, radically redesigned their CPUs but Intel decided to evolve their 16-bit design from their 8-bit CPU. This meant it was easier for software developers to produce products to run on their new CPUs. This has been a policy that Intel has followed ever since. The first 16-bit processor from Intel was the 8086. Code written for this processor will run on Pentium processors available now. This is good for migration from one generation of the architecture to the next but can adversely affect performance, as compromises need to be made in the design.

The 8086 had 16-bit registers, a 16-bit data bus and a 20-bit address bus. This gave the processor the ability to address 1 MByte of memory. (Note that the memory unit addressed was 8 bits long despite a 16-bit data bus. This enables 8-bit data operations as well as 16-bit operations to be executed. In the case of 16-bit operations, the addressed byte and the following byte form a single 16-bit data item.) This processor was followed in 1979 by the more cost-effective 8088 that had an 8-bit data bus. A block diagram of the 8086/8 CPU is given in Figure 5.3. The only difference between the 8088 and 8086 internally was that the 8088 was limited to a 4-byte instruction queue. A description of the registers in the bus interface unit and Execution unit are given in Section A4.1.

TQ A4.1   The 8080 had a 16-bit address bus, so what was the maximum amount of memory it could address?

To be able to address 1 MByte of memory the 8086 used *segmentation*. The 8086 had four 16-bit segment registers, any one of which may form the most significant 16 bits of a 20-bit address (the least significant four bits being filled with zeros).

Figure A4.1 Simplified Intel 386 pipelined architecture showing 32-bit internal data paths

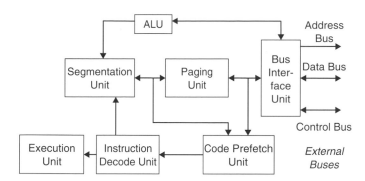

This provides the start address of a 64 KByte segment to which is added a 16-bit offset to form the effective address. This technique is discussed further in Section 5.1.3.

In 1982 the 80186/80188 was introduced. This was basically an 8086/8 with a number of functions that had been performed by support devices brought onto the CPU chip. These functions include a clock generator, direct memory accessing (DMA) and interrupt controllers, programmable timers and local bus controllers. This *integrated* CPU underwent its own development independently of the rest of the family.

The successor to the 8086 is the 80286 processor introduced in 1982. This CPU introduced a 24-bit address bus and 1 GByte of *virtual memory*. Descriptors provide 24-bit base addresses and memory can be swapped to and from virtual memory on a segment basis.

The Intel 386 processor (the initial 80 seems to have been dropped at this stage) introduced in 1985 had 32-bit registers and buses. It maintained the segment addressing of the 80286 but could also support a 'linear' 4 GByte address space (segmentation unnecessary). An application transparent paged virtual memory system was introduced offering a virtual memory size of 64 TBytes. The 386 had six parallel stages that form a sort of *macro pipeline* to improve performance. The stages were the bus interface unit, code pre-fetch unit, instruction decode unit, execution unit, segment unit and paging unit (see Figure A4.1).

The Intel 486, introduced in 1989, added 5-stage pipelines to the instruction decode and execution units. An 8 KByte on-board *first level cache* was included along with a Floating Point Unit (FPU), which had previously been a separate chip (80x87). Later versions of this CPU included support for power management. This was necessary to support the growing demand for battery-powered devices. The Pentium processor, introduced in 1993, added a second execution pipeline to achieve what Intel called *superscalar* performance (two pipelines operating in parallel). There were now two on-board caches in the *Harvard architecture* style (see Section 4.3.2). *Branch prediction* was added to increase performance regards looping constructs. Internal data paths of 128 and 256 bits were added to speed-up internal operations. An Advanced Programmable Interrupt Controller (APIC) was added to ease the construction of dual processor systems. Later versions of the CPU included multimedia extensions (MMX). These extensions included additional instructions and 64-bit registers that allowed a single instruction to be executed on multiple integer data items packed into the MMX registers. This form of execution is referred to as single instruction, multiple data (SIMD) and is particularly useful in multimedia applications where the same operation needs to be performed on many items of data.

In 1995 Intel modified the underlying architecture of their Pentium processors. This new micro-architecture was referred to as P6. The processors in this family were the Pentium Pro, Pentium II, Pentium II Xeon, Celeron, Pentium III and Pentium III Xeon. The Pentium Pro had enhanced parallel features that included three parallel instruction pipelines, five parallel execution pipelines, multi-ported cache and a 64-bit external data bus that could handle multiple overlapped requests. The address bus was extended to 36 bits. The Pentium II processor was the first P6 CPU to include MMX technology and came in a new form of a single edge contact cartridge (SECC). The Pentium II Xeon was intended for higher performance systems and thus included support for higher speed buses and multi-processor design. The Celeron, on the other hand, was designed for the budget market and to keep costs down used a plastic pin grid array (PPGA) and less on-board cache. The Pentium III processor introduced Streaming SIMD Extensions (SSE). The SSE added a new set of 128-bit registers (known collectively as the XMM registers) and the ability to perform SIMD operations on packed single precision floating-point values to the MMX technology.

For the recently introduced Pentium 4 the P6 architecture has been reworked to improve performance and scalability principally through supporting greater parallelism and is now called the NetBurst micro-architecture. The Pentium 4 also includes an enhanced form of SSE (SSE2), which has a new enhanced instruction set, 128-bit SIMD integer arithmetic and 128-bit floating-point operation. The bus speeds have been improved by up to three times that of the Pentium III.

A4.2 The programmer's model

In the introduction we were considering the physical aspects of the 80x86. What we will do now is consider the processor from the programmer's perspective. The execution environment of a Pentium 4 processor consists of

(a) Basic program execution registers

- ▶ eight 32-bit general purpose registers
- ▶ six 16-bit segment registers
- ▶ one 32-bit Flag register
- ▶ one 32-bit instruction pointer

(b) Floating point registers

- ▶ eight 80-bit floating point registers
- ▶ 16-bit control/status and tag registers

(c) MMX registers

- ▶ eight 64-bit registers

(d) SSE and SSE2 registers

- ▶ eight 128-bit XMM registers
- ▶ one 32-bit MXCSR register

Details of the six-segment registers are given in Table A4.1. If this is compared to the table of segment registers available in the 8086 you will notice the addition of two registers which have no specific function but can be used to increase the quantity of memory available to the program at any one time. The segment registers were introduced in the 8086 CPU to enable addresses to be formed from 16-bit values to be placed on a 20-bit address bus as discussed earlier.

Table A4.1   P4 segment registers

CS	Code Segment	start address of segment containing executable code
DS	Data Segment	start address of segment containing program data
SS	Stack Segment	start address of segment containing a stack data structure
ES	Extra Segment	start address of a general segment
FS	General purpose segment register	
GS	Start addresses segments of no default function	

Table A4.2   P4 general-purpose registers

EAX	accumulator for operands and results data
EBX	points to data in the DS segment
ECX	counter for string and loop operations
EDX	I/O pointer
ESI	pointer to data in the segment pointed to by the DS register; source pointer for string operations
EDI	pointer to data (or destination) in the segment pointed to by the ES register; destination pointer for string operations
ESP	stack pointer
EBP	pointer to data on the stack

Although the eight general-purpose registers can be used to store any data or address they also have a special function in some instructions. The registers and their special functionality are listed in Table A4.2. This table should be compared with the table of 8086 general-purpose registers (Table 5.1). These registers can also be used as 16-bit registers to maintain 8086 compatibility. The 16-bit registers can be divided into two 8-bit registers. Table A4.3 lists the registers and illustrates how they are divided up into smaller units.

Table A4.3 Alternate general-purpose register names

31 16	15 8	7 0	16-bit	32-bit
	AH	AL	AX	EAX
	BH	BL	BX	EBX
	CH	CL	CX	ECX
	DH	DL	DX	EDX
	SP			ESP
	BP			EBP
	SI			ESI
	DI			EDI

Appendix 5
IEEE 754 floating point format

In Section 2.7, floating point (FP) representation was considered in a general way. In this appendix we will look at the standard format IEEE 754 for FP numbers.

A FP number such as $-0.100100101 \times 2^{+1001}$, has four components we need to consider; the mantissa (0.100100101), the sign of the mantissa $(-)$, the exponent (1001) and the sign of the exponent $(+)$. As the numbers represented within the computer system will always be binary the base (2) can be ignored.

Let us first consider the exponent and its sign. The IEEE 754 standard uses a method of representing the exponent using a *bias*. If the number of bits used to represent the exponent is e then the bias will be $2^{e-1} - 1$. If eight bits are to be used to hold the exponent then the bias will be $2^7 - 1$ or 127_{10}. The *biased exponent* is determined by adding the true exponent to the bias. As the smallest value, which can be represented in eight bits, is zero, and the largest is 255, then the range of true exponents is -127 to 128.

Let us now consider the mantissa. This will always be in the form 0.1mmm .... where m is a bit of the mantissa. It is thus unnecessary to store the 0.1; we only need the following bits. When we come to do the arithmetic then the 0.1 can be reinstated. If we have an 8-bit mantissa and we wish to store a FP number with a mantissa of 0.100100101 then the value stored will be 00100101. The sign of the mantissa will always be held in the most significant bit (1 for negative, 0 for positive). Note that, unlike the way negative integers are represented, neither the mantissa nor exponent uses two's complement notation. The exponent is biased and the mantissa is sign and magnitude.

IEEE 754 defines a 32-bit format and a 64-bit format for FP numbers. In the 32-bit format there is an 8-bit biased exponent and in the 64-bit format there is an 11-bit biased exponent. The layout of the two forms is shown in Figure A5.1. Figure A5.2 shows how the number $-0.100100101 \times 2^{+1001}$, will be stored in IEEE 754 32-bit format. Note that the exponent is 9_{10}. Add this true exponent to the bias (127) giving 136_{10} or 10001000_2.

Figure A5.1   IEEE 754 (a) 32-bit and (b) 64-bit floating-point standard

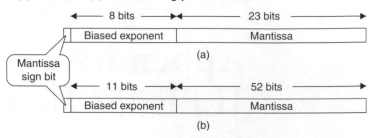

(a)

(b)

Figure A5.2   IEEE 754 example

$$-0.100100101 \times 2^{1001} \text{ floating point notation}$$

1 10001000 00100101000000000000000 IEEE 754 format

Acronyms

ACL	Access Control List
ADSL	Asymmetric Digital Subscriber Line
ALU	Arithmetic and Logic Unit
ANSI	American National Standards Institute
APIC	Advanced Programmable Interrupt Controller
ASCII	American Standard Code for Information Interchange
ATM	Asynchronous Transfer Mode
AUI	Access Unit Interface
BCD	Binary Coded Decimal
BIOS	Basic Input–Output System
CD-R	Compact Disk-Recordable
CD-ROM	Compact Disk-Read Only Memory
CD-RW	Compact Disk -ReWritable
CISC	Complex Instruction Set Computer
CMOS	Complementary Metal Oxide Semiconductor
COM	Communications
CPI	Clock cycles Per Instruction
CPU	Central Processing Unit
CRT	Cathode Ray Tube
CS	Code Segment (Intel 80 x86)
CU	Control Unit
CWP	Current Window Pointer
DAT	Digital Audio Tape
DDR-RAM	Double Data Rate Random Access Memory
DES	Data Encryption Standard
DIMM	Dual In-line Memory Module
DLP	Digital Light Processor
DMA	Direct Memory Access
DNS	Domain Name Service
DOS	Disk Operating System
DRAM	Dynamic Random Access Memory
DS	Data Segment (Intel 80x86)
DVD	Digital Versatile Disk
DVD-R	Digital Versatile Disk – Recordable
DVD-ROM	Digital Versatile Disk – Read Only Memory
DVD-RW	Digital Versatile Disk – ReWritable
EDC/ECC	Error Detection Code/Error Correction Code
EEPROM	Electrically Erasable Programmable Read Only Memory
EIDE	Extended Integrated Drive Electronics
EPROM	Erasable Programmable Read Only Memory

FAT	File Allocation Table
FCFS	First-Come-First-Served
FCS	Frame Check Sequence or Frame Check Sum
FDDI	Fibre Distributed Data Interface
FIFO	First-In-First-Out
FP	Floating Point
FPU	Floating Point Unit
FR	Flag Register
FSB	Front Side Bus
FSK	Frequency Shift Keying
FTP	File Transfer Protocol
GB	GigaBytes
Gb	Gigabits
GUI	Graphical User Interface
HDA	Hard Disk Assembly
Hex	Hexadecimal
Hi-Fi	High Fidelity
HLL	High Level Language
HTTP	HyperText Transfer Protocol
IC	Integrated Circuit
IDE	Integrated Drive Electronics
IDEA	International Data Encryption Algorithm
IEEE	Institute of Electrical and Electronic Engineers
I/O	Input Output
IP	Instruction Pointer also Internet Protocol
IPC	Inter Process Communication
IRET	Interrupt Return
ISA	Industry Standard Architecture
ISDN	Integrated Services Digital Network
ISO OSI	International Standards Organisation Open Systems Inter-connect
ISP	Internet Service Provider
KB	KiloBytes
Kb	Kilobits
LAN	Local Area Network
LCD	Liquid Crystal Display
LED	Light Emitting Diode
LEP	Light Emitting Polymer
LLC	Logical Link Control
LRU	Least Recently Used
LSB	Least Significant Bit
MAC	Media Access Control
MAR	Memory Address Register
MB	MegaBytes
Mb	Megabits
MBR	Memory Buffer Register
MICR	Magnetic Ink Character Recognition
MIDI	Musical Instrument Digital Interface
MIPS	Million Instructions Per Second
MMU	Memory Management Unit
MMX	Multi-Media eXtensions
MODEM	MODulator DEModulator

MSB	Most Significant Bit
MS-DOS	Microsoft Disk Operating System
NIC	Network Interface Card
OCR	Optical Character Recognition
OLED	Organic Light Emitting Diode
OS	Operating System
PC	Program Counter or Personal Computer
PCB	Printed Circuit Board
PCB	Process Control Block
PCI	Peripheral Component Interface
PDA	Personal Data Assistant
POST	Power-On Self Test
PPGA	Plastic Pin Grid Array
PROM	Programmable Read Only Memory
RAID	Redundant Array of Independent Disks
RAM	Random Access Memory
RAS	Remote Access Service
RD-RAM	Rambus Dynamic Random Access Memory
RIMM	Rambus In-line Memory Module
RISC	Reduced Instruction Set Computer
RIU	Ring Interface Unit
ROM	Read Only Memory
RR	Round Robin
RSA	Rivest, Shamir and Aldeman
RTL	Register Transfer Language
RTN	ReTurN from subroutine
R/W	Read/Write
SCSI	Small Computer System Interface
SECC	Single Edge Contact Cartridge
SIMM	Single In-line Memory Module
SIMD	Single Instruction Multiple Data
SIPO	Serial-In-Parallel-Out
SMM	System Management Mode
SMTP	Simple Mail Transfer Protocol
SPEC	Standard Performance Evaluation Corporation
SPARC	Scalable Processor ARChitecture
SRAM	Static Random Access Memory
SS	Stack Segment (Intel 80x86)
SSE	Streaming Single instruction Stream-multiple data stream Extensions
SVGA	Super Video Graphics Array
TAS	Test And Set
TB	TeraBytes
Tb	Terabits
TCP/IP	Transmission Control Protocol/Internet Protocol
TLB	Translation Look-aside Buffer
UDP	User Datagram Protocol
UPC	Universal Product Code
URL	Universal Resource Locator
USB	Universal Serial Bus
UTP	Unshielded Twisted Pair
VLAN	Very Local Area Network

VLIW	Very Long Instruction Word
VLSI	Very Large Scale Integration
WAN	Wide Area Network
WiFi	Wireless Fidelity
WORM	Write-Once Read Many times
WREM	Write-Read-Erase Memory

References and further reading

Abel, L. IBM PC Assembly Language and Programming. 5th Ed. Prentice Hall 2001.

Crusoe Processor Product Brief. Model TM5800. Transmeta 2003. Downloadable from www.transmeta.com.

Hamacher, Vranesic and Zaky. Computer Organization. 5th Ed. McGraw-Hill 2001.

Kingston Technology, Ultimate Memory Guide. Kingston Technology 2001. Downloadable from www.kingston.com.

Lister, A.M, Eager, R.D. Fundamentals of Operating Systems. 5th Ed. Macmillan Press Ltd 1993.

Mano, M. Digital Design. 3rd Ed. Prentice Hall 2002.

MIPS R5000 Microprocessor. MIPS Technologies Technical Backgrounder. Downloadable from www.mips.com.

Simha, S. R4400 Microprocessor Product Information. MIPS Technologies 1996. Downloadable from www.mips.com.

Sparc Architecture Manual. Version 9. Downloadable from www.sparc.org.

Stallings, W. Operating Systems. 4th Ed. Prentice Hall 2002.

Tanenbaum, A. Structured Computer Organisation. Prentice Hall 1999.

White, R. How Computers Work. 6th Ed. Que 2001.

Intel publications (all downloadable from www.intel.com.):

8-bit HMOS Microprocessor. Intel 1990.

8086 16-bit HMOS Microprocessor. Intel 1990.

80186/80188 High-Integration 16-bit Microprocessors. Intel 1994.

Intel Pentium 4 Processor in the 423-pin Package data sheet. Intel 2001.

Intel Pentium 4 Processor with 512KB L2 Cache data sheet. Intel 2001.

IA-32 Intel Architecture Software Developer's Manual. Volume 1: Basic Architecture. Intel 2001.

IA-32 Intel Architecture Software Developer's Manual. Volume 2: Instruction Set Reference. Intel 2001.

Websites

www.arstechnica.com
www.crucial.com/library
www.howstuffworks.com
www.intel.com
www.mips.com/content/Products/ProductInfo
www.rambus.com/technology

www.searchstorage.com
www.sparc.org/resources.htm
www.spechbench.org
www.transmeta.com/technology/specifications/index.html
www.unicode.org
www.whatis.com
www.xs4all.nl/~matrix

Index

Index

Index